DINING
WITH
HEADHUNTERS

DINING
WITH
HEADHUNTERS

JUNGLE FEASTS & OTHER
CULINARY ADVENTURES

BY RICHARD STERLING

THE CROSSING PRESS   FREEDOM, CA

I wish to send my thanks to professors Charles Muscatine and Maxine Hong Kingston, both of the University of California, Berkeley, for teaching me the art of letters; and to my inspiration, the late M.F.K. Fisher, who now sups with the muses.

Edited by Dave DeWitt
Cover art, book design and illustrations by Lois Bergthold
Production by Deborah Beldring

Printed in the United States of America

Library of Congress Cataloging-in-Publication Data

Sterling, Richard.
    Dining with headhunters : jungle feasts and other culinary adventures / Richard Sterling.
        p. cm.
    Includes index.
    ISBN 1-89594-775-7 (pbk.)
    1. Cookery, Southeast Asian. 2. Asia, Southeastern—Description and travel. 3. Sterling, Richard—Journeys—Asia, Southeastern. I. Title.
TX724.5.S68S83 1995
641.5959--dc20   94-48017
                                                          CIP

There is in some few men of every land a special hunger, one which will make them forego the safe pleasures of their own beds and tables, one which initiates them into that most mysterious and ruthless sect: the adventurers.

—Mary (M.F.K.) Fisher

I have eaten your bread and salt,
I have drunk your water and wine.
The deaths Ye died I have watched beside,
And the lives Ye led were mine.

—Rudyard Kipling

This book is merely a personal narrative, and not a pretentious history or a philosophical dissertation. It is a record of several years of variegated vagabondizing, and its object is rather to help the resting reader while away an idle hour than to afflict him with metaphysics, or goad him with science. Still, there is information in the volume.

—Mark Twain

CONTENTS

INTRODUCTION

T HIS IS A BOOK ABOUT HOW I LIVE, how I travel, and how the art of cuisine sustains me. Thackeray wrote that next to eating good dinners, a healthy man likes reading about them. And Homer, in an oft-repeated refrain, breaks his narrative to tell how the Greek heroes laid down their arms and feasted during their wars and travels. The message for us is that feasting and adventuring are inextricably intertwined; cuisine is an integral part of the landscape, a character in the tale.

I subtitle this book *Jungle Feasts* because the dinners you will read about here don't take place in the rarified, sterilized atmosphere we are accustomed to in food writing. They occur in seemingly unconducive places like warships, brothels, trains, among ghosts, in war and, of course, in jungles. Too often, I think, we take the subject of food out of its context and treat it as some discrete activity unconnected to real life. Or, we insist that it be kept in a realm of gentility and refinement—far removed from daily life, adventurous life, or life on the raw side.

I cannot pluck the Muse of Cuisine from the continuum in which she lives. And she sits not only at the tables of the refined, the wealthy, and the well-scrubbed. Like any other art, like any other thread in the pattern of life, she thrives also in the back streets, dark alleys, and the kitchens of the profane. Wherever people invoke the Muse of Cuisine, there she is.

And, this muse has guts. The slick food and travel magazines might prefer life to be all sweetness and light; no dirt, no sex, no pain, no struggle. But I say to you that this muse does not shy away. I tell you that she is wherever people feed thoughtfully, feelingly, and joyfully. She will even attend runaway boys if they know a good dinner when they find it. As in the case of Tom Sawyer and his friends devouring their food on an island in the Mississippi: "It seemed glorious sport to be feasting in that wild free way in the virgin forest...and they said they would never return to civilization."

I come to you now from such a forest and scores of others like it, and I bring you the record of the feasts. For many years now, I have been collecting the recipes I encountered on my adventures. I picked them up the way an actor might hold on to the script of the play he was in, or the musician the score of the concert he played. When I return home, I can prepare the recipes and relive the moment. Unlike a photograph that captures only the image, or the other remembrances that simply jog the powers of recall, I can re-experience the time physiologically. Through the feast, I can taste, smell, see, and consume the past event. And my guests, through my food and my stories, can be there with me. Now, you can too. So come with me and feast!

A Note to Cooks: The unusual ingredients found in many of the recipes, from fish sauce and chile paste to lemon grass and kaffir lime leaves, are readily available in Asian markets in the United States and other countries.

PART I

NAVY DAYS

I WENT TO SEA AS AN UNTUTORED AND UNFORMED YOUNG MAN. I knew very little of life and the world, but I was an eager student—especially if I didn't have to be in high school anymore. I longed for foreign and exotic shores, for women who looked nothing like the ones I knew at home, adventures to have and stories to tell. It never occurred to me at that callow time that food would eventually be a part of my longings.

I grew up in a rural environment, where nearly all that one could expect to eat could be seen in a glance around the kitchen garden and the barnyard and in what men brought home from the hunt. All the ways to eat these foods I knew before reaching the age of eight. Food was a fact of daily life and, while pleasant, little more than that. We fed the animals, and then we fed ourselves. Not much difference between the two. We never pondered the power of food. We never thought about the connection we affirmed with the world when we consumed and assimilated a portion of it. We did not acknowledge the relationship between the food we eat on a given occasion and the people and events that attend the eating.

My sailings would come to teach me otherwise, through lessons that would run the gamut from the seemingly insignificant morsel to the grandest feast. My travels would teach me that the staff of life is something the soul leans on as well as the body. Love would creep into my heart through sharing at the table. Philosophy would stir within through the medium of a humble cup. And I would partake of the most memorable adventures by feasting.

CHAPTER 1

THE DRAGON AND ME:
HOW I QUIT SMOKING AND
SURVIVED THE BOMB

*B*ECAUSE OF STILL CURRENT SECURITY CONSIDERATIONS, *the name of the ship on which this story takes place cannot be revealed, and the names of crew members have been changed.*

AT SEA, TUESDAY, 20:00 HOURS

Before turning in for the night, I called the Messenger of the Watch on the bridge. "This is Petty Officer Sterling," I said, "in compartment Bravo-37-87. I need a wake-up call at 03:30 tomorrow morning."

"Why so early?" the messenger asked. "You got some early lookout?"

"Yes," I lied.

Then I called Corporal Durum of the ship's Marine detachment. "I need the usual guard at the Special Weapons Office at 04:00 tomorrow."

"Till when?"

"About 04:30."

"And who'll be with you?"

"Seaman Henderson."

"Very well."

The Marines never ask why, they just do. I had made these arrangements because I had to take the Dragon's temperature. Periodically we, in the missile battery, had to measure the temperature and humidity of the nuclear warhead magazine, and it was my turn. We usually did it in the wee hours because the Dragon's presence on board was Top Secret. I was taking Ricky Henderson with me because a nuke magazine is a No Lone Zone, and the Two-Man Rule is in effect. No one is supposed to be left alone with the Dragon.

WEDNESDAY, 04:00 HOURS

We arrived at the office door and found the two Marines already posted; their boots, buckles, and weapons were gleaming. We showed them our access passes, pinned on our film badges, and signed the log. They passed us through the portal, and the door closed behind us. No one else would enter.

"You really need me to go down with you?" Ricky asked.

"Nah. Stay here and read your skin mag. Just don't answer the phone if it rings. And don't make any noise."

We moved the office desk and exposed the scuttle—a small, circular hatch just wide enough to allow a man to pass through. Pausing to remember, I dialed the combination on the lock, opened the scuttle, and looked down the shaft that sunk three decks to another locked scuttle. Beneath that lay the magazine, three fathoms below the waterline, at the very bottom of the ship.

I slipped down the hole, and Ricky closed the scuttle after me. Descending, the hard soles of my safety shoes rang on the flat steel rungs of the ladder, echoing in the shaft. Only the dim shaft light shone from above. By the time I reached the next scuttle, I was in half-darkness. I noticed that the roll of the ship was reversed now, indicating that I was below its fulcrum, the waterline. The scuttle had been battened down tightly and I had to use a dogging wrench, a lever, to break the closures. Straining, I lifted the heavy portal and eye-squinting light shot through the hole, driving a column of it up the shaft like a fountain. I held my face over the streaming light for a moment, to adjust my eyes, then dropped down inside.

Everything was white: the deck, the bulkheads, the overhead, the lights, the fixtures...and the warheads. All were white, white, white; pure white, cold white, death white. Melville would have known this shade of white. Twenty-four nuclear warheads rested in two rows of six on the port side and two rows of six on the starboard with a four-foot-wide aisle between them. Each one was lying on its side in a steel cradle frame, strapped in with a steel belt, and they looked like eggs—three-foot-long eggs—Embryos of the Apocalypse. A few of them had thick, black electrical monitoring cables snaking out of their aft ends, giving them the look of huge spermatozoa, perhaps the gametes of Mr. Melville's leviathan.

I stood at one end of the aisle and regarded them for a moment. Then I listened to the silence. A warship is usually a noisy place. Engines thrum, chains clank, men shout, machines whir, and wind and wave sing their song or roar in anger. But the magazine was a quiet place. The only sound was the the soft whisper of the water slipping past the hull a fraction of an inch below my feet. And although Death slumbered here, it was not the quiet of the grave. This was a womb. This was a holy place. The End of the World slept here. This was Destruction's chapel, and we were his altar boys. At the other end of the aisle, a shelf jutted out from the wall. On it lay the open, black-bound log book. Above the shelf, like two candles mounted on the wall, were the thermometer and the humidity gauge: A Pulpit for this worshipful cure of Nukes.

Walking down the aisle to take my readings, I stopped at warhead number W-18. It was a tactical device, small by nuclear standards, its power in the kiloton range. In it were half, maybe three-quarters of a million kills. A Nagasaki. I ran my hand over its perfect, seamless skin. It was smooth like pearl and perfectly symmetrical. The thing was superbly designed to slice through the atmosphere at two and a half times the speed of sound at the tip of a surface-launched guided missile, one that even I might be called upon to fire. I admired the magnificent craftsmanship, the skill, the talent, the care—yes, even the love that had gone into the making of so perfect an artifact. "Who are the gnomes," I wondered, "that hammer away in the secret smithies of Bendix and the nuclear agencies? And what should they be called? Armorers? No, too archaic and not powerful enough. Nuclear Device Technicians? No, too clinical. Death Smiths? Yes, that's what they are, Death Smiths."

I took my readings, and as I was writing them in the log I noticed a bit of ash at my feet. I picked it up and smelled. Correli and Morgan had been smoking dope in here again. I checked the electronics aperture in the rear of a few warheads to see if they had stashed their supply in one. It was, after all, the safest place on board. The only people besides us Missile Men that even knew this place existed were the Captain and a few of his officers, none of whom ever came here.

My search yielded a pack of Salem cigarettes (had to be Arnie's; he was the only one who smoked them), a lighter, and a deck of cards. Some of the guys liked to play cards here. They would place a board across two of the warheads, then sit on the adjacent ones. Arnie always made it a point to fart on the one he sat on. He said it was how he showed his "contempt for war." A. K. Douglas and Ricky Henderson would rub their groins against a couple of Doomsday's Children and then pretend that they "glowed at the gonads." They'd say things like, "Look out wimmin! Nuclear love!" or, "Ooh! A one-hundred-and-twenty-kiloton orgasm, comin' at ya. Yahoo! Measure my virility on the Geiger counter."

I pocketed the goods, took one last look at my charges then ascended, out of the light, through the darkness, and up to the light again. Ricky and I closed and locked the scuttle and replaced the desk that covered it. We secured the office and notified the Corporal of the Guard that he could dismiss his two Marines. On Friday we would return. In obedience to the faraway councils of naval command, our ship would rendezvous under cover of darkness with an ammunition ship at some secret point on the map of the South China Sea. There we would haul Death's Cocoons out of their chamber, pack them in individual drums, and send them by the highline across the water to the other ship. A very delicate operation. What a time for me to quit smoking.

WEDNESDAY, 10:00 HOURS

After breakfast, we met in the Missile House to confer on the warhead movement. We assigned stations and duties to every man: magazine, ammunition lift, topside, etc. We would prepare the goods for shipment, then turn them over, one at a time, to the Chief Bosun's Mate and his deck crew for highlining.

During a highline operation, two ships, displacing, say, fifteen thousand tons each, steam alongside each other, close enough for the crews to yell out when they see old buddies on the opposite deck. When the ships are in position, a bosun on one vessel fires a shotline to the other. The shotline gun is like a shoulder-held flare gun. It fires a tennis-ball-sized wad of compressed, tightly bound nylon cord trailing a slender, white line. It looks like a big, white tadpole. The men on the other ship dodge the speeding wad and grab for its tail. When both crews have a hold on the line, one crew ties a heavy line and a smaller line to it. The other then pulls the two lines back across. The heavy line is wrapped around a pulley on each ship, and ten to twenty men grasp it at each end, as though in a giant tug of war. As the ships roll and pitch, straining or slackening the highline, they pay it out or haul it in, keeping a constant tension on it. A hook and pulley are hung from the highline, the smaller line is tied to that, and both crews can pull it back and forth like clothes on a line. You can hang anything from the hook: pallets, drums, bags, people, even a flexible pipeline to carry fuel or water; or as the Navy saying goes: "Beans, bullets, and black oil."

Highlining is a complex and delicate dance in which every man and machine has to perform without error. Even the elements have to cooperate. Cross currents, rogue waves, or sudden gusts of wind can carry as much disaster as faulty mechanisms, inattention on deck, or a twitch in the helmsman's arm. Ships that carry bands usually muster them on deck and have them play during highlining. It's a tradition, and it calms nerves.

On one memorable occasion we were alongside a thirty-thousand-ton replenishment ship. She suddenly lost command of her rudder, and it jammed left. The movement ripped apart the highline tackle and threw its handlers to the deck. She bore down on our starboard side like a moving mountain of gray-painted steel. Many of our men ran like hell for the port side. On the flying bridge, the Captain and his seventeen-year-old phone-talker stood fast as the runaway monster loomed. Relaying orders to helm and engine room through the cherubfaced phone-talker, the Captain masterfully conned the ship out of danger. Everyone on deck cheered. It was a very close call, as the two ships nearly kissed. We liked to say that the plucky young phone-talker's beard grew out the next day.

WEDNESDAY, 21:00 HOURS

That evening I lay out on the main deck near the anchor chains, smoking. The month was July, and we were in tropical seas. The wind was abaft, about the same speed we were making, so the relative air drifted slowly. The moonless sky was clear but dazzling with stars that swung easily back and forth with the slow rolls of the ship. They glistened and twinkled as if alive, inviting me to linger. The ship yawed, and the stars spun on the axis of the zenith, as though changing partners in a cosmic dance. I heard the splash of flying fish as they leaped out of the water and raced ahead of the prow. The warm and fecund smell of the sea bespoke its countless living things. And the ship, as all good ships, felt alive with the low thrum of her engines and her quickening shivers as she met the rolling swells. The bitter smoke of my cigarette smelled of ashes and death.

I had been smoking since my early teens, and I was thoroughly addicted to tobacco. I smoked two packs of cigarettes a day while aboard ship and up to three while ashore where I had plenty of beer to cool my burning throat. In the mornings, I lit up before heaving out of my rack, and it was the last thing I did at night before getting into it. I smoked between courses in restaurants, and I smoked before and after sex. I smoked in my dreams.

For the last year my health had been deteriorating. I couldn't walk far without wheezing badly. I often had a cold. Lately my heart had been "fibrillating," as the doctor said. To me, it felt like an engine freezing up for lack of oil, trying to continue but stripping bearings in the effort. I was always tired. I took up cigars and a pipe to wean myself away from cigarettes, but I ended up smoking those *and* cigarettes. I would smoke a satisfying eight-inch Manila cigar and as soon as it was out I would light up a butt. Like most smokers, I had already quit many times—but only long enough to know what nicotine withdrawal was like. Ricky Henderson would laugh and say, "Anybody can quit smoking, but it takes a real man to face up to cancer." I feared I wouldn't live long enough to face cancer.

I knew, I had known, and on this starry night I accepted, that I would die of tobacco if I did not forswear it. I held my cigarette close to my face and gazed at the blushing ember. I didn't want to quit smoking. I loved tobacco. My body demanded it. I loved the mellow tar and honey smell of cured pipe tobacco and cigars. A cigarette in my hand, fiddling with it, rolling it between my fingers, had the same effect for me as worry beads in the hand of an Arab. I loved to take a great lungful from a

Marlboro and then let the smoke curl slowly out of my nostrils and form a wispy, gray wreath around my head. After smoking, I often smelled my hands, and they smelled good to me.

Tobacco soothed, like a friend. It was sharp and pungent and masculine and familiar, a constant companion. And sucking on the instrument, whether pipe or cigar or cigarette, was as good as nursing at a breast. A good cigar was better than a kiss. "A woman is only a woman," Kipling wrote, "but a good cigar is a smoke." With the effusive and aromatic stem of a pipe, I could tease the nerve endings of my mouth as well as any lover's tongue. And it would never say no. Tobacco was another kind of Dragon, and we had each other by the throat.

But this Lover/Dragon would kill me. It would consume me even as I consumed it. And all the fine nights of dancing stars would be darkened and made void. I reached for the metal, Navy-issue ash receptacle, the kind that looks like a funnel set into the top of a beer can. I looked at my glowing Marlboro one more time. Without taking another puff, I crushed it out against the side of the funnel, smashing its cherry head into tiny sparkles that sifted down into the hole and disappeared. The crinkled butt followed. "That's the last one," I said lowly. I did not feel very good.

I told no one I was quitting. If I did, there would always be some asshole who would blow smoke at me and say, "Sure you won't have one?" I went to the berthing compartment, let down my rack, and crawled in. I was hoping I might sleep through the worst of the withdrawal. Since I had already been up since 03:30, I managed to force myself to sleep, but not without my head beginning to buzz for want of nicotine.

THURSDAY, 20:00 HOURS

All day I fought off thoughts of smoking. Every time my hunger for tobacco gnawed, I found something to do, something to read, someone to talk to, something to eat, something to think about. Repeatedly throughout the day I automatically reached into my empty shirt pocket for a cigarette. Several people offered me one, and I made excuses. By evening all my mental energies were occupied with keeping my thoughts away from smoking. My eyes began to blink spasmodically. I had vague, unpleasant contrary feelings, like the cold chills that accompany a high fever. I felt at once drowsy, as though from barbiturates, and wired awake with amphetamines. I felt no single discernible physical sensation, and yet I felt profound discomfort. I went wearily to bed, hoping for and dreading my smoky dreams.

FRIDAY, 02:00 HOURS

Typhoon Sally had been running a course parallel to ours. By midnight she had shifted our way and soon engulfed us. I awoke with the sea change. I assumed the highline operation would be rescheduled due to the rough weather. Just sending a pallet-load of groceries over a calm sea is risky enough business. But to sling a thousand pounds of doomsday under a single line in the midst of a gale would be folly, I thought. I went back to my feverish sleep and dreamed of tobacco.

FRIDAY, 04:00 HOURS

A messenger woke me up. I was in a sweat, both from the weather and from withdrawal. The Brass had decided to go ahead with the operation. We were keeping to the edge of the storm where the winds and the seas were lower. The weather would give us the cover the Brass wanted for what was, after all, a secret operation. The deck crew boasted some of the finest practical seamen in the navy. They wouldn't know what they were transferring, and they wouldn't ask, but they were confident they could do the job. They respected Howling Sally, but they did not fear her.

FRIDAY, SUNRISE

The winds and seas were high, and the temperature was a steamy eighty degrees when the ammo ship hove into view. She was coming up from behind us, her fat prow plowing through white water and rain. The eye of her blinker fluttered on the signal bridge, telling us to keep steady, and she would come alongside. She moved gradually through the froth, giving us a coy, wide berth at first. Our ship drove its prow into a wave, shipped eleven tons of water and hurled it skyward in a tower of spume.

We and the opposite crew stood on deck and watched each other through the twilight and flying foam. We watched to gauge the roll and yaw of the two ships to see how closely they would swing toward each other in the churning sea. The ammo ship yawed and swung her stern teasingly away and then dangerously toward us. We adjusted our courses to put the oncoming sea more closely behind us to even out our keels. Gingerly, rolling, yawing, and pitching, the two big ships eased closer together, narrowing the frothing gap between them.

When the two shipmasters judged that they were as close as they dared, they gave the signal. Our bosun stood on the rolling deck and aimed his shotline gun through the spray. The gun recoiled and barked, its report bouncing off the steel flanks of the ammo ship. The shotline sang out. It streaked across the abyss and draped its tail over the deck. A perfect shot—the bosun had laid his line right between her stacks. The two ships were coupled. If all went well, they would remain in their tenuous, thrashing embrace until the one had emptied its terrible seed into the other. The deck crew sprang to their tasks. The Marine guards took up their posts. We, the Missile Men, struck below.

We prized open the warhead magazine. We opened up the ammunition lift shaft that ran from topside all the way down to the magazine. A squad of our men took the lift topside and rolled out the specially designed, nondescript-looking drums that would each hold one nuke. Three men handled the lift. Others stood by as runners and relief. Gunner Cassidy, Ricky Henderson, and myself manned the magazine.

The end of a seesaw travels much farther than a part closer to its fulcrum. A rolling, pitching ship is like two seesaws, one across the other, with its fulcrum in the middle at the waterline. The farther from the middle, and the farther from the waterline, the more travel when the ship rolls or pitches. The magazine was as far down from the waterline as it could be. And it wasn't very close to the middle. That day the magazine traveled like some nightmarish amusement park ride. It could have been mocked up as a huge box of dice being shaken and tumbled by a gambling titan: "Come ride the Giant Nuclear Crapshoot!"

Our first task was to attach the warheads' nose cones. Each warhead comes equipped with two, and while in storage, they are bolted to the rear of the cradle. For launch or transit, one is removed and attached to the leading end of the head. In transit the spare is packed along in the drum. The nose cones are extremely sharp and smooth, as they are designed for supersonic flight. If a man were to fall on one it would pierce him like a spear. The task of attaching them was simple, but I had a hard time concentrating. My nicotine withdrawal was fast approaching its worst stage.

After the nose cone attachment, we began the warhead movement. To facilitate this, the ceiling of the magazine was criss-crossed with slotted tracks. The central track ran fore and aft down the center of the room. Branching out from the central track ran shorter ones. They each hung over warhead locations. Into the slotted track we fitted a hoist that we could slide to a position over any single warhead. Once the hoist was in position, we could unbolt the steel strap that held the nuke down, lower the hoist, pick up the monster, and slide it over to the lift shaft. There we could transfer it to the lift, send it topside, and the men there would secure it in its drum. The drum would be rolled out past a cordon of Marines and highlined to the ammo ship, which was named after a volcano—I won't say which one.

Ricky and I took ratchets and began to unbolt the strap of the first warhead. Gunner handled the hoist. A buzzing sound penetrated my ears. It circled counterclockwise around my brain and made me dizzy. The dizziness moved like a slow current down to my stomach and nausea flickered; the nicotine withdrawal was taking my sea legs.

"How embarrassing," I thought. "They'll razz me for sure." A seasick sailor is like a cowboy afraid of horses. A slow fire burned in my lungs, and they demanded nicotine to quench it. I took huge breaths and held them, hoping to fool my lungs into feeling that they were full of smoke. My right hand, of its own accord, rose up to my face, and covered my nose. I sniffed hungrily for the aroma of tobacco but smelled only soap.

We loosened the bolts, and through the buzzing sound in my head the ratchets sent their raspy clicking. The hoist whined when Gunner lowered it. The hooks clattered as we attached them to the warhead. The hoist whined again, and the chain rattled as the little behemoth arose from its resting place. It cleared the cradle, and Gunner stopped the hoist. The inchoate thing hung three feet off the moving deck, smooth and white —its nose cone glistening. Its nose bobbed up and down slightly, like a hound picking up a scent. It began to swing, straining at its chain leash, a dog of war eager to be let slip. But we were taking this one to kennel.

We drew it out to the middle track. In my distraction and dizziness, I failed to note the arc of the warhead's swing. The ship gave a roll. The heavy weapon swung my way. The tip of the nose cone hit me in the right thigh, just below the hip, all one thousand pounds of its terrible weight concentrated behind that one, tiny point. It pierced the skin to an eighth of an inch, and withdrew. Blood seeped from the wound and made a purple stain on the blue cotton trouser cloth.

9

We regained control of the weapon and slid it to the forward bulkhead. We slipped it onto the lift and secured it, then sent it topside. The process took about ten minutes. Twenty-three warheads to go.

Moving on to the next one, Gunner said to me, "Better watch yourself, Dick. Those things are sharp."

"Is that a 'Broken Arrow'?" Ricky joked. That was one of the code words we were to use in the event of an accident. "Broken Arrow," if we dropped a warhead and cracked it open; "Bent Spear," if we just dropped it. Who in blazes thinks up these code words, anyway?

Ricky and Gunner walked easily by me on fluid sea legs, their bodies never deviating from the vertical, as though they were hung from gimbals. I steadied myself by grasping onto protruding nose cones and followed. We worked mechanically for a long time, one weapon following another and another and another. In the process I got stabbed again, this time in the left leg. It was a glancing blow, leaving more bruise than wound, but it tore my trouser leg. I didn't think about it. I couldn't think about anything except standing up straight on a heaving deck and the maddening craving for a smoke. A smoker's longing for tobacco is like thirst—insistent, unceasing, and steadily worse. I swallowed repeatedly, hoping to satisfy the clutching in my throat. I clenched my teeth and bit down hard. I pinched myself. I sweated. My eyes ran. I sucked in air like a man who could get none. I suffered, goddamn it.

As we were setting another warhead into the ammo lift, I heard a loud sophomoric giggle from above. I looked up the shaft to the next deck and saw A.K. Douglas, Ricky Henderson's "nuclear love" mate from Arkansas with a silly grin on his face. He had just opened his fly and was shaking his "glowing gonads" at us. "You want some of this?" he asked with a "Yuk, yuk, yuk." He was inordinately proud of his tool, though I have to admit it could take your breath away seeing it for the first time. It hung in elephantine fatness halfway to his knees, and the bulbous crimson head resembled nothing so much as a big meaty strawberry, ready for plucking.

A.K. never referred to his unit as his penis or his tool or any of the many Anglo-Saxon appellations for the male equipment. He called it "The Ol' Arkansas Strawberry." And he never said that he made love to a woman, or fucked a woman, or enjoyed female embraces. He always said, "I took her to bed, you know, and then I give her the Ol' Arkansas Strawberry. And she liked it real good, too. Yuk, yuk." He always made a sharp jabbing motion with his arm when he said, "I give her the Ol' Arkansas Strawberry," and he ejaculated the words rather than spoke them.

As I stood there looking up the shaft in my misery he repeated, "You want some of the Ol' Arkansas Strawberry there, Petty Officer Dick? It's nukified. Yuk, yuk." Ordinarily I would have made some pat remark, like "Don't point that thing at me when you don't know how to use it." Then he would have proudly holstered his gun having once again demonstrated its mighty caliber and that would have been that. But I had no sense of humor at the moment. And A.K. saw I had no sense of humor. He wagged the Ol' Arkansas Strawberry at me every time I brought a nuke to the shaft. I knew if I told him to zip up and shut up it would just encourage him.

So, I began to think about strawberries. I thought about my grandmother cutting them up to make jam. I thought about the robins and other birds that used to peck at the strawberries we grew at home in Mendocino. Their sharp little beaks left deep wounds in the flesh, which turned an unappetizing brown. My frustration with A.K. began to subside. Finally, I thought about piña coladas and margaritas I had seen bartenders make with strawberries—how they whipped and beat them in a blender till they were reduced to a blood-red puree. In my mind, I concocted such a cocktail, and named it An Ol' Arkansas Strawberry. My agitation with A.K. disappeared, and he noticed and finally repackaged himself. I was free to go back to being merely miserable.

Halfway through the operation, word came down from topside to hold up for a while. Packing a warhead is not simply a matter of sticking it in a drum and putting a lid on it. Everything has to be done by the book, and it takes time. We were stacking them up, and they didn't want them rolling around on deck.

"Jesus Christ, let's put some hustle on it and get this thing over with," Ricky bitched. Gunner calmly sat down on an empty cradle. I, wobbly at the knees, made my way over to W-18, the small tactical device, sank to the deck next to it and lay my head against its smooth side. I held on to the cradle to steady myself and curled my knees up to my chest.

"You seasick, Dickie?" Gunner asked with some surprise. Still, no one knew.

"Uh huh," I moaned.

"Ha!" Ricky yelped. "What a non-hacker. Ho ho."

I didn't care. I was, indeed, a little queasy, though I wouldn't call it *mal de mer*. I was just plain miserable. A taut string ran inside my skull from the top to the bottom. At one end a screw turned, and with each passing minute tightened that strainful cord. It was now so tight it began to sing in a piercing, painful note. The ship kept rolling. The deck rose and fell. I pressed my head against the bulbous Death of a City and hung on.

We had had no breakfast that morning. Because it was so early, we hadn't bothered. Somebody sent down a couple boxes of C-rations to snack on. They were the kind where all the food comes in a can: canned meat, canned vegetables, canned fruit, canned pound cake, canned bread, canned peanut butter and jelly, and canned crackers. Also a pack of instant coffee and sugar, six matches, one stick of gum, a little P-38 can opener, a wad of toilet paper, and a pack of three cigarettes, all packaged in olive drab. "You want anything, Dick?" Gunner asked, as he and Ricky went through the contents.

"Nah, I'm not hungry," I said through a now-snotty nose. I sniffed and thought about those three cigarettes. The string in my head strained to perilously near the breaking point.

"Well, here. Take these then," Gunner said. From one of the boxes he handed me two thick, round soda crackers - the kind you'd see in a cracker barrel.

"Ha!" Ricky yelped again. "Non-hacker!" Nibbling on a soda cracker is a remedy for ordinary seasickness. Gunner was doing me a kindness in giving them to me, but still it was embarrassing. Determined to put my best face forward, I said, "Well, gimme the goddamn peanut butter then, too!" Gunner handed me the flat can of peanut butter, three inches in diameter and three-quarters of an inch high.

With shaky hands I unfolded the can opener and removed the lid. The roasted peanut smell rushed into my nose. The roasted, slightly burned, almost smoky smell filled my nostrils and half-clogged nasal passages with a swirling cloud of relief. To my smoke-starved senses the rich, mellow, sometimes sweet aroma was almost like pipe tobacco. I sucked it in like snuff. I snorted it like cocaine. Like a diver who breaks the surface after too long under water, I gulped in the smell as though it were life-giving air.

With a forefinger, I dug into the peanut butter and scooped out a gob. I scraped it off onto my lower teeth. With my tongue, I maneuvered it to the middle of my mouth and pressed it against my palate, gluing my mouth closed. A buzzing, tingling feeling spread through my lips, as though sensation were returning after a long absence. As I breathed, the air in my windpipe moved past the back of my tongue and picked up the roasty, toasty aroma and channeled it back and forth through my nose. With my tongue, I smeared the peanut butter in circles against the roof of my mouth, melting it, dissolving it, driving it into my taste buds, and intensifying the flavor and making my salivary glands gush. The whining string in my head eased ever so slightly.

I used one of the crackers as a knife to scoop out the peanut butter and spread it on the other cracker. I put the two crackers together and made a thick sandwich. I took a crunchy, creamy bite. I held it in my mouth and sucked on it like the end of a good cigar. In time, it dissolved into a starchy, sticky paste which I tucked into my cheek like a great pinch of Copenhagen snuff. That one bite lasted several minutes. It didn't satisfy any of my body's craving for nicotine. It didn't quench the fire in my lungs, nor still the buzzing in my ears. But it gave me just enough of a tobacco-like sensory fix to keep the brain string from snapping. It was no substitute for a Marlboro, but I would make it suffice. It would be my Marlboro sandwich; my Nuclear Marlboro Sandwich.

I sat there holding the cradle with one hand and my pacifier with the other. I heard Gunner and Ricky start to work again. They let me sit it out for a while. Finally, they came over my way. Standing over W-18, Gunner said, "It's time for this thing to go." I took another chaw of my plug and stuck the remainder into my shirt pocket. I chomped down hard and pulled myself up. I took a moment to steady myself, then held out an open hand to Ricky, who handed me a ratchet. I took a strain on one of the strap bolts and broke it free. We uncradled W-18, hoisted it out and sent it topside. We continued working, and I kept a piece of my Nuclear Marlboro Sandwich in my mouth at all times, making sure to pass the aroma through my nasal passages often. Sometime during the remaining hour or so of the operation, I got nipped again by the Great White Beast, in the right knee. It hurt and it bled, but I ignored it as best I could.

When we had sent the last of the Dragon's children topside, we unhooked the hoist and put it in the lift to send it to its storage place above. I was about to activate the lift, when Gunner said, "Dick, you look like death warmed over. Go ahead and ride up with the hoist. Get those punctures on your legs bandaged. Me and Ricky'll secure."

"Thanks, Gunner," I said, and climbed into the lift and sat down next to the hoist. As I reached for the "Up" button, Ricky got in one last jibe.

"Just a non-hacker," he said grinning. "Just a non-hacker. Ha!"

"Oh yeah?" I challenged him, indicating the three bloody spots on my trousers. "How many guys do you know who have been wounded three times by nuclear weapons and lived to brag about it?" I punched the button and rose up. And I never smoked again.

NUCLEAR MARLBORO SANDWICH FOR QUITTING SMOKING

To this day, I have not lost my desire to smoke, nor my fondness for tobacco. Like an addict to any drug, the craving can visit me at any time. Making a peanut butter sandwich can still help me deal with it. Sometimes just thinking about it, and remembering the relief it brought me that day long ago, is enough.

2   large round soda crackers
1   flat can peanut butter
1   sharp object

Spread enough peanut butter on one cracker to make a very thick sandwich. Place the remaining cracker on top. Take healthy bites, but don't chew; just suck on them till they dissolve. If the desire for a smoke is still too strong to resist, take the sharp object and stab yourself in the legs three times, or until the craving goes away.

AN OL' ARKANSAS STRAWBERRY

A.K. Douglas could be a boor, but he was also one of the best storytellers I've ever met. He could make up the wildest tales extemporaneously and hold his listeners rapt through the longest nights at sea or evenings in tavern. He also had a large repertoire from which he could respond to requests. My favorite Douglas tale is not printable in any medium and would suffer from the lack of his interpretation. I'll just say that it involved wild animals and a trip home to Arkansas during the winter. Sipping the drink he inspired always brings his stories to mind.

3   ounces Arkansas Everclear or other clear grain alcohol
2   cups sliced strawberries
1¾   cups sour cream
1¾   tablespoon brown sugar
1   ounce Triple Sec
2   cups party ice
2   large, very red, whole strawberries, hulled
1   banana, peeled and cut in half crosswise

Combine the Everclear, sliced strawberries, sour cream, brown sugar, Triple Sec, and ice in a blender and puree. Pour the mixture into iced goblets. Using toothpicks, affix the two hulled strawberries to the business ends of the two banana halves. Use them to garnish the goblets.

Yield: 2
Serving Suggestion: Give her an Ol' Arkansas Strawberry

CHAPTER 2

DAVY JONES' CUPPA JOE

*T*HE SUSTAINING POWER OF A MERE MORSEL *was one of my earliest gastronomic lessons. I was not surprised, therefore, when I later read tales of survival in which people kept their spirits alive, and hence their bodies, with only a mouthful. Or when Pearl Buck's Wang Lung, in her novel* The Good Earth, *endures his craving in the famine with a few dried beans. Given the power of something small to eat, there should be no wonder in the power of something small to drink.*

*T*HEY THAT GO DOWN TO THE SEA IN SHIPS, *that do business on great waters; these see...wonders in the deep.* —Psalms

On the light cruiser *USS Oklahoma City,* the famous "Gray Ghost of the Vietnam Coast," we were crossing the Java Sea, bound south for Jakarta that morning. The equatorial waters were so warm and still that we seemed to be on some quiet pond rather than the farthest reaches of the Pacific. Only our ship disturbed the glassy water. In the distance, clouds rose and formed, and metamorphosed and puffed and spread with startling rapidity. They were mottled with pink, and the color fell shining on the sea. The blue of the water, in turn, reached up to the clouds, where the colors mixed and mingled and unravelled the horizon, confusing the distinction between sea and sky, making the world a billowy sphere of pink and blue and white for us to glide through.

The sphere was composed of two perfectly matched opposing hemispheres, each reflecting into the other. The ship's ripply counterpart shimmered upside down, an undulating alter ego. The ship's eye hung forward and above the prow where the water was yet undisturbed, and to stand there at the eye and look down was to see the sky in the sea and the sea in the sky, and yet both still in their proper places, too. One's own face stared up at one looking down and yet still looking up, each into the other, into the other, "stretching out to the crack of doom," as Macbeth said. To fall in at that place might be to fall into infinity or the looking glass or oneself. We sailed in a cosmic house of mirrors, where, after a time, the real and the shade were indistinguishable. The perfect calm had made this dizzy, delirious thing possible. Only a sudden gale or other rough weather could have spun this tangled scene apart and torn the real from the tendrils of illusion.

Joseph Conrad called this the "Shallow Sea" because of its submarine mountains and plateaus rising up within an anchor chain of the surface. Our Captain had said that if we found a shallow enough spot we would drop anchor for a few hours and have a swim in the sea and a barbecue on the fantail. And that would be fine. The ship's cooks would bring out their best. The band would play jazz and show tunes. We'd sun ourselves and swim and eat and talk about all the beer we'd drink in Jakarta. And the whores. Beautiful Java whores lolling beneath their big umbrellas or beside their little shepherd's tents, scattered along the beaches like starfish. "Venus' little starfish," we called them.

"I'm gonna fuck a ton o' whores!" bantam Sammy Seacrest crowed.

"How many whores in a ton?" I demanded, as ritual prescribed.

17

"Two thousand, unless they're small, ha ha!"

"Then I'm gonna fuck two tons of whores, yo ho!"

"Yo ho!" a chorus answered.

The ship's sonar fathometer was in working order, but still a bosun's mate stood on the fo'c'sle taking soundings with a plumb line. Standing above the prow, like David about to slay Goliath, his watery reflection mimicking him, he swung the weighted end of his line into a blur and then sent it flying from his hand. The little stone arced through the air and raced ahead of the ship, trailing its slender line. Then, like a fisher bird, it dove through the surface and sought the bottom. As the ship made way the bosun hauled in the line till it hung vertical and called out to the navigator, "By the mark...five!" Five fathoms, thirty feet, from the keel to the bottom. Should we have two fathoms he would call, "By the mark...twain!"

Sam "Malibu" Robinson and I were standing at the lifeline, drinking mugs of the bad and ubiquitous Navy "joe." Coffee to a landsman. Black as night, bitter as death, and hot as hell. Despite its deservedly rotten reputation, it seems at times that the U.S. Navy is fueled on this terrible, biting brew. Anyone can tell you that aboard ship, no man is ever more than sixty seconds away from an urn full of it. I have heard people joke that it's made from what the coffee dealers sweep up off the floor. Joke or not, I believe it happens sometimes. It really is bad stuff, but American sailors drink gallons of it.

Sam and I were drinking our mugs of mud, making our obligatory complaints about it and trying to look through the sea for the bottom when we heard Seaman Simms holler from aloft, "Go fuck yourself! Eat shit, you motherfucker, eat shit and die! Eat a mile of shit and die!" He bounded down to the main deck and continued his argument with another seaman. I couldn't tell what the argument was about, but it didn't matter; Simms argued about anything. He was always arguing. He was always right, and the whole goddamn world was wrong and it could all eat shit and die.

"You know, I hate that sonofabitch," I said to Sam. "I really hate his fuckin' guts."

"You and me and a hundred other guys. If he was in our division we'd have to give him a little 'extra military instruction.'"

"I wish something bad would happen to him," I said, still hearing him bitching at his shipmate. "I hope he gets injured. No, no, I hope he fuckin' drowns today. I hope the bastard goes swimming and drowns!" And I meant it.

Simms finished his tirade and stomped past us. He was twenty years old with blond beach-boy good looks and a muscular frame. His face was red and had a look of angry disgust. His eyes bore an injured expression, as if to say, "What's the matter with these assholes? Why don't they shut up and get off my case?"

He stopped near the lifeline and quivered a little. Simms didn't enjoy being angry—he just was. And he always wanted to do things his own way. Whatever he did, he would do a good enough job, and he didn't want anybody telling him how to do it, when to do it, or who to do it with. Simms was uncooperative. And that's a maritime and military sin. On shore, individualism is often valued. On a ship, you need cooperation. A ship's company is a family business.

Simms went back aloft to the cable winch he'd been working on and glared at it. That's how he always started a job; he got mad at it. A slow, sustained, internal rage, that was his style. "Bitter as Navy joe" is how a bunkmate described it. He stripped off his shirt with determined speed, picked up his tools and began again on the offending winch. His lower lip pouted, and the muscles of his arms bulged as he forced the machine to submit to his will. He stripped off its protective plates and ripped at its insides. When he found the guilty piece he was looking for, he tore it out and flung it on the deck. Then, still bare-chested and snorting, he paced deliberately back and forth in front of his quarry. He nudged it with his toe. Satisfied that he was alive, and it was dead, he picked up the corpse and tossed it overboard.

About midday the bottom came to the mark three. The engines reversed, sending a shudder through the cruiser, and then stopped. The ship glided to a slow halt. Chief Bosun's Mate Smith directed the anchor crew as they dropped the massive hook, and the chain thundered through the chute.

I changed into swimwear and met Sam and three others on the main deck. Sam was dressed in his Malibu jams, Sammy Seacrest was buck naked, and the rest of us were in Government Issue. As cooks set up barbecue grills on the fantail, and the ship's band prepared to play, about twenty-five men gathered on deck in a holiday mood and were waiting for the lifeboat to be lowered before we went into the water. Hearty, beer-bellied Chiefs made jokes and slapped each other on the back. A couple of shy junior officers on their first cruise wondered if they should act decorously in front of "the men" or let their hair down and enjoy themselves. Seamen and apprentices were skylarking and playing grab-ass. And we petty officers admired the scene and told ourselves that it was "us that operate this goddamn ship, ain't it?"

A gunner's mate, sitting on one of the ten-foot gun barrels of the forward turret, hollered up to the flying bridge, "Captain, Captain, fly the Jolly Roger!" Captain Butcher leaned over the rail and beamed and gave the high sign. He liked playing pirate too. He gestured to his yeoman. Seconds later the Skull and Crossbones flew up the signal mast and caught an upper-level breeze.

"Hurray!" we all shouted. "Shiver me timbers! Hurray!"

Another flag ran up alongside the Roger and snapped open. It was Captain Butcher's personal standard: Popeye with cutlass in hand and an eye patch, and the motto "Press On Regardless."

"Yahoo!" we cheered and applauded.

"Press On, Press On Regardless! Yeah!"

"Haze gray and under weigh, this motherfucker is A-OK!" we chanted.

"She's the Gray Ghost of the 'Nam coast!"

"Fuckin-ay right!"

Senior Chief Howard, oldest man on board, veteran of the battles of Japan's Iwo Jima and Okinawa, Korea's Inchon, and a score of duels on Vietnam's Yankee Station, spilled over with delight and danced a hornpipe. Others jumped up and down, laughing, cheering, exulting.

The lifeboat was in the water now. It was manned by a cox'n in the stern and a swimmer amidships. And in the bow, armed with an M-14 rifle and watching for sharks, was bosun's mate Al Trevino, who had a Purple Heart and whose uncle was Lee Trevino the golfer. Waving his rifle and shouting, he signaled all safe and secure. Several men leaped in and made a great splashing.

19

"Let's play abandon ship!" Sam yelled.

"Yeah!" the five of us shouted in unison. We raced to the prow to stand above the eye of the ship and ran through the Navy drill.

"All hands stand by to abandon ship!"

"Ship's position is...."

"Nearest land is...."

"Your mother's name is...."

"Steady men. Go in feet first in case you hit some flotsam."

"Cross your legs to protect the family jewels."

"Arms crossed in front and elbows up to protect your handsome face."

"Eyes on the horizon to keep you vertical all the way down."

"Now, leap through the flaming oil and swim under it to safety, just like it says in the book. Away!"

The sea rushed up and swallowed us with a gulp. Breaking the surface in a froth, we swam aft to the stern. Treading water there, we could see through the ocean's perfect clarity to the ship's huge screws. Sammy took a great breath and dove down to the ship's keel, where he "tickled her belly." We went forward again to investigate the anchor chain.

Equatorial seas are delicate and changeable. The reflecting half-domes of the Java Sea are as fragile as the mirrors they imitate. They can shatter and take new form suddenly, from placid calm to churning torment without warning. I felt the sea-change before I was consciously aware of it. Then I saw the ship swing on her anchor as she would do in harbor when the tide shifts. A swell of water, from nowhere, rose up under me, lifting me with it, then dropped me back down into a trough. The next swell rolled heavily over my head, forcing brine into my mouth. I heard some shouts of the other men, but I could see no one among the sudden hillocks of water. The current was carrying me toward the starboard quarter of the ship so I went with it, rising and falling with the sea, till I was alongside the hull. There I found I had to swim hard against the growing mountains of water just to stay put. "Hey," I hollered to the main deck, trying to sound calm. "Somebody throw me a line! Hey, hey, someone on deck. Somebody, help!"

A swell came from behind. It lifted me up. With the sound of the surf it rushed toward the ship and bashed my body against the steel hull. The flowing water pressed me against the ship, forcing air out of my lungs until the wave was spent. As it receded, it took me back with it. Salt burned my eyes. I tried to lift my head to breathe, but the next wave fell on me, tumbling me over, and throwing me against the ship again. As the steel hull came at me, I held my arms out to cushion the blow, but several tons of rushing water bent them like sticks. My lip split against the shock of steel. I drank blood and brine and vomited underwater. A throbbing, spinning buzz filled my head. I clawed the air to rise to it. I could hear the shouting of others as the ocean swirled around them too, but I could now see only shapes and swirls of light and dark.

The ship continued to swing on her anchor till she was nose into the sea. Then the swells dragged me along the side of the hull. They rolled me, scraped me against sharp little barnacles that lacerated my body and cut to the kneebone. I tried to swim against it. I swear I tried with all my might. But I just couldn't swim up those hills of water.

They took me beyond the ship. My body ached from blows and fatigue, and blood seeped out of my scraped arms and legs. The swells wouldn't let me have any air. When I tried to breathe, they forced brine down my throat, and I vomited and my mouth and nose burned. The waves hurled their monstrous weight on me and beat me down into the troughs. I couldn't move. My strength was gone. I was sleepy. I had always thought that in a matter of life or death I could huff and puff and gather the strength to do whatever was needed. But I couldn't even open my eyes.

To me the world became quiet. The thunder of the sea was muffled and distant. I heard no more shouts. The hammering of the waves became a gentle undulation. I became aware that I could see the depths. I saw where the clear blue water near the surface began to darken and then turn black and become void.

"I'm dying," I thought with bemused disappointment. "I'm only twenty-two, I've never even loved a woman, and I'm dying. I've never loved a woman and I'm dying...I've never loved...."

In my soul's eye I looked down upon a white sand beach. It was perfectly clean. No driftwood washed up on it. No fire rings dotted it. No sculpted sand castles and no footprints betold my passing. I slid sadly, gently, painlessly down toward death. The sea rolled easily over me now. I began to feel cold. It started at my feet and moved slowly up. But it was an easy cold. It didn't make me shiver.

Suddenly, I heard a splashing sound, like a hooked fish fighting for life at the end of a line. Someone pulled my head up out of the water, and I began to hear the sea again.

"Okay? Okay?" I heard him say above the roar. My body wouldn't move—it still belonged to Death—but my eyes half opened of their own accord. I recognized the hated Seaman Simms. He had me about the waist in a bear hug. My head leaned against his, and we rose and fell with the waves.

"We're gonna swim together back to the ship, okay?" he shouted.

"No," I murmured. To murmur was to use up all the strength I had. If he would cheat death of me, he would do it alone. He hesitated. Maybe he thought of leaving me. He looked past me, through the hostile sea to the ship. A hue of melancholy softened the ever-present anger in his eyes as he judged the task ahead of him. I can't tell you exactly how a man reaches down to the bottom of his soul for strength. But I can tell you that at that moment, Simms did. The muscles of his face set, and I know—I can swear to it—that he had prepared himself to keep me afloat even if it had to be for the rest of his life. He hugged me very tight and began to swim against the murderous swells. He swam with conviction for three hundred and fifty yards. He swam without the use of his hands, pushing my dead weight before him. He was wearing fins, but they were speed fins, giving him little advantage. He swam mainly on faith and commitment.

I slipped back into darkness on the way home, but I came to as we reached the starboard quarter. Crewmen had hung a cargo net over the side for men to climb up, but I still had no strength. Simms grabbed a line that somebody had thrown down and tied it around me. Then he slipped, exhausted, under the water. Trevino came by in his boat and caught him by the hair and pulled him aboard. A man on deck began to pull me up out of the water. I don't know who he was. All I could see were his arms, big, muscular, tattooed black arms. I decided that's what angels look like.

They laid me on the old-fashioned teakwood-covered deck. I lay there motionless until two men picked me up and carried me below to sick bay. They put me in a bunk in a dark, quiet corner, covered me, and left. I lay there between sleep and waking, between death and life, hearing, feeling, and thinking nothing. No sound, no smell, no sensation penetrated my senses; no time elapsed. I floated in oblivion or infinity. After a long time an old, familiar sensation ran through me. I heard and felt the comforting, caressing thrum of the ship's engines as they came back to life. Then the grinding windlasses lifted the anchor from the bottom and pulled it snug into its socket. The Gray Ghost shivered slightly as she gathered way and pitched easily as she shaped her course southward, away from the maelstrom. Then I slept.

When I awoke, I smelled coffee. Not the coffee you smell in the morning at home or in restaurants. It was the heavy smell of Navy coffee, sharp and burned and bitter. The Navy's favorite saying is that there's the right way, the wrong way, and the Navy way to do anything. That goes for coffee as well as anything else. I opened my eyes to see a hospital corpsman departing, having just given Seaman Simms a mug of joe. Simms was in the bunk across from me.

I wriggled my toes, and they hurt. I wriggled my fingers, and they hurt. Anything I moved hurt. Every muscle in my body ached, and the now-bandaged barnacle cuts burned. I felt empty, like the sea had torn the kernel out of me and thrown back the useless chaff. I gave a little groan, and Simms looked over at me. His usual suspicious, hostile expression was back on his face. I took a little comfort in that, thinking that at least I'd be dealing with the devil I knew. He looked away and took a slurp of his coffee. He rolled it around in his mouth and swallowed, smacked his lips, and sniffed. He looked askance back at me.

He didn't say anything, but he got up and came over to me like he had something to say. He stood there for a moment, suddenly confused or unresolved. He looked like a man standing naked and not knowing what to do with his hands. He sat down on the edge of my bunk, then stared into his coffee for a moment. He looked up at me and, still saying nothing, offered me the big, Navy standard, blue-trimmed, white china mug.

I struggled to sit up and took the mug from him. I could see and smell that the coffee was made to the usual strength: strong enough to wake the dead and scare the living. Some people would call it cowboy coffee because it's said that you could float a horseshoe in it. The aroma was powerful, almost stingingly bitter and burnt. This was not coffee a man would offer to his wife. But I could feel that the smell alone was bringing my senses back to life. I took a cautious sip. It was hot and thick and strong, and it glowed down to my gut, sending out life-giving rays of heat. Its bitterness almost made me shiver, and I caught my breath. I heaved in a huge gulp of air. The burned-black coffee taste clung to my tongue, and my taste buds resonated, singing like vibrating harp strings with the old familiar flavor. The powerful potency of the brew was softened ever so slightly by the traditional Navy cook's method of preparation. He had added a tablespoon of clean sea water to the five-gallon urn. There is some debate as to whether the sea water should be added before or after brewing, but either approach will take some of the snarl out of the coffee. It's not enough sea water to taste salt, only enough to alter the flavor.

I continued to sip the coffee, and with each swallow, the empty feeling inside me filled up a little more. I marveled that coffee so bad could be so good. I drained the cup and finally Simms spoke.

"You want some more?" he asked. I nodded. He took the mug and returned with it filled.

"I put a little sugar in it," he reported. "Cook said it would give you strength." With that, Simms left. I wrapped my hands around the hot mug and hugged it to me. I breathed in the good, bittersweet vapors.

"Not a bad guy, that Simms," I thought. "Not a bad guy."

NAVY JOE, OR COWBOY COFFEE

This is the way I usually make coffee when camping or sailing. If the morning is a quiet one, the first sip never fails to remind me of Simms and the cup of coffee he gave me, and to cause me to ponder the question, "What is good?"

Navy cooks use a percolator, but I find that the following method approaches the true flavor more closely. It is easy to make and is best done in camp or on a boat.

5   heaping tablespoons ground coffee
1   quart cold water
    pinch of salt

In a fireproof pot, mix the coffee with the cold water and salt. *Do not* use gourmet coffee or boutique coffee or anything else with claims to high quality or social standing. Put the pot on the fire and bring it to a boil. Remove from the fire and let the grounds settle for a few minutes. If you don't like a lot of body in your coffee, strain it through a paper towel when pouring it into a mug.

Yield: 4 Cups

ROYAL NAVY GUNFIRE

Gunfire is the British sailor's equivalent of American Navy Joe. In Hong Kong, British and American sailors have traditionally formed waterfront alliances (drinking fraternities) to regale each other with their sea stories and see who can drink the most and talk the dirtiest. Complaints about the chow and junior officers are routine. A British petty officer described making Gunfire as follows.

2   **pints water**
8   **tablespoons very cheap tea**
8   **tablespoons sugar**

Combine the water, tea and sugar in a pot. Put it on a fire and bring it to a boil. Remove from heat and let the leaves settle. God Save the Queen.

CHAPTER 3

PIPER·NIGRUM

DINING WITH THE
HEADHUNTERS

"IN ALL THE DREAMS OF ALL THE POLITICIANS and merchants, sailors and geographers, who pushed back the limits of the unknown world, there is the same glitter of gold and precious stones, the same odour of far-fetched spices." —Sir Walter Raleigh

Entili, chief of the Iban tribal village in the heart of Borneo, sat cross-legged and bare-chested, his big tattoos animated by his rippling muscles. Through our interpreter he commanded me to stand up and give account. He demanded to know who we were and why we had come to his domain.

"Good question," I thought as I stood before the assembled tribespeople. "Why in the Sam Hill have we brought ourselves into an uncharted jungle peopled with headhunters? We don't even know if we're in Malaysia or Indonesia; we've gone clean off the map!"

One of many reasons for this mad quest was my interest in spices, an abiding passion I first acquired during my naval service in the Far East. With thirty-six days leave, I was pursuing black pepper, that ubiquitous, taken-for-granted necessity of virtually every kitchen on earth and ship's galley at sea. I had come to find its source, where it grows wild in profusion; where it is used in food, magic, love potions, and healing; where it expresses itself in ten genera and over a thousand species.

Of its many varieties, the best known is *Piper nigrum*, the dried berry (a peppercorn) of a woody perennial vine native to tropical Asia. Over 100,000 tons are shipped annually from Asia and Brazil, almost a third of it to the United States. It accounts for fifty percent of the world's spice trade. It finds its way to the table, into processed foods, perfumes, and medicines.

Pepper's curative powers are reflected in virtually all the ancient pharmacopoeia. Hippocrates prescribed it for feminine disorders and Theophrastus as an antidote to hemlock. (Socrates should have consulted Theophrastus.) My experience in Borneo would become further testimony to its medicinal value.

Its most dramatic impact on human affairs has been in its trade. Until modern times, it was so precious that it was sold not by weight but corn by corn. Pliny complained that Romans spent more than 50 million sesterces on it. In A.D. 412, Rome was ransomed to Alaric and his Visigoths for gold, silk, and 3,000 pounds of pepper. Columbus and others were in search of a route to the Indies where Marco Polo had told them they would find the source of pepper. It was used as a medium of exchange in medieval Europe. A pound of it could set a serf free in France or buy a slave in the Levantine bazaar. In the Spice Islands, pepper fiefs sprung up like Colombian drug baronies, and nations went to war for it. Except for gold, no other commodity has been so prized, so fought over, or has brought so much satisfaction to so many people.

And so, we went off to find it in Borneo, the largest of the Spice Islands. My friend Mack and I left our ship in Hong Kong and followed the spice route to the Land of Pepper. We arrived at the town of Sibu at the mouth of the muddy Rajang River in Sarawak, Malaysia. From there we traveled upriver by scheduled passenger boat, then by motor launch, then dugout canoe, and finally, by foot. Along the way, we stopped at the little settlement of Kapit. This village was the farthest reach of the old spice traders. Here they were met by the jungle dwellers who brought them pepper, game, and tree resins. This spot was the jumping-off point into the unknown, into the immemorial pepper forests.

Our luck was good in Kapit, for we met David. Half Chinese and half Malay, he was working at some fetch-and-carry job, and not only could he speak a pidgin-style British English, but also Iban, the local dialect.

In the voice of strong young men on a mission we told him, "You come with us, pal. We're on an adventure." (We were even wearing pith helmets, I swear.) David didn't think twice. He threw a toothbrush and a shirt into a bag and said, "We bloody go!" That was his favorite word, "bloody," and it rhymed with "body."

David advised us to bring some presents for the native people we would meet in the interior. He suggested a case of whiskey, five pounds of tobacco, printed tee shirts, and a few cans of food and an opener. He said the people might not care for the food but would appreciate the "bloody" cans.

With all our supplies, we set out for "Indian country." As we traveled, Mack and I often sang. Our favorite was the theme from "Rawhide." We tried to teach it to David, but he just giggled and looked extremely amused. After strenuous jungle travel, somewhere upriver, we met up with one of the jungle dwellers. He wore a loincloth and had gorgeous tattoos all over his body. Some were floral designs, others geometric, and still others resembled an intricate paisley print. Each one represented an enemy slain, a child fathered, a successful hunt, or a rite of passage. He carried a blowpipe with poison darts. We told him that we were friendly and that we came bearing gifts. He told us his name, which sounded a bit like Jerry, so that's how we addressed him. He took us to his slim and pretty wife, whose name was Eetwat. She wore a sarong and also had tattoos, like all the other men and women of their tribe, and she looked at us with large-eyed delight. The look on her face was like that of a young girl who has just been given a new Barbie doll or a kitten, and she adopted us on the spot.

They led us into their village, where the people dwelt in a longhouse by the river. It stood on stilts to accommodate the river's flood and was divided into apartments of roughly equal size, with a large common room in the center. A veranda ran the length of the structure. Jutting out from the common room was a deck of bamboo poles laid about an inch apart. Beneath that was an enclosure containing some two dozen very large pigs. The pigs were fed when somebody simply walked out onto the deck and dumped refuse through the bamboo poles.

A great commotion erupted when we arrived. Most of the adults seemed to be aware that there were palefaces in the world, and a few had even seen them, but the children had never even heard of such critters, and they fled at the sight of us. We were introduced to the chief, Entili, and a few of the elders. Entili was taller than most of his fellows, about five-seven. He had the body of an iron pumper, hard and sinewy. His eyes gazed coolly from a face that bore a look of calm satisfaction. The face seemed to say, without boasting, "I can lick any man in the world." We hauled out our presents, which the chief gave a cursory examination. He declared them to be good and us to be welcome, for the time being. He told us to stay with Eetwat and Jerry, which seemed to please them.

28

As all this was in progress, Eetwat began to prepare food according to the Iban custom of hospitality. We were invited to sit on the ground and wait, and I watched as she cooked a fish over an open fire. She was obviously taking great care with it, as she turned it and sprinkled it with some kind of seasoning which she took from a section of bamboo, crumbling it in her palm and letting it sift through her fingers. The spice was red warrior ants.

Eetwat presented her offering to us with smiles and cooed some sort of happy incantation. The people crowded around to watch, sure in the knowledge that the pale strangers had never before tasted a dish so fine. The tattooed men clutched their blowpipes and rested their hands on their knives. The tattooed women watched us wide-eyed, their bare bosoms heaving with the excitement of the event. The ants were only barely crumbled, just enough to break up the major body parts. I hesitated.

"Mack," I said under my breath. "It's ants; they're feeding us ants!"

"I was trying to pretend they were paprika. Do you think they'd mind if we scraped them off?"

I looked at the tattooed multitude. I looked at the expectation on Eetwat's face. I looked at Entili, who seemed to calmly say, "Eat it or I'll kill you." I looked at the post in the village quad where they hung up the heads of their vanquished enemies. "I think we better eat 'em," I said. "And I think we'd better smile, too. They're starting to look unhappy."

"I'm smiling, I'm smiling!"

I took a large piece of fish with lots of ant parts on it. Hoping none were in a condition to bite back, I put it in my mouth and chewed, smilingly. "Mmmm," I said, nodding to our hosts.

"Yum!" said Mack, patting his tummy.

The heads and jaws of the ants crunched audibly between my teeth. I saw David chewing calmly, glancing askance at us with a sardonic twinkle in his eye. I had expected the bitterness of gall, but to my surprise the ants tasted good. The formic acid that coats their bodies tastes like a mixture of lemon and tarragon, giving them a sort of bearnaise flavor. Once I got past the idea of the wriggly little critters in my mouth, Eetwat's fish made a pretty good meal. The only thing I didn't quite get used to was the crunch. I made a mental note to suggest to Eetwat that she mash the ants in a mortar and use them like pesto.

The day after our arrival, Mack went hunting with Jerry and some of the other braves. An avid hunter, he was pretty excited at the thought of a primitive chase. "I'm gonna get a wild boar!" he announced. "I'll borrow somebody's blowpipe and some poison darts and get a wild boar! Maybe they'll teach me how to make my own poison. Or do you think that might be some witch doctor's secret?"

I went with Eetwat and some others to help gather wild pepper, which they harvest for their own use as well as for trade. On a hillside not far from the longhouse the vines rioted, creeping and climbing everywhere we looked. They sported large, philodendron-like leaves, and they climbed up trees and curled around rocks higher than a tall man's head. The berries grew in slender clusters that hung from the vines like jewelry, each bearing fifty or sixty gems. The immature ones were green, and the ripe ones red.

As we gathered berries, Eetwat introduced me to the pleasures of betel nut, the fruit of an Asian palm tree. Crumbling about a teaspoon of the soft nut meat, she wrapped it in a leaf of the pepper vine's cousin, *Piper betel*, and smeared it with lime paste. Then she would hand it to me and coo something in Iban. As I chewed the prepared wad, the three ingredients mixed and turned the bright red that stains the mouths of millions of Asians. Soon my salivary glands gushed, and I had to swallow repeatedly or the juice would overflow my mouth and stain my chin. The taste was pleasant, sour and a little fruity, like an acidic wine or a tart berry. Some people spit the juice, but I like to swallow it. It's mildly intoxicating due to the alkaloid arecoline. In exchange for this initiation, I taught her how to play tic tac toe, which she thought wonderful and later taught the whole village to play.

With several baskets full of both ripe and unripe berries, we returned to the village, where the women processed them. To produce black pepper, they spread immature berries on mats to dry. As they dry, their skins wrinkle and turn black. They are then ready to use whole or ground.

White pepper is a more involved process. Ripe berries are soaked to soften the skins and then threshed, like grain, in order to extract the white core. They are then left in the sun to dry. To thresh the berries, the Iban put them in a wooden trough and pound and knead them with the ends of heavy staves. White pepper is less aromatic and more biting than black because the nonvolatile piperine, the hot stuff in pepper, is concentrated in the core. The volatile oils that are the aroma constituents are more plentiful in the skin.

The Iban can produce another kind of white pepper by rubbing the skins off dried berries using a wooden mill that resembles a hand-operated millstone. The result is "decorticated" pepper. It's the same color as white but tastes more like black.

Toward the end of the day I sat on the longhouse veranda relaxing, and Eetwat brought me a handful of prepared betel. She smiled and cooed in her winning way, and we played tic tac toe, scratching our marks on the wood of the veranda. She seemed to think that Mack and I were a pretty agreeable sort of strangers. Sometimes she would reach over and pinch me on what to her was my big nose, and then she'd giggle and chatter about who-knows-what. I'd tell her things like, "If you ever get divorced, I'm going to come back here and marry you, and we'll have two-point-seven children and a Ford station wagon, ha ha." Of course she didn't know what I was saying, but I think she got the gist of how I felt.

When Mack returned from the hunt, he had a long face. "What's the matter, mighty Nimrod, no luck?"

"Worse! You know those bamboo sections they carry, the ones we thought were for water?"

"Yes," I said through the betel nut buzz.

"Well, they're not for water! As they go through the jungle they catch bugs. Then they pull off their wings and their legs, and they put them in the bamboo. Then when they get hungry they have a nice, fresh snack!"

"No!"

"Yes!"

"Did they...?"

"Yes!"

"Did you...?"

"Yes, I had to. I'm not gonna refuse anything from a head hunter on his own turf."

"How did they taste?"

"I don't know. I didn't want to chew them, so I took only small ones and swallowed them whole."

"You mean they died in your stomach?"

"Yes. And they gave me heartburn. And gas. And now, every time I burp, it's like one of their spirits gets caught in my throat."

Poor Mack. I gave him the biggest chaw of betel I had. "Here you go, buddy," I said, "cop a buzz. No telling what we'll have for dinner tonight."

On another day, Mack and I went for a walk in the jungle. David was nowhere to be found. The Iban have some interesting sexual mores, and he was taking full advantage. We learned that they refer to the amorous pursuit as "hunting." David was proving a very mighty hunter, and not disposed to hunting in a pack of, say, three. We bitterly regretted our inability to speak the language.

As David hunted that day, we went on a gathering expedition. We were seeking a local fruit that I have never seen anywhere else in the world. It's the color and size of a lime and is shaped like an egg. It has a rind the thickness of an orange, but it breaks easily. If you hold the fruit in your hands and give it a twist, the rind will break in a clean line around the circumference. Then you lift off one hemisphere and see, shimmering inside, what looks like a golf-ball-sized Thompson seedless grape with the skin removed. It even tastes like the grape, and might have made a monster raisin. We had no idea what the thing was called, so we called it "grapeyfruit." We ate gobs of them, but the Iban use them for making liquor.

We were out in back of the village and had gathered up a lot of grapeyfruit. I was sitting under a tree relaxing and Mack was throwing stones at a leafy, bushy hillside. Suddenly we heard a crashing sound and then the gurgle of running water. One of Mack's stones had hit a precarious little clay pipe that the villagers had rigged up to bring clean water from a spring into the village. They had had it pouring into the pigpen beneath the deck, next to the chief's apartment.

"Uh oh," we both said.

"Mack, you've destroyed the people's water supply."

"Do you think they'll take it hard?"

"They won't take it easy. Their lives are in peril now." Mack knew I was kidding him, but didn't know how much.

"Maybe we could fix it," he said hopefully.

I told Mack that in cases like this, they strip the offender naked and give him an hour's head start into the jungle. If they catch him, they hogtie him to a pole and lug him back to the village like so much meat. There they lash him to a stake. All the kids get to throw stuff at him while the men beat drums and chant. When they get to a fever pitch they bring out the women, who torture the unfortunate sod with hot firebrands, taking care not to neglect the family jewels.

"Jungle justice ain't pretty, Mack. But it's effective."

31

Like I said, Mack knew I was teasing him. But he was starting to sweat it. We were, after all, in Indian country. And the cavalry was very far away. Mack kept touching his crotch, just to reassure himself, I guess.

We started trudging back to the longhouse with our harvest of grapeyfruit. "Hey," Mack said brightly, "we don't have to tell them. We could just play dumb. Maybe they won't even notice."

"I dunno, Mackie. Seems to me the men will be pretty thirsty when they come back from the hunt. And if they haven't had any luck, they won't be in a very good mood."

We were getting pretty close to the longhouse and Mack said, "Maybe I'll just confess. Be up front, you know? I'll bet they'd cut me some slack."

"Or cut your throat. You never know with headhunters."

Mack laid low all that afternoon and chewed an awful lot of betel nut. I saw two guys notice the dry pipe. They went up the hill, the water started flowing again, they came down the hill. And that was the end of it. But I didn't tell Mack. I was having too much fun. I kept making up and telling him of newer and better tortures that the natives might perpetrate on offenders. Like the one where they chop off a piece of your living body every day, then cook and eat it in front of you. After a month you're nothing but a blind and tongueless basket case stinking of gangrene. You wish they would just make a roast of you and have done with it. But instead, they let the kids use you as a football. Boy, did I have fun. And boy, did I get mine later.

That evening Eetwat and Jerry decided to give us a feast in their apartment. They killed a chicken (I think it was a chicken), picked some strange-looking vegetables and got out a great quantity of rice which they grew in a small field nearby. They also invited four or five youths and maidens of the tribe. David told us that this was "big bloody honor." We hadn't seen David for some time, but he was joining us now to rest up from so much "hunting" and to fuel up for further pursuits. The way he eyed the girls in the apartment made it clear who his next quarry would be. (And he would stalk them alone, the bastard.)

Eetwat put all of her ingredients into a black iron pot with some ants and herbs and made a stew. Nothing much of it was recognizable, but it tasted good and Eetwat seemed to love playing hostess. Jerry looked on proudly. I told Eetwat that her husband was the luckiest guy in town. I think she understood me, too, even before David translated.

After we had all eaten our fill, Mack and I sang "Rawhide" and they all liked that, although David giggled all the way through. I then took out my camera and snapped a flash picture. The Iban froze for a second when it went off, then laughed till their faces hurt. They thought it was the funniest thing they ever saw. They made me take several more just so they could have some more laughs.

We were all having a high old time when one of the men of the tribe came through the door in great excitement. He announced that we were summoned to the presence of Entili. "Chief say you come," David translated. "You have dinner with him."

"Great. When?"

"Right now."

"Tell the chief thanks, but we're stuffed."

David looked at us like we were joking or stupid and he couldn't tell which. I think the survival instinct returned to Mack and me simultaneously when we both blurted, "But we'll go, we'll go! Oh yeah!"

David looked relieved and Eetwat and Jerry looked like they derived some kind of honor from having their guests invited to the chief's table. (Actually, they sit on the floor and eat with their hands.) The youths and maidens looked excited.

The messenger conducted us to the chief's apartment where an old woman met us at the door. She took over from there, ushered us in, and seated us next to the chief on the floor. A gray-haired elder and the chief's dad sat with us. Chief Entili addressed both of us as "Tuan." David said, "That mean bloody good chap."

We were all sitting cross-legged in a circle, and the old woman set a big dish of rice in the middle. Then Entili brought out two cans of the food we had brought and opened them, using the new opener with a satisfying expertise. We tried to eat sparingly, but he kept pushing food at us and calling us "Tuan" and smiling a lot.

When we had forced down all the food, we were finally able to call it quits. I tell you my head was spinning, I was so full. With a certain gravity the chief presented the empty tin cans to the elder. He seemed to offer him advice or instructions on their use, and they turned them over and examined them carefully. That done, the chief held up one finger and made some kind of announcement. He called to the attending woman, and she brought us a bottle of liquor. It wasn't the whiskey that Mack and I had brought; we could tell from the old reused bottle. It was grapeyfruit moonshine.

The woman brought a couple of glasses, two coconut shells, and a clean empty can. With great ceremony the chief poured us each a measure. I could smell a strong odor of grapeyfruit—almost overpowering—spicy sweet and alcoholic, like grapeyfruit perfume. The tribesmen knocked theirs back neat, rinsing their mouths with it before swallowing, so I did too.

I want to tell you that stuff tasted like piss! And searing hot piss, too! And those headhunters sat there smacking their lips and called for another round. Jesus, Joseph, and Mary, I don't know how I got the next draught down. And on my full stomach, too. It's a wonder I didn't just puke on the spot. Maybe the first round just knocked my tastebuds down for a count of eight, and that's how I survived the next shot.

I looked over at Mack, and he seemed a bit shaken too. Then the chief made another announcement, and David and the tribesmen heartily approved. David said, "Hey, big news. Entili say we have big party, all for you blokes. Bloody good news, eh?"

"Now?" Mack wheezed.

"Right now."

"Oh, God."

We were taken to the common room where the people were gathering. Some old women rolled out a big ceremonial mat in the center of the room. The thing was woven from several different grasses and had the most intricate designs that were similar to the people's tattoos. David said it belonged to the chief and was used only on special occasions. In a corner, another woman attended a small cast-iron brazier that smoldered with a heady incense. She replenished it from time to time from a bag of leaves, twigs, and pepper berries.

33

When all the tribal members had arrived, they sat around the walls in ranks three deep, leaving the center space empty. The chief made a big announcement and all the tribe nodded agreement. David translated: "Entili say you tell your story."

"Eh?"

"Chief want for you to stand up and say who you are, why you come, what you want." You may find it curious that we had been in the village for some days, and no one had asked us our story before. The answer is simple: people who are still happily living in the Stone Age are just not in a hurry for much of anything. At least, that's my theory.

I looked at the people of the tribe. They were all very quiet and expectant, eager to hear whatever we might have to say. I wondered what they would do if they weren't pleased by what they heard. I looked at Entili and I couldn't tell if his eyes were cool or smoldering.

I looked at Mack. "Maybe you ought to make a speech, Mack," I said as casually as I could.

"No."

"C'mon."

"No."

"You're bigger than I am—maybe they'll be scared of you."

"You're older, and it was your idea to come here in the first place."

I was stuck. Mack was adamant, and the folks were starting to stir. I stood up, hoping for the best. Drawing a deep breath, I began: "My friends, and I hope you are my friends." I waited as David translated. The people nodded. "We come from America," I continued, "a land far away. We come in peace."

Mack choked on a giggle.

"And we come because we heard that you are all nice folks, that you have the best pepper in the land, and we wanted very much to visit you." I smiled hopefully all around. Mack waved. The people seemed to approve, and I warmed to my subject. Nodding to David to continue translating, I proudly said, "We are two men who travel far. We are men of the United States Navy." I waited for the translation and the good impression that would surely follow.

"Hey, what you think?" David chided. "I can't say that."

"Why not? It's true."

"I can't say navy. They got no word to say navy. You look. You see ship? Ha ha ha."

"Oh, yeah. Okay, tell them we're military men."

That wouldn't do either. They'd never seen an army, but the chief and a gray-haired elder had an idea of the word "army." The chief had seen British colonial troops during a trip downriver in his youth. And David said the old guy had taken the heads of five Japanese soldiers who had gotten lost in the jungle during the Pacific war. "But nobody know military. Ha ha ha. They don't even know bloody ocean!"

"Well," I said, taking a little linguistic license, "say we're warriors."

"Okay," he said with that sardonic twinkle in his eye. "They know that word."

"And do the best you can with ocean."

34

And so it was. To the people of the village, we were warriors who went about in a big canoe, on the big water, way downstream. And our tribal name was "Merica." The chief was satisfied, and so were his people. Entili announced that a party should commence, that liquor should flow, that drummers drum, musicians play, and the people dance and sing as much as they desired.

The first thing they did was bring out more of that grapeyfruit paint thinner and start pouring liberal draughts for men, women, and children alike. As full as I was, I didn't want to drink any more, but this was a party in our honor. The stuff had started to go down a little easier, though. Partly due to previous exposure and partly due to pride, I couldn't let those women and children outdrink a Warrior of the Big Canoe. They were knocking that stuff back like Gatorade between puffs on their home-rolled cigars. They make them from some kind of wild tobacco that I'm sure would make a strong man weak. I was just glad I had quit smoking and didn't have to match them stogie for stogie.

A couple of the braves came over to us and asked to see our tattoos. Obviously, to them, we would have to have some, since we were warriors. After all, they had them. Now, I have never had a tattoo and have never wanted one. But how does a Warrior of the Big Canoe explain that to a guy who wears his bravery all over his body? This, my friends, this is where I got mine. Mack, the son of a bitch, does have a tattoo.

And his is not even a worthy tattoo. Compared to the graphic scenes on the chests of mariners, the Louisville Slugger labels on their penises, and the grinning faces on their buttocks, his is miniscule. He has a little tiny chain around his left ankle. B.F.D.! But, he has one more than I do.

He told everybody that each link in the chain represented an enemy killed in battle. He said that when you got your chain to link up like his then you became an official Great Warrior. I was sick. I was sick, I tell you. Everybody made a fuss over Mack, the official Great Warrior. They poured him more grapeyfruit, which was starting to taste okay by now. And the women all wanted to wear his pith helmet. I showed them the scar on the bottom of my left foot where I stepped on glass and had to have stitches when I was six years old. I told them an enemy soldier had bayonetted me there when I tried to kick him. But nothing was as good as a tattoo. Yeah, I got mine all right. Yessiree. And Mack, if you're reading this, up yours! I had some more grapeyfruit to soothe my injured ego, and I was starting to feel better, when two of the tribal maidens were brought over to us by a delegation of young men. David said that they were going to honor us now with a song. And, as it was a ceremonial song, it had to be done in proper form. We were to sit on our heels with hands on knees. One of the girls would sit in front of each of us and look shyly at the floor. She would then tap us lightly on the hands to indicate to whom she was singing. Everyone had hushed and was listening to hear the song the maidens would sing to the Warriors of the Big Canoe.

Mack got his song sung to him first because he was the goddamn official Great Warrior sonofabitch! Damn! And I was his senior in rank. Was I in a snit. David said the song was about a great warrior, and I listened carefully for any word that might sound like "official." When the one girl finished, the other girl sang the same song to me, so if Mack was official in their eyes so was I, and I told him so.

Everybody liked the singing and wanted more. So the chief said that Mack and I should sing a song. I was ready for this. I sang "Moon River," as they lived on the river bank. I sounded pretty good too, I don't mind telling you. I put lots of feeling into it. And I didn't forget any of the words, even though the grapeyfruit cocktail was starting to go to my head.

"Top that," I told Mack. "Mr. official-ass Great Warrior."

Ha! He couldn't think of anything to sing. He asked me for a suggestion. "How about the official-ass Great Warrior song—there must be one." But then I relented. I figured we were even. "Do you know the 'National Anthem'?" I asked him.

"I can't sing that very well."

"How about 'America the Beautiful'?"

"Oh yeah. I can sing that." And so he sang it with gusto, and it was well received.

The best was yet to come, including more grapeyfruit, which was going down like water by now. Two guys brought out these one-stringed instruments, one of them plucked, one played with a bow, and a third fellow had a drum. Everybody settled into their seats around the wall, three ranks deep, and the guys started playing.

They played a haunting melody, rhythmic and simple, but lovely. It was a graceful tune, that's what it was. And it bespoke something very, very ancient. It calmed the people like a narcotic mist. They made little sounds that emanated from the backs of their throats, and they swayed at the shoulders and hips. Then one of the maidens of the tribe got up, almost in a trance. She moved to the center of the room and began dancing. Her dance had only a few steps, but like the tune, it was simple and graceful and haunting. She looked like a piece of silk, hanging in space and undulating in a drifting air. She spoke with her hands, a little like a hula, and turned slow pirouettes. She was a flower, blossoming to the time of the music.

Three of the maidens took turns dancing as the people murmured quiet approval and also poured more grapeyfruit. Suddenly the music changed to a banging, drumming sound and the girls ran back to their seats. The tallest man in the village (about five-eight) leaped into the center. He was waving an ancient-looking sword that they call a *parang* and he was wearing a robe made from the skin of a Malaysian bear stuck with eagle feathers. The drummer drummed and the banger banged and the dancer whirled around with his parang, doing battle with unseen foes. Everybody made ooh and ahh sounds and drank more liquor.

After winning his battle the dancer and the tune changed, and he started doing a masculine version of the maidens' dance. He had the same kind of simple steps and grace, and it actually looked pretty easy. I said, "Hey, Mack. I bet I can do that."

"Why don't you go cut in?"

So I did. I knocked back another noggin of grapeyfruit nectar, then got up, walked over to the guy and pantomimed that I wanted to try his dance. Everybody loved the idea and the band played on. The dancer gave me his bearskin, but he kept the *parang*.

I found that I could imitate the dance perfectly, but I threw in another step of my own just to amaze them. They were fascinated! They bent forward for a better look, taking careful note of my intricate footwork. They exchanged many remarks. They were obviously pleased to learn that people of the Merica tribe could do a proper dance. I said, "Mack! Quick! Take my picture. I'm dancing among the headhunters." He got out my camera and took a good shot of me in that bearskin.

Then they made Mack get up and dance. He kind of jumped around the floor for a while, and they couldn't decide if that was art or not. Then I did an Irish jig, thinking to broaden their experience. I don't think they understood it. So Mack then tried out a square dance on them. He do-si-doed with an imaginary partner and tried to dance a square with only one corner. The people seemed to think it looked kind of dumb, and since I still have a picture of it, I can tell you they weren't far off the mark.

By this time, a dozen or so of the people had risen and were dancing variations of the maidens' dance. Mack and I each had another pull of the grapeyfruit, this time right from the bottle, and Mack said, "I know. Do your fish face for them." I sucked in my cheeks and brought my lips together vertically, then moved them up and down like a perch. I was getting sort of blind by this time, so I don't know how the people took it, but I was having a great time. I borrowed somebody's blowpipe and pretended that I was hunting for wild boar or the neighboring tribe or who knows what. I shook it at some imaginary enemies and issued a few dire threats to them.

Since the pipe was about the length of a rifle with a bayonet on it, I started going through the manual of arms. But I kept bogging down at position number six. I couldn't remember if it was parade rest or port arms or what. So I just held it up at right shoulder arms and went marching around the room singing, "Hut two three four." I thought I could give the tribesfolk the flavor of the military life that I had been unable to express by means of vocabulary. Mack started singing "Oh we oh, we ohhum," like the witch's guards do in the *Wizard of Oz*, so I marched around to that for a while too, weaving in and out among the dancers. Then I thought I would use the blowpipe to demonstrate the art of pole vaulting, but Mack warned me I might break it and the owner would get sore.

I decided to show them backward somersaulting instead. Now I have to take Mack's word for what happened next, because I sort of blacked out. He says that I was doing a pretty good, though wobbly, backward somersault, when I reached the position where you're standing on your hands, ready to curl up for another roll back. I was right near the chief, fairly vertical and head down when I sort of tipped over sideways and twisted forward and fell on my face and belly in an attitude of genuflection or kowtow in front of Chief Entili. It must have looked pretty good, like I'd done it on purpose. And I'm sure the chief thought the Warriors of the Big Canoe were putting on a good show. But when I didn't move afterward, it was pretty obvious that the grapeyfruit had got me.

Mack says that's when I began to vomit. He says that I began to push up a mole-hill of undigested rice, red-flecked with ant bodies, right there in front of Entili. Worse, I was doing it on his swell ceremonial mat. Now remember that I hadn't told Mack that the water pipe situation was okay. He was afraid that might still be a hot issue, and here I was desecrating something that might even be sacred.

Mack will tell you himself that he was pretty scared. He started scooping up my vomit in his hands and running to the windows to throw it out. He kept saying, "I'm sorry! I'm sorry, chief! I'll clean it up!" Then he'd run back for more, all the while saying, "I'm sorry, please don't be sore." For all I know, he broke down and confessed to wrecking the waterpipe, too, and threw himself on the mercy of Entili. But the chief wouldn't have understood, and David had long since disappeared for a liaison with one of the dancing girls.

Mack got up as much puke as he could, using only his hands. Then he picked me up by the collar and dragged me out of the building to clean me up. He is a real pal. I know he took me down to the river, because I woke up in it. But only briefly. After that I remember the sound of voices and feeling many hands carry me. That is the end of my personal record of that evening.

I woke up the next day on the floor of Eetwat's and Jerry's apartment. A herd of water buffaloes was stampeding somewhere between my ears. The world was spinning, and I can honestly say that I've never felt worse in my whole life.

My bladder was about to burst, and excuse my language, but I had to piss like a racehorse. Nobody was around, and I was afraid to stand up so I struggled, slowly, to my hands and knees and crawled out of the apartment. On the way out I smelled some of the grapeyfruit firewater from somewhere and went into the dry heaves. Shaking and weak, I dragged myself, half-blindly, down the walkway and stopped when I found myself on the big terrace that overhangs the pig pen. I collapsed face down on the bamboo poles and lay there gasping for breath. And it didn't smell too good either, above those pigs.

I really had to go something terrible, but I just could not move. It is a tribute to the human mind that I was able to devise a plan, even under those stressful conditions. I reached down with only one hand, and unzipped my pants and pulled out Mr. Happy. I then stuffed him between two of the bamboo poles, then relaxed and let go. I don't know how the pigs took this because I passed out again, in midstream. When I came to I was in a position of coitus, as you might say, with the bamboo. Mr. Happy was dangling like a piece of bait above the swine, who were only about two feet below. I was glad that pigs are not generally taught to sit up and beg. I pulled myself together, as it were, feeling very sick but proud of my achievement.

I crawled into the common room then, and propped myself up against a post. I sat there in a daze until Eetwat came and found me, having discovered that I was gone from the apartment. She said, "Oh, tsk, tsk, tsk," and patted me on the shoulder. It's curious how "Oh, tsk, tsk, tsk" sounds the same in almost any language. She ran and got me some water to drink and a pile of betel nut. She wrapped up several chews for me, then she straightened my hair and wiped my sleep-sodden eyes out with her bare fingers. She made signs that said Mack and David had gone for a hike or a hunt and would be back later. I couldn't hold back a belch, and it became obvious to Eetwat that I had a bellyache, lots of gas, and heartburn. She went and got two dried peppercorns, which she crushed between two small stones, then wrapped in a betel leaf to make a fat pill which she gave me with some water, and soon my stomach felt much better. The rest of the day I did nothing but sit against that post and chew betel and swallow pepper pills. Sometimes I found enough strength to moan, but I had to husband my resources. Later in the afternoon, when the sunlight was slanting and highlighting the dust particles in the air, the men of the tribe came back from forest and field, and they all trooped into the common room where they saw me. The chief pointed down at me and said something, and they all laughed. Somebody else said something, and they laughed again. They went chuckling off to their apartments, two of them marching and singing "Oh we oh, we ohhum."

"Ya lousy savages," I thought miserably. "I'd like to get you in a Hong Kong cocktail lounge and see how you stand up to a dozen frozen margaritas. Ya goddamn cannibals." I swear, I felt like I wanted to cry. But soon Eetwat returned. She said, "Oh, tsk, tsk, tsk," and she patted my shoulder, and she cooed a little Iban coo, and I soon felt better. She nursed me all day and into the night. Sometimes she even put the pepper pills into my mouth with her own fingers and let me spit the spent, dry betel pulps into her hand. That woman was the soul of human kindness. And ever after, I called her "Doctor Pepper." If she wandered down to the Big Water, she could always count on me for a hand.

There are a lot of things that I have eaten and drunk around the world. Most of them I have enjoyed and hope to enjoy again. But Chief Entili's rotgut grapeyfruit Borneo booze just isn't one of them.

INDIAN LOVE POTION FOR MEN

The original use of pepper, as with any spice, was not culinary but mystical. The special properties of spices were believed to be governed by the stars and planets. Pepper was said to belong to the planet Venus, and many love philtres were concocted with it. The Indian sage Kalyanamalla recommended this as a sure aphrodisiac.

1   ounce black pepper, finely ground
4   pepper leaves or substitute bay leaves
1   cup raisins
1   cup honey

The directions, according to Kalyanamalla, are: "Take and grind all together in a mortar. The man who rubs his lingham (nether parts) with this mixture will succeed in bringing even a very old woman into the right frame of mind for love."

Yield: Enough to stimulate an entire barracksful of lusty gentlemen
Heat Scale: Ask her
Serving Suggestion: Use only as directed. Immoderate application could be dangerous.

MOCK GRAPEYFRUIT

4   cups vodka
1   cup white grape juice
1   tablespoon bay rum cologne

Combine all ingredients and be thankful you don't have to drink it.

EETWAT'S PEPPER PORK

The day Jerry and Mack went hunting together they had no luck, so Jerry butchered one of the pigs he had been raising in the pen beneath the longhouse. Eetwat cooked it in a black iron pot over an open fire with fresh green peppercorns, an oniony herb, and a curious little citrus fruit that I have never seen outside of Borneo. I have adjusted the cooking technique to a stove and substituted scallions and oranges for her native ingredients.

1   pound pork chops
    Dredging flour, seasoned
2   tablespoons peanut oil
2   scallions, thinly sliced
    Juice of 1 orange
2   tablespoons green peppercorns (packed in brine), rinsed.

Dredge the chops in the flour. Heat the oil in a skillet to medium high and brown the floured chops. Remove the chops and reduce the heat slightly. Saute the scallions until soft. Return the chops to the pan and add the orange juice. Cover and reduce the heat. Simmer until the chops are barely, barely pink. Uncover and reduce the sauce to the desired thickness. Add the peppercorns, stir, remove from the heat and let sit for two minutes before serving.

Yield: 4 Servings
Heat Scale: Pungent
Serving Suggestions: This dish goes well with wild or brown rice and winter squash or broccoli. A dry Gewurtztraminer is the perfect foil for the slightly smoky young peppercorns.

EETWAT'S FISH OF WELCOME

There is no real substitute for large red warrior ants. Small ones have little taste and black ones are bitter. I'm sure the ones used by Eetwat were dead, because they never ran over her hand. I don't know how she killed them, but you can slaughter yours easily by putting them in the freezer. If, despite your searchings, you can't come up with the right kind of ants, use this recipe. Except for the lack of crunch, it tastes remarkably like the real thing.

1	freshwater fish, 1 to 2 pounds, cleaned
2	tablespoons butter
	Juice of 1 lemon
2	teaspoons dry tarragon or 1 teaspoon fresh
1	teaspoon paprika
	Salt and pepper to taste

Grill the fish over coals. While it cooks, melt the butter. Add remaining ingredients and cook, stirring, for 3 minutes. Drizzle the butter sauce over the grilled fish.

Yield: 4 Servings
Serving Suggestion: Serve at any feast of welcome for Great Warriors or ordinary Joes.

STEAK AU POIVRE (PEPPERED STEAK)

This dish works best if you crush whole black peppercorns between two stones, as Eetwat did in her role as Doctor Pepper. If you haven't got the stones, use the cracked pepper available in most stores.

2	tablespoons crushed black peppercorns or cracked pepper
1	trimmed, 1-inch-thick beefsteak, fat trimmed and reserved
1	teaspoon salt
1	tablespoon lemon juice
1	teaspoon Worcestershire sauce
2	ounces whiskey

Sprinkle half the pepper on a cutting board. Lay the steak on top and press down with the heel of your palm and knead the steak in order to work the pepper into the meat. Repeat the process on the other side.

Rub a skillet with steak fat and sprinkle it with salt. Heat to very high. Add the steak and sear on both sides. Reduce the heat and cook to desired doneness. Remove the steak and drain the fat from the pan. Return the pan to the stove and add the lemon and Worcestershire to deglaze, scraping up any brown bits with a wooden spoon. Return the steak to the pan and add the whiskey. When it begins to sizzle, touch a flame to it and flambé, shaking the pan until the flames die.

Serves: 1
Serving Suggestion: Corn on the cob, green salad, and a cold beer make a perfect ensemble.
Variation: Before deglazing the pan, saute a handful of diced onion.
Heat Scale: Pungent

CHICKEN MADAGASCAR

The first time I enjoyed this dish was at tableside in the revolving restaurant of the Hong Kong Hilton Hotel. It is simple and makes for a great show. You can prepare it at your table over a chafing dish, backpack stove, or a can of Sterno. As you put it together, entertain your guests with true stories of your foreign adventures—or with colorful lies.

2	tablespoons sweet butter
1	pound diced chicken meat
2	scallions cut on the bias into 1/4-inch pieces
1	ounce peppermint schnapps
½	cup heavy cream
2	tablespoons green peppercorns (packed in brine), rinsed
	Salt to taste

Melt the butter in a skillet over medium heat. Brown the chicken. Add the scallions and cook for about 10 minutes, stirring occasionally. Add the schnapps. When it begins to sizzle, touch a flame to it and set it alight. Shake the pan until the flames die. Add the cream and peppercorns and bring to a boil. Salt to taste. Serve at once.

Serves: 4
Serving Suggestion: Serve on a bed of white rice with steamed asparagus on the side.
Variation: Use pork loin instead of chicken and sour cream instead of sweet cream.

PRE-COLUMBIAN CURRY

Long before Europeans brought the chile pepper to Asia in the sixteenth century, Indians were making curry. The chief firespice available to them then was the venerable *Piper nigrum.*

2	tablespoons butter
1	onion, thinly sliced
3	cloves garlic, chopped
1	teaspoon minced ginger
2	teaspoons freshly ground black pepper
1	teaspoon white pepper
1	teaspoon turmeric
8	ounces lentils, washed and drained
3	cups water
	Salt to taste

Melt the butter in a saucepan and saute the onion, garlic, and ginger until tender and brown. Add the black pepper, white pepper, and turmeric and cook for one minute. Add the lentils and cook, stirring, for 1 minute. Add the water and bring to a boil. Cover, reduce heat, and simmer. Salt to taste. The lentils are done when they are reduced to a porridge, about 40 minutes.

Serves: 4
Heat Scale: Pungent

SICHUAN HOT AND SOUR SOUP

The Chinese use white and decorticated pepper extensively in noodle dishes and soups. This soup is an excellent one for a cold winter's night in Sichuan or even a warm day in west Texas.

5	cups pork or chicken stock
4	wild mushrooms, such as chanterelles or morels, soaked in 1 cup water until soft and then coarsely chopped; reserve soaking water
½	pound julienned pork or chicken
½	pound straw or white mushrooms or both, sliced
1	tablespoon white pepper
2	tablespoons white vinegar
3	tablespoons soy sauce
1	dash dry sherry

1   tablespoon cornstarch dissolved in a little water to make a paste
1   egg, beaten
¼   teaspoon sesame oil
2   scallions, minced

Bring the stock and mushroom soaking liquid to a boil. Add the meat and all the mushrooms, cover, and simmer 15 minutes. Add the pepper, vinegar, soy sauce, and sherry and simmer for 5 minutes. Thicken with the cornstarch paste. Slowly add the beaten egg, stirring gently. Sprinkle with sesame oil and minced scallions.

Serves: 6
Heat Scale: Pungent

QUEMADO

The word *quemado* is simply the Spanish for "burned." No one knows exactly where this concoction originated, but all agree it is one for lovers, for it mimics their passion. It is wonderful served beside a campfire.

4   whole black peppercorns
     Juice of 2 lemons
2   teaspoons sugar
4   cloves
1   stick cinnamon
⅔   cup light rum
⅔   cup brandy
6   tablespoons 151 rum
1   woman's handful slivered, toasted almonds
1   man's handful chopped, fresh fruit, such as strawberries and peaches

Combine all the ingredients in a fireproof vessel. Let steep for 30 minutes at room temperature. Gently heat the liquid in a well-ventilated place to body temperature in order to volatilize the alcohol. At arm's length, touch a flame to it and admire the furious, passion-blue fire. When the flames subside to a slow and flickering burn, ladle it into bowls or wide-mouth mugs. Enjoy with a spoon.

Yield: Too much for one, not enough for three
Heat Scale: It all depends on you
Serving Suggestion: Feed it to each other.
Variation: Omit either the fruit or nuts.

CHAPTER 4

THE FEASTS OF FATIMA
AND THE SULTAN

*A*ND SO WE COME TO LOVE, *brief and hot with deep and heavy scents. The belly and the heart, finding their way, each entwined with the other. The feast has no better spice than love; and love no finer venue than the feast.*

A little warning to the reader: This is a Sea Story. And we say of Sea Stories that some are truer than others. But this one is too true. I was serving on board the light cruiser *USS Oklahoma City* in the early '70s. She was a WESPAC ship, "forward deployed to the Western Pacific," as they say. That is, she lived in Asia. From 1967, she would not return to the United States until she was decommissioned in 1980. She was known as the "Gray Ghost of the Vietnam Coast," or sometimes as "The Ghost Ship." We who sailed her were the Ghost Men. Being seamen, and forward deployed, we had little opportunity to meet the nice kind of ladies you'd like to bring home to Mom. To be blunt, the only women with whom we could find sure association were the port women in the various waterfront establishments. Now I'm not making excuses, nor am I voicing regrets, I'm just stating the facts. We had two choices: take vows and become maritime monks, or consort with whores. The whores won, by a big margin.

So let me tell you right out, in case you want to screen your reading, this is a story about a certain Ghost Man and a certain whore.

THE FIRST DAY

We sailed to the island of Penang, down near the line, the equator. It belongs to Malaysia these days, and it used to be a part of British Imperial Malaya until about 1950. It sits at the western mouth of the Straits of Malacca, right where the Pacific and Indian oceans meet. It's about ten miles across.

Now, my story takes place in the days before they built that long causeway to the mainland and started selling those noisy, smoky, two-stroke motorbikes that rip the air and turn it blue and stinky. Until that time, the principal means of getting around were foot and pedicab. Autos were few, and many of those that existed were vintage '40s or '50s. The pedicabs were sometimes called trishaws because they had three wheels. Two passengers, three if they were small, sat on a love seat mounted on two of the wheels, one at each end. Behind that was attached a half a bicycle contraption on which the driver sat above and behind his passengers and pedaled. They all had those ringy, chingy little bicycle bells and were painted in bright colors.

It was a magic place. There's just no other way to say it. An Island of the Gods, where all the world's great religions and civilizations meet and live in harmony under the law willed to them by the Empire and the enlightened rule of the Sultan. About a third of the people are Malays, a third Chinese, and the remainder Tamils, Sikhs, Thais, and Europeans—mostly Brits and Aussies. Most of the people lived in the principal community of Georgetown.

We were coming in for R&R, Rest and Rehabilitation; although we called it Rape and Riot. If we had our way about it, that was something closer to the truth. And in Asia's fleshpots, we did have our way about it. We came into port that day as ready to invade as to visit.

47

But the instant we rushed ashore, we could tell the Penang difference and we slowed like a sea wave coming up the beach, dissipating till it soaks into the sand. There were no neon signs. Didn't need them either; the place was colorful enough with all of God's houses. There were none of the usual waterfront people waiting on the docks to sell us worthless junk, do our laundry, save our souls, or pick our pockets. Life in Penang went on, as usual, uninterrupted. The air was slow and silky. And there were sounds, like the music of *gamalangs* and the chants of *muezzins*, but there were no harsh sounds, no grating sounds, no clanging-banging sounds. No one seemed to be in a hurry.

I heard the "ring ring" of three of those little bicycle bells as their pedicabs rolled up. Their drivers had fixed umbrellas over the love seats, for it was hot that day. Two of them smiled; the other was stoic. Six of us got in and had an easy rolling trip into the town. My five mates were: burly, Castro-bearded Sam Robinson; curly blond Ricky Young; Al, the preacher's son; Jack "Tarkus" Wells, who was a misfit seaman although his dad was a Navy captain; and Tiny Rowan, the yeoman.

We rolled past money changers and jade dealers sitting cross-legged on the ground, their goods spread out on lengths of cloth laid on the walkways. I saw the mosque of Capitan Kling, sprouting peaked, red tile roofs, yellow domes, and filigreed minarets. The walls of Indian temples, simple of design, extruded gods in sculpture, and their portals spilled them forth in deluge. On a street corner, a huge urn on wheels sent wisps and puffs of sandalwood incense up to heaven. A church bell rang somewhere. And I can tell you of the Taoist Snake Temple. There, live pit vipers are kept sedated during the day by heady incense, and the faithful bring their prayers to them. At night they wake, eat the tiny bird's eggs left for them, then go into the bowels of the earth, where the gods live, carrying the people's prayers.

Throughout the streets of Georgetown the smells of cookery floated like a current that carried an olfactory melody. Garlic was always in evidence, a steady base or rhythm in the melodic culinary texture. Over it a wide spectrum of spices, meats, poultry, noodles, breads, soy and shrimp sauces, aromatic leaves, and countless other ingredients rolled up and down the scales, ever-changing, singly and in combination. It was a chef's fugue, played ceaselessly from dawn till midnight every day. It gave the air of Penang a quality I can only decribe as "timbre," or tone color.

I think the essence of the magic of Penang is in the uniqueness of its air. It is more than a vehicle for aromas and breezes. It is a character that lives there. It is like a drug in its ability to dissipate tension. It's thick, it's moist, it's warm. It is a tactile sensation. It has a viscosity like some unknown element between air and water. You could reach out with your hands and take scoops of it. As in the warm waters of tropic seas, it bleeds off harsh sounds and anxiety. You have to move slowly through it but you can glide through it like a boat on a still pond.

As we sailed in our little three-wheeled vessels through the viscous and scented air, someone said from one of the other cabs, not altogether sarcastically, "Well, this is all very nice, but I, for one, have had a long voyage, and I'm thirsty."

"Yeah!" We all cheered in unison, as the little wheeled love seats tooled down the road in loose file, their umbrellas swaying.

"Beer." Sam growled, pumping his fist. "Beer."

"Yeah!" We affirmed. "Beer!"

"Well I, for two, have had a long voyage, and I am hornier than a three-peckered billy goat in the spring!" Ricky yelled.

"Yeah!"

"Pussy!"

"Yeah!"

"Naked skin!"

"And don't forget the TLC, I want lots of TL fuckin' C!"

"Arms and legs full of TLC!"

"Affirmative, matey! Pound your breast and smile to overflowing."

"There is nothing like a dame," we sang.

"Tonight my pillow is a woman's shoulder."

"A titty!"

We wanted to swim through a sea of beer to a soft woman for an island. We yearned to leave behind the haze gray and steel, the bark of commands, the uniforms and guns, the great machines, and the smells of men. The sea is a woman; but her embrace is a sailor's last. Life is short, my men, and if you should leave without the smoky memories of women....

And so our little train of love seats went swerving 'cross the town with renewed purpose. I thought we had hit the jackpot when we came to an intersection, and I noticed a street sign I had not seen before that read, "Love Lane."

"Oh, my God!" I yelled. "We've arrived! We hit the jackpot! This has got to be hooker heaven!"

"Hurray!"

But the drivers told us to settle down. The street was just named for a guy named Love. Damn!

The first place we went to was in a cul-de-sac. It looked sort of French colonial and had a terrace on one side. Tables and chairs were set up there, and a boy in a cotton smock served customers while the women entertained them. That place didn't have enough women, so Ricky, it must have been, said, "Let's go to someplace that has more bitches." Like Tiny Rowan and others, he often called the hookers "bitches."

"Damn it, Ricky. I wish you wouldn't do that," I told him. "They're not bitches."

"They're not?"

"No. Okay, some of them, sure. But you're a bitch sometimes too, and so am I and so is the whole goddamn world. So where do you get off?"

Some of these guys like to say that they budget so much for food, so much for drink, and so much for the bitches. They say that they like Thailand because the bitches are good. These guys were my buddies, and I liked them a lot. But I wished they wouldn't call these women bitches. Or LBFMs either, Little Brown Fucking Machines. For Crissake, even Whit Whittington called them that, and he was black!

Ricky muttered something about life being a bitch, and I realized I was preaching a sermon, so I shut up. We went off in search of what I'm sure Ricky and Tiny would still be pleased to call "a more bitchful place."

Our three drivers pedaled us to several different places where we were able to sample the drink, to eye, and be eyed by, the women and unwind after a long and stormy crossing. The drivers always knew of yet another establishment where the beer was colder and the women were prettier; always "just down the road." And so their fares multiplied. At one point we paid them extra to race. And they raced us to a place on Chulia Street.

I hope that memory is serving me correctly here. If there is a Muse of Memory, I invoke her now. I believe they took us to the Chung King Hotel & Bar at 398-A Chulia Street. There were any number of places like the Chung King, and I could have this wrong, but I believe the Chung King was the place. I wouldn't want to give publicity to the wrong establishment. Out in front a little portico provided a space where our drivers parked and waited. A short hallway led into a parlor with rattan and stuffed furniture. The floor was made of little yellow ceramic tiles. On the right was a counter, behind which was a middle-aged-looking Malay, lean and wrinkled but not gray, and kind of dour, bending over a ledger. At the far side, a door led out to an atrium or courtyard, and some narrow stairs went up to the rooms on the next floor. About a half-dozen girls looked up eagerly as we came in. A well-fed, but otherwise nondescript Chinese man introduced himself. I think his name was Tang, and he was the owner. The Malay at the ledger was his "clerk," Ohsman.

Tang must have encouraged a competitive environment, because the girls rushed us. One was a Tamil in a sari, and she was the darkest person I'd ever seen. Two were Chinese, one tall and thin, one short and not so thin. The short one had a broad, smirky face with a few tiny pimples, and her hair in braids, or maybe it was a queue. She was the house's do-anything girl. Trying to outbid the other girls, she said that she would take on three of us at once.

"What about four?" one of us challenged her.

"Okay. Four. But hurry up, let's go. Then I take a shower."

"Forget it, Babe. Well, maybe another day."

I guess a couple of the girls were Malays, and one of them was Eurasian. She had freckles and wore a ponytail. She was half-Portuguese and half a lot of other things. I remember her as a bit shy because being of mixed race, she was lower on the local pecking order. The smirky girl called her "the mongrel." There was one who didn't get up and rush us with the others. She was sitting on a couch wearing a long red velvet dress. She wore no makeup; it would have been superfluous, as her lips were full and well-shaped and her brows were naturally dark and framed her large eyes that seemed to reach out and touch me. She held a book in her hand, on her lap. She was Malay, very dark, but not like the Tamil girl who was inky dark. This girl was stained-wood brown. And red was the perfect color for her to wear.

As the other men were appreciating the ladies and laying their claims and ordering beer, I walked over to the quiet one. She watched as I approached, slowly. When I stood over her, and she was looking up at me, I thought I would say something, but all I did was look at her, hard.

"Hello," she said. And she smiled. A real smile. Not a whore smile; not a stewardess smile or a beauty queen smile, but a real smile with lots of very white teeth.

"What's your name?" I asked.

"Fatima."

She pronounced it FAHtima, not FaTIma.

"What's your full name?"

"Fatima Binti Abdulla."

"That's beautiful. My name's Richard. Sometimes my buddies call me Dick."

"Do you want to sit with me for a little?"

"Yeah, yeah, that would be nice," and I sat down with about a foot of space between us and put my arm on the back of the couch. Her hair smelled of coconut oil, and her skin gave off the faintest suggestion of burnt clove.

"What are you reading?" I asked her.

"Oh, just a book," she said, closing it and smiling self-consciously. Book didn't rhyme with "look," it rhymed with "duke." And the word started at the back of her throat and traveled the length of her tongue to arrive at her parting lips. "Just a book," she repeated, stroking its worn cover.

"What's it about?"

"It's about some people, and they are traveling around the world." She spoke British English with a Malay accent that rolled the R with a musical trill. Her voice was low for a woman and was rich and velvety. When she spoke, her lips didn't simply move but formed, sculpted, and shaped each word. The book was a thumbworn paperback copy of James Michener's *The Drifters*. I noticed that she also had an English/Malay dictionary.

"Do you like reading books?" she asked, her R trilling.

"Yes, yes I do. I read novels. And poetry too. I like Kipling, maybe you've heard of him. And I read *Playboy* and all those other magazines with naked women," I grinned.

She blushed. It surprised me to see a hooker blush, but she did, her cheeks turning from mahogany to rosewood. She brought her book up to her face, just beneath the eye, like a fan, and smiled and blushed at me over its pages. A real smile! Again. The smile melted to a calm, and the blush cooled, and her large eyes danced as they took me in. The book came down slowly.

"You are in the American ship?" she asked.

"Yes." The boisterous voices of the other men and women had grown infinitely smaller. They had moved out to the periphery of some great sphere and were only a hum. A thread had spun between her and me. A thin, tenuous thread, tied one end to her and one end to me, taut. It vibrated, ever so slightly. I believe it was red, like her dress. I could have touched it, but I'm sure it would have broken if I had because it was so delicate, like spider's silk.

She had touched me somewhere and drawn that piece of web. Or maybe it was the other way around, I touched her, or both. Can you touch somebody and not be touched? Does one touch follow the other? Or is one brought into being, instantly, by the other?

"How strange," I thought. "And her a hooker." It's not that men didn't have feelings for, or relationships with, hookers. I knew some who had married their favorites. But they had known them for a long time.

"We just got into port this morning." I told her. "We're only staying a few days this time, but we'll be coming back."

We talked a little about nothing and something. She asked me about my voyages and travels and if I were a war hero or something.

"We're all heroes. Just ask us," I joked. I know I told her a story, but I don't remember everything I said. I was absorbed in listening to that velvety voice of hers and the trill of the R. I was watching her lips purse as they formed words like book that rhymed with duke. She hadn't fondled me or anything, and yet she had touched me. Sometimes they put their hands all over you trying to excite you. In Tijuana they go right for your crotch as soon as you sit down. In Singapore they put their arms around you and rub your shoulders. In Thailand they sit there smoldering and invite you to touch them.

"Yeah, I could do that here," I thought to myself. "Sure. I could do whatever I want with you, Fatima. You are for sale, after all. What's a short-time cost in this place? Five bucks? Chump change. I've got two month's pay in my pocket, and I could buy you till Christmas. I can take you upstairs and strip you naked. I can bend you over or lay you down or whatever I want for five lousy bucks. Four-eighty-nine or so at the current bank rate. Ten or fifteen for the whole night. Yeah, that's what I can do. And you know that. And I could break this thread, too. Easily. Easily." But then, I couldn't. Or wouldn't? I didn't. And the taut, quivering thread hummed.

"Well, are ya?" I heard someone say from the distant periphery. I looked up to see Ricky Young standing over us, repeating his question. "You gonna stay here all day making goo-goo eyes or come with us?"

"You're leaving?"

"We been here a fuckin' hour, man. Where you been?" He took Fatima's hand and shook it saying, "By the way, my name's Ricky B. Young and people call me the Youngster. Maybe you and me will do some business later on, but right now I've got to take Dickie away."

I had to go. You don't separate from your mates when you're on the beach together. Not till the end of the day. It's the buddy system; you take care of your buddies, they take care of you. Nobody comes between you. Two guys got scolded once because they came back to the ship with Tony Farioli all drunk and dropped him off on the mess deck, then went back on the beach. Tony was so bombed he couldn't get into his bunk. He fell down, tearing his ear on a bunk post, and had to have stitches. "You failed to utilize the buddy system properly!" Gunner's Mate Caples told them. "You should have made sure he was safe in his rack before you left him. That's what it's all about."

Then there was the time in Indonesia when sixteen of us took a two-day tour up to the Java highlands. They put us up in a lodge near a tea plantation. They gave us an excellent dinner of rice, curried vegetables, and grilled goat meat. I know it was goat meat because I went into the kitchen and saw the cooks carving the meat from a freshly killed carcass hanging from the ceiling. I told the guys what we were eating, and while one or two gagged, most just laughed. One of our more literate members pointed out that the goat is an ancient symbol of virility and desire and downright horniness. His remarks were fitting because soon after dinner, the staff asked us if we wanted any girls. We all said okay, one each, and they trucked in sixteen girls from around the countryside on an old flatbed military vehicle. None of them spoke more than a word or two of English, so it looked like it was going to be an interesting evening. We all made our choices and were off to our rooms. I think I got the best-looking one. Her name was Mun.

Pretty soon there was a big disturbance, and one of the guys banged on my door saying they needed an interpreter (I had been learning to speak Tagalog, the language of the Philippines and related to the Javanese tongue. I didn't speak well, but I winged it.) All thirty-two men and women were gathered in the main hall, and we could see that there was some kind of strife between Carl Brody and his girl. She was almost in tears and was protesting something to one of her fellows. Carl looked sheepish. Mun looked at me and pulled her lips apart so as to make them look big.

"No good, no good," she said. Some of the other women imitated her, all saying "No good," and shaking their heads. You see, Carl was black. His money was just as green as the next man's, but to them he was "No good, no good."

You may find the coming scene a little disturbing, especially if you're a woman. Let me assure you that there was no gender issue involved here. We simply had a case of Us versus Them; our tribe against their tribe.

There was no question or debate about what to do. We lined the women up against the wall, police-style. It was tough to risk losing Mun, but this was the buddy system and, by now, a point of honor. We made it clear to them—with vivid gestures and nasty looks and a few words—that one of them was going to service Carl, or they could all go to hell. And as it was nighttime and the flatbed truck had gone, they could have themselves a nice, long walk home in the dark and no cash for their efforts. I'm sure none of the women would have come to any harm, but I'm also sure of the depth of feeling for our shipmate, especially Carl's two closest pals. A couple of the women would have received a kick in the ass to start them on their walk.

I guess we thought they would confer briefly and maybe half of them would rise above the color bar, maybe they would even say they were sorry, and figure, "what the hey, its all the same money." But the bitches drew lots. I don't refer to the women of this trade as "the bitches," like Tiny and Ricky and some of the others do. But on this occasion, I say that the bitches drew lots. I don't care if they're racists. All the world is racist. They can cherish all the vanities they like as far as I'm concerned. Hurting our buddy's feelings like that is another matter. I don't know if it was any good for Carl that night. I don't even know if he screwed the bitch, and no one asked him. But his buddies had stood up for him, to a man. That's the buddy system.

I didn't want Ricky, or anyone else, getting his hands on Fatima. So I paid for her, giving the money to Ohsman, and made arrangements to stay in her room on the upper floor that night. I paid a little extra, too, to keep her from having to work while I was gone. "I'll come back later tonight," I told her. "In the meantime, you've got the day off." She smiled that real smile, with lots of teeth and crinkles at the eyes. I left her with the scent of coconut and clove lingering in my senses.

By the end of that evening, only one other man and I were left in the lounge of the Eastern & Oriental Hotel, the E&O. It was only about eleven o'clock, but it was a weeknight, and this island was laid-back. The others had either gone back to the ship or to their hotel rooms. My buddy, who shall remain nameless, had some girl waiting for him, but he was married, and he needed to be well fortified before sleeping with a woman who was not his wife.

"Why don't you just sleep alone?" I asked him. "I won't tell anyone."

"The wife keeps writing me erotic letters. Drives me crazy."

"You're the one who does this to himself, man. If it's going to disturb you like that, why bother? After all, your wife is probably one of the few women back in home port who isn't screwing someone on the U.S.S. Midway."

"Yeah. I hope so anyway. Maybe I'll make this the last one."

I saw my friend to his room in a lesser hotel. The E&O isn't one into which you brazenly bring a hooker. I don't know if they'd throw her out, but they'd charge you extra for sure and probably treat you to an icy stare in the morning. They have a lot of pride in their establishment, which goes all the way back to the British Empire. The great English writer, Somerset Maugham, used to stay there and dine on filet of sole with shrimp sauce, creamed spinach, and parsley potatoes. A lifetime later the American writer, Maxine Hong Kingston, would stay there as a guest of the government. It's a high-class operation. No whores in the lobby, please.

The temperature was still near eighty degrees, and I wore a fine, light sweat as I walked the narrow street that led to Fatima's place. I could smell the asphalt as it gave up the heat it had absorbed during the day. The palm trees lining the street hung their fronds limply in the moist, windless air. Fireflies winked and spun among the ferns and leafy shrubs. I passed the open market as the last of the merchants were closing their stalls. The air was a cloud of ginger, garlic, fish and vinegar, textiles, incense, and cedar.

When I reached the Chung King, it had the only light on Chulia Street still burning. Fatima was sitting on the couch again, the only person in the room. She had changed into a white cotton sarong and was still reading *The Drifters*, slowly, using her dictionary. When she saw me, she marked her place with a ribbon, got up, and smiled. She smiled just as real as before, but this time it was a little smile. Not the broad smile of meeting, but the little kind that says "I know you."

I approached her slowly, like before, and came to within an inch of that thread's length and stopped. It writhed, like the head of a serpent, seeking, and then bit. It sang a silent chord. In her flat sandals, Fatima reached my collarbone. She had a rich black profusion of hair that hung down her back and over her shoulders. Her most remarkable feature, to me, was her skin. It was dark and warm and lustrous, as though she had been burnished or rubbed with oil.

"Ohsman said you're not going to come but I told to him no. I said he's going to come. Richard will come, I'm sure. Or do you like to be Dick?"

I told her, "For you, I'm Richard," because of her luscious trill of the R.

"Got any more beer here?" I was thirsty after the hot walk. She got a bottle of Anchor out of the cooler, from the bottom, nice and cold. When she turned away to get it, I noticed that her sarong was backless, exposing a vast amount of that beautiful shining skin, the muscles and spine working beneath it.

"I'm putting it on your bill," she said as she wrote it down in the ledger on Ohsman's countertop.

"That's nice," I thought. "I've never had credit in a whorehouse before."

"I have something else for you," she told me. "Maybe you were too busy to take your dinner tonight, so I brought you these." From a paper bag, she took out four little pleasantly brown half-moon pastries, each a little larger than an egg. "Curry puffs," she said. "Very popular in my country."

"Did you make them?"

"Yes, I had free time all day."

I broke one open, and it crackled. A heady aroma of garlic and chile escaped, and shrimp meat showed itself bright pink within the deep-fried pastry case. I offered her half.

"No," she said. "You eat, you eat."

So I sat on the couch where we first met, and I took the little meal that Fatima had saved for me. For such a simple dish, the curry puffs were a remarkably sophisticated marriage of textures, flavors, and aromas: a chewy crunchy pastry smelling of good oil; shrimp and bean sprouts and chives bringing together the sea, the shore, and the earth; all knit together in an Indian spice bouquet.

"I didn't know Malayans were fond of curry," I said. "I thought it was an Indian dish."

"My country is many places."

"Oh?"

"Oh yes. Malaya, China, India, Cambodia. Even a little bit of England."

"So I guess you have foods from all those places."

"Yes. Of course, yes. But maybe we make it a little bit different, so it can be ours."

I finished the last puff, and she asked, "Are you satisfied? Do you want more beer?"

"Please," I said, handing her the empty. She brought me another, a large one. Marking it on the ledger, she asked, "Are you ready to go?"

Her room was neat and spare. A plain wooden floor, two wooden chairs, a wood table, a dresser, and two double beds that sagged a little. The sheets were clean but had been through many launderings and were wood-ash gray. The whitewashed walls were bare except for a small hanging of some local design. The room itself was large and airy. Double windows opened out onto the courtyard, and I could smell the pungent, musky-sweet flowers outside. As I pulled up a chair, Fatima handed me a bottle opener and a single glass.

"None for you?" I asked.

"No, thank you. Do you want to relax a little?"

"Yeah, yeah, I will," and I took off my shoes and put my feet on the bed. As she took off her earrings and sandals I asked, "Where did you learn English?"

"Convent school. At home, in Malacca."

"You're Catholic?"

"No, Moslem. Mother sent me anyway."

"How long?"

"Three years. I'm going to close the light now?"

"Sure." And when she had and it was dark, very dark in that room, I could see the white sarong come off and lie across the other chair as though under its own will.

Her dark shape then moved toward the bed and got in, pulling the sheet up to her waist. She was a silhouette, reclining on large pillows and outlined with perfect clarity against the wall. In the darkness of the room, I couldn't tell where her skin and hair met, but her outline looked drawn with ink and a fine pen. Her breasts stood and pointed upward. Her belly rose and fell with her breathing. Her lips moved. I listened. No sound. Yet I could see them move. Was she praying? I thought I remembered reading that Moslems prayed on their knees, although a Turk once told me that you could "pray riding on a horse and God still hears." But he said that the Arabs didn't see it that way. I wondered about the Malays.

I sipped the beer for a few moments as she lay still. Then, looking up from my glass, I saw that she was facing me, her head propped up on one hand.

"Tell me about your family, Fatima," I asked. I had found that people in Asia are very family-oriented. And they like to talk about them, especially if they're separated from them. It's a good way to establish and maintain rapport. They'll tell you about their parents, their six brothers and their eight sisters and their seventy-seven uncles, aunts, and cousins. And they'll show you pictures if they have them. It makes them feel good.

Fatima was tracing circles on the mattress with her palm. "I have my mother, in Malacca. Sometimes I visit her, or send her some money."

"What about the others?"

"No others."

Wrong move. Damn! It could be that her mother was a hooker too. Sometimes it happened that way. Three generations, even. Best I shut up. I sure didn't want to remind her of anything sad. I set about to drink all the beer, even though it was a full liter. I knew that without some sedative I would wake up in the middle of the night, during dream sleep, when my body felt no rocking of the sea.

"Will you come to bed to me now?" she asked as I poured. I hesitated. I was suddenly afraid. I didn't know of what. Of Fatima? How could that be? I had paid the fare, she was mine, I could do what I liked. What's to be nervous about? It was that smile that said, "I know you." I heard it in her voice. It was black in that room, but she could see me. I felt a little like I wanted to hide. But the thread tugged, and it hurt. It was tied around my breastbone, and it hurt with a cutting hurt because it was so fine. I don't think Fatima was pulling on it. It just coiled itself of its own accord and pulled me into bed with her.

Soon, naked, I held Fatima to me. With any other whore I would have rubbed against her till I was erect, then entered her without ceremony. But this time was different. The thread had coiled itself so tight that I found it difficult to move. I lay there for a while not fighting it and breathed in her scents of coconut and clove. At length I brought my hand up to her face. With it, I began to trace the line of her jaw, just with my fingertips. With the back of my index finger, I felt her lips. They were full and bow-shaped. I crooked my finger. The knuckle pressed against her lips, and they parted. My curved finger slid into her mouth, her teeth scraping against it, and she bit down, almost hard. The pressure shot through my whole body. Finger and groin throbbed. Gut shivered.

I uncrooked the finger, and she let it go, sliding out wet. I crooked my middle finger and returned, into her mouth. She bit. Harder. Hard enough that I pulled, and she didn't release. I pulled harder, and her head came off the pillow, my body came off the sheet, and I pulled myself atop her as her legs parted. Her body took mine, I uncrooked my finger, and she released it. And I was one with her.

Her hands were on my shoulders, and I could feel her long nails against my skin. Her knees were bent, the soles of her feet against my legs; my face in her billow of coconut-scented hair. Then, before I began to fuck her, the muscles of her vagina twitched, then flexed and gripped. It felt like five warm fingers, each gripping after the other. And that was a way of speaking, don't you see? She didn't need to make that effort. She might have lain there, quite still, her mind in some cool, other place. It was her prerogative. But she didn't.

Again her body spoke, and almost imperceptibly her hips began to rock. It spoke again. She was saying, "Enjoy. You paid. You bought me for a while, so enjoy. That's our bargain. There, yes, take what you buy. Reach for it now, reach. Farther, farther, reach and take it. Take it all, it's yours for a while. Have it! Seize! Grasp! Now! Take!...all."

About the axis of our bodies, the universe slowly rolled and brought the pillow softly to my head. Fatima's body released mine and gave it back to me. My breath, for a while, came in deep, even draughts. Her fingers twined and untwined through my hair, and they said, 'There. There, mariner. There. And now sleep, for that too comes with the price. It's all in our bargain. And there's a bargain for you.' Though I had no sea to rock me, I didn't wake till morning.

THE SECOND DAY

Before leaving Fatima for the ship I gave her the price of her time for the coming day and night. "Here," I said. "Check yourself out and pay Ohsman when he comes in. I'll be back as soon as I can."

Things were slow on board, and I finished whatever I had to do by ten o'clock. I had worn civvies the day before, but I thought that Fatima might like to see me in uniform. She had asked about my military career. So I put on my best dress whites with new ribbons. I also wore my corfam shoes that shined like patent leather. The suit itself was custom-tailored in Hong Kong and I had one of those belt buckles with the ship's logo on it.

She did like it. She grinned hugely when she saw me come into the Chung King. She took my arm and turned me around for a good look-see, then patted my arm in approval, fidgeted with my collar, and touched my ribbons for luck. She was in black jeans and the usual sandals. She wore a blouse made from that coarse, wrinkly cotton that comes from India. A sort of magenta color.

The day before, I had had a tour of all the bars on the island. This day she was going to show me its less-sordid side. We saw a pedicab whose driver, an old, short, wiry Malay, was lounging outside the house. Fatima negotiated the fare, in Malayan, telling where she wanted him to take us. We got in, and the wizened little man began laboring down the road.

We drove through town toward the west shore. There we turned onto Farquar Street and rolled past the grand old E&O Hotel with its cool, airy lobby and

Humphrey Bogart/Casablanca ceiling fans. A 1934 roadster was parked inside on display. "How would you like to stay in this place sometime?" I asked her. She said nothing, simply blushed, smiled, and touched my thigh.

We continued along the shore to the abandoned British Fort Cornwallis and the huge grassy esplanade that separates it from Government House. We stood on the stone battlement, and she pointed out to sea and showed me the visible line of demarcation where the jade green of the western Pacific meets the inky blue of the Indian Ocean (the Aye Oh, as we call it).

"Is that where the Moslem missionaries came from, about eight hundred years ago?" I asked.

"Yes," she said, looking out to sea. "From India. And some from Arabia."

I decided that we should take a stroll through these quiet streets so she could better acquaint me with the town. I knew Penang was a place I would return to often. It wasn't long before I smelled spicy food and asked Fatima where it was coming from. "Pushcarts," she said, and pointed off to the east.

"Pushcarts? What are they?"

"Places for eating. Very good."

I smelled garlic and curry and coffee and tamarind; fish sauce, onions, broiling meats. Without saying anything, we found ourselves ambling in that direction. We passed a clutch of pedicabs, their drivers all competing to offer us a ride. We declined and continued following our noses. A troupe of Malay women with wicker trays on their heads and dressed in colorful batik sarongs crossed our path. I made what I thought was a Moslem sign to them, touching the fingertips of my right hand to forehead, lips, and then heart. They all giggled, some of them covering their mouths with scarves.

"That's American way to say hello?" Fatima asked.

"Huh? I thought it was Moslem. I saw it in a movie."

"I never saw before," she chuckled.

Quickening the pace, we passed a hole-in-the-wall mechanic's shop, whose smells of grease, oil and metal mingled with those of spices. We rounded a corner where Pitt and Light streets converge, and there we saw, in a one-acre palm grove, dozens of pushcart kitchens, painted in gaudy colors, and operated by cooks from all over the Orient. Each cook was a consummate master of two or three dishes from wherever he—or his ancestors—hailed from. They were Malayans, Chinese, Hindus, Sikhs, Tamils, Thais, and a lone Portuguese. Steam billowed, meat sizzled, woks and spatulas clattered, and conversation hummed. Some of the cooks had electric stoves on their carts, which they plugged into sockets that were wired onto palm trunks. Some were gas-fired and carried small propane tanks. Still others had carefully banked charcoal fires, over which they grilled giant prawns, squid, chicken legs, and skewered beef or pork. Folding tables and chairs were scattered about. All the carts had green plates or orange plates or both. Green indicated that the food the plate held conformed to Moslem dietary laws. The orange ones were for culinary pagans like me.

"Are you hungry?" I asked Fatima.

"Maybe a little. Do you want to eat?"

"Yes, yes! But I don't know what anything is or how to get it. What's the routine here?"

"All right," she declared. "I'm going to take care of everything. You want beer?"

"You bet."

She ordered something from three different carts, a soda for herself and a big bottle of Tiger beer for me. She got the beer first, so I wouldn't be standing around with nothing to do, I guess. As each dish was served up, she took it over to a little table she had staked out beneath a palm by the side of the road.

As we waited while one of the dishes was being prepared, I noticed a big Indian guy, who seemed to be a friend of the cook, standing behind the pushcart. He kept sneaking glances at Fatima. Now you know the kind of glances I'm talking about. You've seen them. They're the glances that say, "I'd like to buy a piece of your ass too, baby. If I had that Yankee's money I'd come around to your dirty little whorehouse and fuck your whore eyes out every time my cock so much as tingled. You little cunt-for-sale."

If Fatima noticed, she didn't let on. But when the guy's glances turned into leering and drooling, I started to get angry, so I stood between him and Fatima with my back to him. I showed him my ass, as it were. I'm sure Fatima knew what was going on by now because she stood close against me, as if to take shelter. But she said nothing, and I didn't want her to have to dwell on it, so I didn't say anything either. We just stood with our bodies close together, as if against a storm, and weathered it. Sunshine returned when the cooks called out that they had done their best for us and "God give you good appetite."

When Fatima got all the food on the table, she bade me attend her feast. One of the dishes was called *bee hoon mee*, very thin fried rice noodles with bean sprouts, tiny shrimp, and vegetables seasoned with soy sauce and diced green chiles.

Another dish was a mild chicken curry, very rich and saucy, made with red chiles and coconut milk and rice on the side. Fatima began with that. She started with a fork, but then said, "You won't mind if I just use only my hand?"

"Huh? Oh yeah, that's your custom, isn't it?"

"Yes."

"And you only use the right hand. Right?"

"Yes," she leaned forward and whispered. "Because the left hand is the toilet hand."

"I'd join you and eat with my hands too, but I'm afraid I'd just make a big mess on my whites."

The last dish was some kind of fish like mackerel. "It's from my city, Malacca," Fatima told me. "We call it *asam pedas Malacca*. How do you find it? Is it too spicy?" It was in a dark, smoky sauce, redolent of ginger, garlic, fennel, and pepper. It lightly stung my nose when I smelled it. Its taste was so spicy hot that it made me break out in a sweat, but I love that stuff. Fatima was surprised; she didn't think the Yanks ate such things. I told her I'd eat anything with four legs except a table and anything with wings except an airplane. She laughed.

"I think you are a man who likes eating very much," she said. "It's good to like eating."

59

"And you? I can see you like to eat. Do you also like to cook?"

"Yes, I often do."

"And what do you like to cook? Tell me about the food of your country."

"Well, we have many things and many curries. We make them with chile. And lemon grass and tamarind, very good. We like to use *kunir*...how can I say...turmeric. And of course, lots of coconut."

"Yes," I said. "I smelled it in your hair, and it made me hunger for you. With all my senses." She said nothing to that but smiled a tight little smile. I thought she would blush again, but she didn't. "Tell me some more."

"We always use *blacan*. It's a paste made from shrimp." She got up and went over to one of the pushcarts and brought back a sample. It was dark pink and pasty, with a deep, powerful aroma. "Often we dry it, then cook it," she said. "It becomes even stronger and makes a good taste and smell in the food. You see?"

She picked up one of the plates from the table and said, "Smell." It was down deep in the dish, subtle but unmistakable. And richly good.

"You have so many different kinds of food, from so many different places," I said. "I bet I could have a different dish every meal all my life and not have anything twice."

"Yes, of course. My country is many places."

It must have been about two o'clock as we finished the last of the fish. I was savoring the slow burn in my mouth and waving to some of my buddies who were passing by. One of them was Eddie Terrel. He had one of those Indian hookers with him, dressed in a sari. She was walking three paces behind him with her hands folded in front of her breasts, eyes down. Ha! He was strutting, making sure the whole world saw him. I'll bet he even had her lighting his cigarettes for him and calling him "Sahib." Ha! What a guy, Eddie Terrel.

Some other crewman had a hooker with him, too. I don't know who he was, but I'm sure he was new. He was holding hands with the woman, trying to cuddle with her like she was his girlfriend back home. Bad form. Bad hooker form, bad Asia form. She looked embarrassed. Decorum is the watchword here. Asians have fairly rigid customs governing the relations between men and women in public. And the commercial relationship between prostitute and client is not without its parameters either.

I had told Fatima that I wanted to visit the market, so she called over to a Malay boy who agreed to go fetch us a pedicab. For this, I gave him half a Malaysian dollar (about a dime). We were soon at Penang's outdoor marketplace, which is a bit like a flea market but more upscale. A kind of traditional Asian mall. But here there are few price tags, and so you get to haggle with the merchants. Haggling is an art, and there are lots of tricks.

I bought Fatima a dress-length of the best batik. She said that she would make the dress herself and would wear it for me the next time I came to Penang. She smiled and smiled. I told her that if there was anything else she wanted, to let me know, and I would buy it for her as long as it didn't break the bank.

We went to a curio stall where I was looking at some odds and ends and comparing notes with some of the men from the ship when I noticed her buying something herself. She took out her wallet and found two old, nicked and dull coins, one copper, one aluminum I think, and paid the seller for two iron-on patches the shape of a Levi's hip pocket. They each bore the logo of Camel cigarettes. She was vastly pleased with them and insisted on paying for them herself; I tried to buy them for her, but she said no, thank you.

To her they were a sample of real American iconography—the genuine article. They represented a fantasy land to her. It was that strange and wonderful land that dominated the world from so far away, the one she was reading about in *The Drifters*. The land that bred these men who were visiting Penang today and who had all that money and all that swagger and called everyone "buddy." These men who were walking through the marketplace and walking on the moon and waging war on a nearby country for no apparent good reason. Her icons represented a dangerous and beautiful creature, arrived here from legend and prowling through the secret gardens of Asia. And maybe they represented me a little bit, too.

Back in her room that evening I sat in the same chair sipping beer while Fatima was in the shower. I could hear the muffled voices of the people downstairs as they partied. I was resting my feet on the bed again, just like the night before, when she came into the room wrapped in a thin cotton towel that clung moistly to her body. At the top, her nipples protruded against it, and at the bottom it conformed closely to her mons and I could see the impression of the thin, dark hairs there. Her glossy skin shone with moisture. She hadn't wet the hair of her head, but it was disheveled and so thick and so long and so wild that it looked like a lion's mane. She was so beautiful it made me ache. I knew that if I spoke just then that my voice would crack. I felt seasick, but without the nausea.

As she knelt to put away her shower kit in a lower drawer, she noticed my attention on her. She stopped what she was doing and exchanged gazes with me. Then she came over to me and stood next to the chair. With the long nail of her forefinger, she began to comb through one of my ear-length sideburns. There are many Asians who seem fascinated with the hair on the body and face of a Westerner. She moved to the hair on my arm, and stroked it, tugged lightly on it, combed her nails through it.

How many children in the Far East had done that with the hair on my arms I couldn't tell you. Children I didn't even know sometimes, if I was talking to their parents or other elders, could not seem to contain their curiosity about it. And they would not be satisfied just to touch it; they had to explore it, play with it, experience it like some exotic luxury. They would spend minutes at it; two, even three kids at a time. On some occasions I have been the first white man a child has ever seen, and often the first up close. I guess the sight must be pretty amazing to them. I've never denied the children their curiosity. Indeed, I've felt honored by it.

At that moment I felt honored by Fatima, the port girl. I swear I couldn't move for fear I would disintegrate. That's when she kissed me. She put her arms around my shoulders and pressed her face against the side of mine, then kissed and inhaled through her nose sharply to take in my scent. I had read about that way of kissing in Malaya, but I had never seen it. She did it again. And again.

You have to bear in mind, now, that prostitutes don't kiss their clientele. It's just not done. It's like an unwritten code of conduct. They may perform any act, natural or unnatural, but they don't kiss. One reason is that many of the clients don't want a whore to kiss them. You never know where her mouth has been. But even more than that, kissing is reserved for affection. It's the one thing she doesn't sell. She has to have something to give, after all. Everybody has to have something to give. What good are you without it?

And so Fatima gave me the one precious thing she had. There's a story in the Bible of the people giving tithes. The wealthy gave a lot of money and were pleased with themselves. Then an old woman who had no more than a penny, gave her penny. The rich people laughed and derided her small gift. But Jesus told them that the old woman had given the greatest gift because it was all she had, and they were ashamed. I was ashamed at that moment, and I felt that if God were looking down on us, He was making a place for Fatima and none for me.

But maybe Fatima didn't see it that way. Her eyes were dancing at me just like that first time we met such a long day and night ago. She sat on the bed as she retucked her towel, keeping her modesty. Her hands she laid on my outstretched legs, unthinkingly gripping and ungripping them. She kneaded them, all the while her eyes dancing at me, dancing. The muscles in her jaw clenched and relaxed, clenched and relaxed. Her liquid eyes came to a tense stop, locking on mine, and her hands held tightly. She was a wound-up spring. Then her face began to soften and her grip to weaken. Suddenly she exhaled a smile and let go of me. She laughed. I smiled. And we embraced. And I kissed her.

THE THIRD DAY

The world was exceedingly, quietly alive when I awoke. It hummed the same note as that taut crimson thread that tethered me to Fatima. Outside the first raven squawked and sleepy pedicab drivers were just coming to their vehicles. One of them chimed his little bell and another answered him from farther off. A pushcart clattered its way to the open market. And Fatima, her face hidden beneath her hair, was just beginning to draw deeper, waking breaths.

As I was dressing she sat up, covering herself only partially now, and looked at me through sleep-narrowed eyes above a subtle, satisfied smile. A cat with a mouthful of canaries. I smiled. My shoes had gotten kicked under the bed, so I sat on the floor next to it to reach them and put them on. As I was tying them, Fatima suddenly loomed over me on hands and knees and barked a sharp, triumphant animal sound. A beast of prey saying "gotcha!" She grinned, exposing all of her white canines.

It was the first time I had seen her naked in the light. Her lion's mane fell around her face and neck and shoulders and down her back. Her limbs were spread out, her hind section cocked slightly back, ready to spring. "Yes, you are a lion," I thought. "A bronze lion. Not a lioness but a lion woman. You're a griffin, you're a sphinx. You're a mythical creature. You're mythopoeic in warm flesh and red, pumping blood and muscle and moisture and breath."

"I imagine a mirror behind you so I can see you there too; see you 360 degrees around. Just like I see your face and your mane; the ripe flesh of your breasts hanging between your forelegs; the small, black pelt between your haunches and the quiv-

62

ering flesh of your rump. And claws? Yes! You have claws, with which to scratch me till I bleed and lick my blood and nourish yourself on it."

She snapped at my ear and caught it and held it between her teeth, the wet heat of her mouth flowing into it.

"Growl!" I said.

"RRRR."

"More!"

"RRRRR...RRRRR...RRRRR," and she twisted her head and she tugged, gently hard. Her lips closed over the ear and her teeth relaxed and she sucked. "RRRR."

And she bit possessively. "RRRR," and she sucked again. Satisfied with my flesh, it slipped from her mouth with a wet kissing sound. Her tongue darted into the canal, and I heard its probing. Covering the ear with her open mouth, she slowly licked the bruised flesh to heal it, then kissed it one perfect kiss. It throbbed with pleasure-pain.

On elbows and knees now, her chin resting on her hands, her body sloped upward to the rear. Looking past her face with its wet lips and through her tousled hair my eye followed the line of her back to the two hemispheres of her buttocks. Then down the thigh to where the bent knee and elbow and the breast came close together. Sculpture. I took a mental picture. "Now I have you forever on film—on the special film of my remembering eye."

Getting to my feet, I suddenly realized that in forty-eight hours I would be leaving. I began to miss her already. "Fatima, listen," I said, rubbing my ear as she got out of bed and wrapped the sheet around herself, togalike. "How would you like it if we go somewhere else tonight, to stay? Someplace nice, someplace very nice."

"To stay for all night? In a very good room?" She trilled.

"The best!"

"With air conditioner?"

"Yes! The best place in all Penang. What is it?"

"No, that's E&O." That was only for fine folks.

"Then it's E&O. For us." She looked a little pensive, and I figured it was concern that she'd be seen and thrown out or otherwise embarrassed. "Don't worry," I said. "Here's what we'll do. I'll go get the room and pretend that I'm alone. I'll come tell you what number it is, and you come later, on the sly."

I pulled out my wallet and started counting out the cost of Fatima's time for the rest of my stay. She watched me in silence. I handed her the wad of colorful little Malaysian notes. She stood there holding her toga wrapped around her, saying nothing. Her eyes danced, but slowly this time. And sadly? "What gives?" I thought.

"Here, take it," and I held it out again. She reached out and lightly tapped the back of my hand and withdrew. It was the old Malayan way of polite refusal.

"You go to the hotel," she spoke in a low voice. "Get the room and you can wait me. Ask to somebody to tell me its number. When the house is closed I'm going to come to you."

I looked stupidly at her and at the money, thinking only in practical terms. "But you'll have to work."

"I'm going to tell to Ohsman that I have a woman sickness."

"Ah. Yeah, sure. I should have thought of it myself," I said with a wink, dropping the money into her purse. She reached in and gave it back to me. She wrapped my hand around it, held that in her two hands and said, "I'm going to come to you."

"Jeez," I thought. "This girl really likes me. Good God, of all the men in her life it's me, me that she's going to give a freebie to. Wow. I'm going to have to dust her down for sure." (That was our term for leaving the woman all your unspent cash when you left; it was customary if she had treated you especially well.)

I had a lot of things to do on board that day, so I wasn't able to get away till the afternoon. As soon as possible, Ricky Young and I went to the E&O and I got a room fronting the beach. It ran about $100 Malaysian (roughly $20 U.S.). Ricky agreed to tell Fatima which one. But first, we had to have a drink in the hotel pub.

The E&O pub was so English that it seemed somehow incongruous there on that most Asian of Asian isles. It was built into the hotel to give a bit of home away from home to those British Empire types who had come out here to serve the Crown. It was richly paneled, had a swirled marble floor, and lots of stuffed furniture. Very cozy. When we walked in, it was already half full of patrons, a few behind a painted folding screen, put there for people who wanted to be anonymous, I guessed. I could smell stout beer, limes, sausages, and the sharp odor of Burmese tobacco. I wished I could have brought Fatima with me. I bet she would have liked it.

Sitting at the bar was a tall, distinguished-looking European with silver-gray hair reading a copy of the *Straits Times* of Singapore. He wore gold-rimmed glasses and closely resembled Woodrow Wilson. He had an aristocratic nose that seemed designed for looking down, and I imagined him practicing that maneuver in the mirror. He looked too haughty for this century.

As we sat at the bar, I couldn't help but smile at him. He noticed, we exchanged greetings, and he introduced himself. He was Wing Commander Bertrand W.D. Stanbury, Esq., R.A.F. (Ret.). "Pleased to meet you," Ricky said, and offered his hand. "I am Petty Officer Ricky B. Young of the U.S. Seventh Fleet (active), and this is my buddy, Dick."

"Hi."

"Welcome to Penang, gentlemen." He spoke with the richest of English accents, the mumbly kind. "Mmm, you, George," he said to the well-groomed Chinese bar-man, waving a finger at him from the wrist. "These gentlemen are with the Seventh Fleet. Let's give them whatever they like, mmm?"

"Hey, thanks a lot, Commander," I said.

"Oh, I'm not a commander any more, you know. I'm only a Mr. Stanb'ry now, only a Mister."

"You're just being modest. I'll bet you've got lots of war stories. Were you ever wounded?"

He had been. And he did have a lot of war stories. He was a wonderful old soak from an upper-crust British family and had started out in life as a journalist. In 1939 he volunteered for the RAF because, as he put it, "this Hitler fellow simply had to be stopped." He flew bombing missions over Germany throughout WWII. He got bored with peacetime, so in the 1950s he volunteered for the British military mission to the long-lived "Malayan Emergency," the communist insurgency that was sort of their Vietnam—but they won. When the troops went home, he stayed on as a special advisor to the Sultan.

Now he lived in boozy retirement, had a local wife, and spent his days in the pub in the E&O. He shunned the lounge. He said it was "fit only for Frenchmen."

Despite the diversity of their separate backgrounds, exiles and wanderers know when there's another one in the room. We swapped stories for several rounds. I was so charmed by the way he spoke, I figured that it had to be a practiced way of speech, and if I woke him up in the middle of the night, he would talk just like I did. I was compelled to ask him, "Commander, in what part of England did you uh, cultivate your...rich accent?" He drew himself up erect and looked down his nose just like I had imagined him doing in the mirror.

"My dear boy," he said, mumbling each word deliberately, "I don't have an accent; you have an accent!"

We laughed, and he smiled triumphantly.

He said that he liked Americans, but still he was "glad we got rid of the damned Yanks! They were always such a troublesome colony." We talked about British and American military prowess, and he said with great conviction, "You've really no reason, you know, to celebrate that bloody battle of Bunker Hill. It was the British who won, after all."

"Well, that's true, Commander," I said. "We lost the bloody battle. But we still own the bloody hill!"

After three or four rounds the Commander said, "I think it's time for a nibble. Would you like to join me for a little satay?"

"What's that?"

"Well I'm sure you chaps might call it Malayan-style 'barbecue,' but it transcends mere burnt flesh slathered with a sticky sauce. You there, George. Bring us a plate of satay. These gentlemen must be educated."

George adjusted his bow tie, then fetched a tray of bite-sized bits of beef threaded on bamboo skewers. They had been grilled to perfection with dark brown, carbonized edges, yet were still pink in the middle, and they exuded smells of meat and spice that did not mingle but somehow remained separate and enhanced each other greatly. On another plate, he poured a deep red chile and tomato sauce and spread it evenly to cover the plate. On top of that he poured about half as much of a peanut-based sauce and let it settle into a second concentric circle.

We dipped the skewers into the sauce plate, swirling them to mix the sauces. Biting into the meat made it burst with juice, and the flavor of coriander seed and cumin from the marinade came through, but didn't overpower the meat. The sweetness and heat and the richness of peanuts in the sauces acted as a frame rather than a cover for the whole. Every taste and smell was distinct, nothing masked. Like the curry puffs, a simple dish was in fact a complex composition. Like a jazz ensemble, each instrument played something different and distinctive, yet none distracted from the others. I was beginning to learn that this was a distinguishing characteristic of Malayan cookery. Its culinary styles, and their individual dishes, like the people who have come from many places, have not melded or fused into one new style or culture. Rather, each has retained its own character, making those adjustments necessary to fit with all the others.

65

By early evening, it was time for the Commander to go home to his wife, and Ricky had to give Fatima my number on his way to meet Sam and the others in yet another house of one-night wives. I went to my room to shower and change for dinner. I had decided that I would dine in the main dining room of the hotel, wearing my best civvies, and rub elbows with all the local potentates. And maybe I would pretend that Fatima was with me, and that I was showing her the time of her life. In my fancy, I'd throw lots of money around and command the waiters with an easy confidence. I'd read from the French side of the menu while she looked on admiringly. I'd see that the staff called her "ma'am" and treated her with the deference due to the Lady of one of the Ghost Men. She'd be thrilled and would demurely sniff her corsage.

The dining room at the E&O was very formal, very English. The tablecloths and napkins were stiffly starched and so were the waiters, but weren't overbearing. The silver was so heavy you could use it for ballast in any small ship. I sat at the same table that Somerset Maugham used to frequent. They told me that if I came back the next night, I could be served by the same waiter that used to serve him! I was very impressed. Actually, at the time, I didn't really know who Maugham was. But I knew that he was famous and highly regarded, especially at this table. I ordered the same meal he used to have, plus oxtail soup. And I decided that as long as Fatima was dining with me in fancy, I would invite the great man of letters as well. He said he was already engaged with some "perfectly boring" expatriates, but he would try to get away, at least for a drink. "I'd love to hear your stories, my boy," he said. "I want to write them all down." Fatima offered her hand for him to kiss.

I can say without reservations (no pun intended) that the E&O is still my favorite hotel in the whole world. I've spent so many days and nights there, met so many interesting people, and have so many stories about it—like the incident of The Sultan's Feast.

On my first trip to Penang, I was on leave and had taken the train from Singapore. I was staying in another hotel, but I wanted to have dinner at the E&O. I was flush, so I was going to order the best on the menu, tip very large, and feel like a sultan. I put on the best clothes I had, including my white calfskin shoes, custommade in Hong Kong. I even wore a tie, very formal for these parts. Was I gussied up!

When I got there, the first thing I did was go to the lounge for a drink—gin and tonic, of course. However, I had come to the E&O by walking along the beach, not the road. I knew I could take a short cut into the place by using the rear entrance into the dining room and go through there into the lounge. As I came abreast of the hotel, I could smell the tantalizing spicy bouquet of chile prawns, a local specialty, rolling out from the kitchen. The aroma was so powerful that it seemed to be the only thing cooking. I resolved to have it for dinner and maybe order two portions.

The dining room was empty except for two waiters. All the people were in the lounge. "Must be a thirsty day," I thought, and went into the lounge with the others. The place was really crowded, and everybody was dressed to the nines, just like me. A waiter came over and asked me if I wanted a drink.

"Sure," I said, "gin and tonic." He went away and came back with the drink and before I could pay him, he left. "OK," I said to myself, "maybe he's in a hurry. He'll come back." I milled around like the other people, and the drink went pretty fast. As I finished it, the waiter came back and asked if I wanted a refill. "Sure," I said, "one more time." Again he brought me the drink and left before I could pay him. That's when I noticed that *nobody* was paying. The bartenders were pouring liquor and beer like it was Kool-Aid, and nobody was collecting any money.

Then this guy in a turban, I guess he was a Sikh, stood up on something and hollered, "It's almost the time! Everybody, it's almost the time!" Everybody perked up and looked eager.

"Please, the gentlemen with the golf clubs." And these four guys with putters were lined up shoulder to shoulder at the doorway with their clubs held up at "port arms." Now, I happened to be standing there, and so these four guys with raised clubs were facing me, and they look a little more perked up and eager than the rest of the crowd.

Then the Sikh yelled, "Now the gentlemen with the tennis rackets." So four more guys came over, with tennis rackets at "port arms," and start lining up facing the golfers. "Would you mind stepping aside, sir?" the Sikh said to me.

"Sure thing. You bet," I said, and I moved over to a place where I was at least a couple club lengths away, looking down the corridor these eight guys have formed next to the door. "Is this some weird Asiatic game of Lacrosse?" I wondered. "Do they get liquored up and then go at each other with clubs and rackets? After all, in the supper clubs of Thailand, they like to roll out the mat and do a little kick boxing. Maybe it comes down from some ancient blood sport, formerly played with scimitars, but the British made them quit it and use lesser implements of destruction. I hope it doesn't turn into a wild scrimmage, and I get clobbered in the confusion."

Suddenly the Sikh hollered, "Now!" The eight guys lifted their weapons up above their shoulders and crossed them, forming a guard of honor. The band struck up "Happy Birthday," and everybody started singing. In walked the Sultan of Penang, who I recognized from a military parade I had attended! Behind him were people who I take to be two of his wives, a teen-age daughter, and three guys in uniform, one of whom I recognized as the superintendent of police.

Remember where I stood—looking right down the muzzle of this cannon that's going to shoot the Sultan straight at me! He shook a couple of hands as he came my way, smiling and highly pleased at this display of affection by his people. And there I was, standing like a schlep with my jaw hanging, the Sultan and the top cop coming at me, the fool who has just crashed a private party for the biggest bigwig on the whole damned island! I started singing "Happy Birthday." With feeling.

When the Sultan got to me, he reached out and shook my hand and said, "Good to see you," and he moved on.

"Happy birthday, Your Excellency," I sang. Wife number one was next, and she looked at me as if to say, "And just who the hell are you?" Fortunately the momentum of the train behind her pushed her on, and she followed the Sultan, accepting the greetings of the people. Wife number two looked through me to someone else and waved, and that was A-okay with me. The teen-age daughter smiled, and I felt better. But then the police chief gave me the same look as the senior wife, and he seemed to be making a mental note to check me out as soon as things settled down.

Everybody went into the dining room for the main festivities and a fine dinner of chile prawns with the Sultan, so I decided it was a good time to make my exit. Some old English couple grabbed me and said, "No, no, this way, this way."

I said, "Sorry folks, but I've got to go to the gents. I'll be right back, I swear."

"Don't be late," they chirped.

"No way."

I went out the door the Sultan had just come through and walked past a guy who had a guest list. "Sir, excuse me," he said. "What is your name, please?"

"Eh?"

"Your name, sir."

"My name?"

"Your name, sir. I need to check you off so you can come back in."

"Oh. Yes. Of course. Well, I'm not coming back in. Personal emergency, you know. Got to run."

I went through the lobby past that 1934 roadster and out the door and didn't come back for days.

I meandered through the streets, relieved at my escape, but quite hungry. And it was those damned chile prawns I wanted! "If the Sultan can have 'em, I can have 'em," I thought furiously. As though in answer to a gastronomic prayer, that distinctive aroma came snaking up the street. I followed it across the lane and through an alley till I came to a hole-in-the-wall restaurant called the See Kong Hooi. The place had about four tables with no patrons, a beer cooler, and a plump, surly waiter in a threadbare tee shirt and Bermuda shorts.

I took a seat and without looking at the menu told the unshaven half-dressed servant, "Chile prawns, for the Sultan and me." He looked a bit startled but said nothing and hollered at the cook, who set to work. In minutes the waiter returned, still looking a bit perplexed, and set the dish in front of me. "Thanks," I told him. "His Highness and I shall enjoy these immensely. It's his birthday, you know." He pulled nervously at his tee shirt and tried to smile, but he seemed not to be used to it, and it only deformed his face. Then he nodded and muttered something in Chinese and shuffled away, leaving me to the birthday banquet.

The cook had peeled and butterflied giant prawns, and they had curled back on themselves in cooking to expose the white flesh of their undersides. They swam in a sauce of chile, fresh tomato, and bamboo shoots. It was all wokked together with garlic, ginger, scallions, soy sauce, wine, and sesame. It was sweet, sour, salty, bitter, and hot all at the same time. The prawns were chewy, the bamboo crunchy, and the sauce silky.

I called the waiter over, and to his further confusion I ordered two beers. I told the man to pour them into glasses and set one at each end of the table. Picking up mine, I toasted the Sultan. "Happy birthday, Your Highness." The poor waiter averted his eyes, but the Sultan and I dined well together in my fancy.

So anyway, back to matters at hand. There I was at the E&O, pretending to dine with Fatima. The oxtail soup came, and it was the best I've ever had—rich and thick and made with Madeira wine. Somerset Maugham's sole was a fat fillet sauteed and topped with a thick sauce of pounded shrimp, sweet butter, tomato, chives, and tarragon. The creamed spinach was made with nutmeg and genuine heavy cream and tasted almost like a sweet. I had sherry trifle for dessert. I had never heard of it before and I pronounced it "triffle." The waiter chuckled.

"Well, that's how we say it in California," I explained to the imaginary Fatima. She nodded knowingly and sniffed her corsage.

I finished the meal with a glass of Sandeman's Ruby Port—red, rich, heavy, and sweet—a glass of liquid jewels. Just like Somerset Maugham, the famous guy. I was there, right there at his table. Me, a twenty-two-year-old sea-blown bum from Mendocino County, California. Just a nobody. But I was a somebody here. And I had a date with one of the loveliest women on the island. I toasted her, and she blushed sweetly.

After dinner, I walked along the beach to my room. The moon was rising and glittering the sea to the west. The ocean seemed to sigh contentedly. The moist, warm equatorial breeze ran ahead of me as if to lead the way. It beckoned me along and whispered from the fronded tops of the palms along the beach. The wind is like that in the tropics. It's always...familiar. And it's always warm and soft, even in typhoons, when it's the most dangerous.

In temperate zones the wind always seems cold and violent. It's something that strikes you, stings your ears and fingers, and makes your nose red and runny. It's on the rampage in the temperate zones, and out to blow away your newspaper, deposit leaves on your lawn or dust in your eyes.

But in the tropics, the wind is a woman. A sensuous, lascivious woman who titillates your nerve endings and whispers in your ear. It is Aphrodite.

I entered my room and called room service for coffee. After it was served, I sat down to sip and to wait. Just as she said she would, a little after midnight, Fatima tapped on the sliding glass door that opened out onto the beach. I slid the door open and the breeze billowed in, carrying her coconut and clove scent. Wisps of her black hair reached up and touched my face. She looked up at me and smiled a little nervously. I kissed her lightly on the lips, and she pressed her face against my neck and smell-kissed me, in that Malayan way.

"Did anyone see you come?" I asked as she entered the room.

"No. I came around the back."

She wore a red batik sarong kebaya.

"You have been swimming?" she asked, pointing to the swimsuit I had changed into.

"No, but I thought you and I might go. It's such a warm night."

"But I have nothing to wear."

Raising my brows and smiling, I asked, "Have you ever heard of skinny-dipping?"

"Skin dipping?"

"No. Skinny-dipping."

"Mmmmm, no," she said cautiously. "This is something from America?"

"It's going swimming with nothing on," I grinned conspiratorially.

"Oh. Well, anyway, I don't swim."

"Well, you don't have to swim. You can just play in the water. That's why we don't call it skinny-swimming."

"You do this?" she asked, looking at me askance.

"Of course. Everybody does," I said, turning out the light.

"Women too?"

"With their men."

I climbed out of my suit and picked up a towel.

She stood thinking a moment, looked out to the beach to see if anyone was there, then quietly slipped out of her sarong. She followed me out the door, staying close, to hide behind me. I looked up and down the beach. Satisfied that we were still alone, I took her hand, and we walked past the palms, where the breeze whispered in the fronds, toward the gentle Indian Ocean surf. In the light of the full moon, her darkness stood out against the white, sandy beach. The luster of her skin caught the moonlight and reflected it so that she looked like a luminous shadow. We stood there for a while and felt the sensuous breeze caress our bare bodies with its humid fingers.

We waded into the dark, silky sea and played and splashed and spoke in laughing whispers. The water glistened as it ran down her face and hair in rivulets. It made a sheen on her breasts, and I tasted the salt on her nipples. The moon was so bright I could see into her eyes, and I looked into them, holding her shoulders, for a long moment. She gave a little laugh, and the breeze echoed it high up in the palms. We walked arm in arm to a place under a palm and lay down. I nuzzled my head against hers and smelled the sea in her wet hair, long, thick and black, clinging in arabesques to her brown face and shoulders. She bit my arm gently. The sand gave way like pillows beneath our bodies. Warm flesh melded. The moon peered mischievously through the palm fronds and the breeze, Aphrodite, flowed warmly over us.

When at last we rose, we walked silently into the sea and bathed each other. Then I carried her in my arms back to the palm, and we sat on the towel and watched the sky until the moon, chasing the horizon, caught and joined with her. The only sounds then were the sighing of the ocean, Fatima's murmurs as she nestled her head on my shoulder, and Aphrodite, giggling in the palm fronds.

When it was very late, we went back to the room to sleep a little.

THE LAST DAY

The sun was up, and Fatima woke with a start. Her motion woke me and I heard her give a little cry. I opened my eyes to see her dressing hurriedly.

"What's the matter?"

"I have to go," she said tersely. Then under her breath, "Already I will get five slaps."

"Huh? What?"

"Nothing."

"No, wait a minute. You said five slaps. What do you mean five slaps?"

"Five slaps of the face," she said, looking in the mirror.

"Why are you going to get 'five slaps of the face'? And who the hell is going to give them to you?"

"Ohsman, of course," she replied, quickly brushing her hair.

70

"Ohsman? Tang's errand boy?"

"Ohsman is Mr. Tang's manager of the house." She seemed surprised at me.

"So why is Ohsman going to slap you?" I demanded as I got out of bed.

"Because I left the house without permission."

I stood staring at her, not wanting to comprehend.

"We're not supposed to leave without getting permission," she explained. "Especially for visiting a man. I have to go now."

She turned to the door but I caught her by the arm, pulled her back to me, and said, "Now wait a minute! Just wait a minute. You mean to tell me that he's just going to go ahead and hit you, slap you, five times?"

Seeing that I was getting upset, she tried to calm me. "Oh, don't worry. He's not going to hit me hard. If he does, then I will be ugly, and nobody will want me. He's only going to do it for the noise."

"I don't believe I'm hearing this! Listen, I don't care what that bastard's intentions are. I'm going there with you, and if he feels like slapping somebody, he can try it on me. Then we'll see what he gets for his trouble!"

"No! If you go to see Ohsman it's only going to be worse for me. Please...no...you stay here, Richard. It's our rule. I broke the rule. It's all right. I wanted to see you for a while, so I came here. I know the rule. So, all right, please, stay here."

"No! I won't. A guy that slaps women around needs to get some of it himself. And that's just what's going to happen if he tries anything. Listen now, don't you worry. He's not going to touch you as long as I'm there."

"But you're not going to be there always! You're going to leave with your ship. And you don't have to worry. And maybe you don't come back." Her eyes were misty and she said, "And maybe you come back and you want another girl. Then I'm alone with Ohsman. And he tells Mr. Tang, and he will make me leave the house. Then they're going to tell everybody that I make trouble, and I won't get another job, so stay here. You have to stay!"

She picked up her bag and went out into the hot morning, down the beach, without turning back, her five-foot, red-clad frame moving slowly home to Ohsman. I stood there, naked, looking after her.

Slowly, realization sank in. "Oh my God. Oh no, no. Fatima, I'm sorry. I didn't realize. I didn't think." For all my high-flying sentiments about not calling hookers bitches, I hadn't considered Fatima's feelings, her life, the constraints she lived in. As fond as I was of her, as much as she had charmed me, I realized that I had been thinking of her as a toy, or a playmate. I had looked upon her as an audience to strut my uniform for, a partner for some laughs, a good lay, whatever you like, but not as a creature who could feel pain.

Fatima had come to me that night a complete human being, not simply a warm body for hire. She had affections and fears and hurts. She liked me. And she wanted to have just one little night with me as one woman to one man. Something clean. Something, if not pure, then at least approaching it. Christ, she deserved at least that, the poor girl. The poor darling. "Yes!" I cried out to myself, to the air, to the gods, to whoever might listen. "She's a human being, goddamn it! She rates more!"

At four in the afternoon, I opened the Chung King's door loudly. Ohsman was at his counter. Fatima was standing near the other girls. They all looked my way as I came in. I looked aside at Ohsman, and he glowered at me, his sour mouth puckered up like a prune. Yeah, he was pissed; we had cheated him out of a few bucks. I locked eyes with Fatima and slowly walked toward her. She stood rock still. She was wearing her white sarong, the backless one, and was ready for work. I could feel Ohsman's eyes on me as I passed by him. I refused to acknowledge him, but his glare was boring a hole in my head anyway. Nearing Fatima, I looked for signs of violence against her and so far saw none. "He couldn't have hit her. He wouldn't. No way." Then it occurred to me that he could have hit her on the back of the head, or somewhere on her body.

That wouldn't leave any marks. "Nah! No way." I stopped at a thread's length from her.

In her left eye, the little weblike blood vessels were broken. The eye was blood-shot. I looked closely for marks on her face and there were none, but the texture of the skin on her left cheek was different. It had no luster. It was dull, about a hand's width, and it wasn't smooth. She saw that I had seen and looked at the floor.

He had hit her. The son of a bitch had hit her. My mind cried out. Anger pumped up my chest. My hands made fists without my bidding them to. Arm muscles throbbed, bicep, tricep, and forearm. Power trembled in them. I would break something in him. "I'll break his face! I'll hit him in the gut, and I'll open up his face. And if I can't do it alone, I'll get some guys, and we'll all stomp the shit out of him."

I jerked my head his way. He looked at me, his gaze unwavering. The wrinkles of his mouth shifted over to one side, and it curled itself into a tiny, scornful smile. The smirky Chinese girl sniggered. My chest heaving, I realized that if I made a move on Ohsman, he'd just call the cops. He'd probably dealt with guys like me before. Maybe he even had a weapon. And even if I did slug him and get away with it, he would simply take it out on Fatima. A weasel like him would. "Damn! Damn! Damn!"

I turned back to Fatima, realizing that I was causing a scene and embarrassing her. But I was still angry, and yet unable to take action on it because it would just come back on her. I thought, "I'll give her some money," but I couldn't do that either! That pig Ohsman would just take it away from her, saying she owed it to him. "Damn!" My ears started to ring. "I'll have Sam bring her the money in an envelope," I thought. "With a note, a letter."

What the hell else could I do? Take her on board as a stowaway? Send her a monthly allowance for life? Float her a big loan or send her home to my mother? I couldn't help her. I couldn't do one stinking, infinitesimal fucking thing! It was her life, and she was stuck in it.

There was a groan or a cry in me wanting to get out, when Fatima reached out toward me and said shyly, "I want to see you again." Her long-nailed fingers reached my abdomen and traced five lines down my shirt. My insides screamed at her touch, "What the hell's the matter with you?" I thought. "Don't you have any buddy system? Don't you have any rights? Don't you have anything?"

Tears were rising up from the bottom. They would soon be at my eyes. I couldn't let that happen in front of Ohsman or those smirking, slutty whores. Or in front of Fatima, for they were coming to her also.

I took a step back and croaked, "Well, we're leaving in the morning, you know."

"Wait," she said, and grabbed her purse and dug through it. It didn't take long, there wasn't much in it. She drew out those two Camel patches that she had fancied so much. "Here." She handed them to me, sniffling and trying to smile. "For a little remembrance," she said, rolling the R.

I swallowed and took them, forcing my hand not to shake. I took another step backward. Holding the patches in one hand, I waved a few fingers at her with the other, then turned, kind of half-saluted, and left while I had time. On the way out, I heard human sounds through the buzzing in my ears, but I don't know what they were.

I walked out onto the street. The sun was dropping, and I walked toward it. The esplanade lay in that direction; there was privacy in a large space. All the colors of Penang swirled around me: people in their batiks, gaudy pedicabs, pushcarts, dogs, ravens, jade dealers, money changers, all coming, going, doing, being—a maelstrom of people, colors, sounds, and smells. I was nearing the esplanade, and the tears were making a movie on my remembering eyes. In it was Fatima, dressed in her white sarong, the backless one, ready for work, and the next man; a bruised eye; and Ohsman.

After a couple of hours, I went back to the E&O Hotel. I had checked out of my room, but I got several sheets of their letterhead stationery and an envelope from the reception desk. I went into the pub, ordered a pint of beer, and sat down at a table, off to the side. I counted out my remaining cash. I kept enough to see me through the evening and set aside the greater part for Fatima. It must have been about fifty or sixty dollars—for her a month's pay, easy.

I started to compose a letter to her. I wanted to tell her all of my feelings about her, how I was sorry she had the life she had. I wanted to tell her that the next time I came to Penang, I would buy her out of the house for the entire period of my stay, right up front; that we would have lots of fun together. I would buy her nice clothes that would make her look like a regular woman, so nobody could tell that she was a whore, and we would stay at the E&O every night, and that no one would abuse her. I had to tell her that I wasn't coming to see her that night because…because why? Because I couldn't bear to see her in the snare she lived in? Because I had the blues? Because I was too angry at Ohsman? At the world? At her?

I wrote, "Dear Fatima, here is some money for you. I hope to see you next time around. Take good care of yourself. Lots of luck. Love, Richard."

I sealed it up with the money, and later on I gave it to Sam or Ricky or somebody to give to Fatima—on the sly so Ohsman wouldn't see.

After that, I "went on the grog," as the Aussies say. I went from bar to bar all night drinking gin and beer. Several hookers tried to chat me up, but I told them to leave me alone. Eventually I ran into some of my friends in one of the bars and decided it would be better if I partied with them, at least for a while. I began to feel a little more lighthearted, and thought that maybe I would go see Fatima after all. But then I realized that it was late in the evening. As it was our last night in Penang, every man who didn't have duty was on the beach drinking and whoring enough to last till the next port. Fatima was probably engaged by now. She had a living to make.

I got the blues again. Somebody asked me, "Hey, what's with the long face? It's party time. Where's that foxy little hooker you had? She didn't clap you up, did she?"

"Hey, don't talk about Dickie's hooker like that. She's his darling true-love. Ha!"

"Uh oh. Petty Officer Sterling has deep feelings for one of the ladies of the land. Ho ho!"

"You gonna dust her down?"

"What's the story?"

I told them to go fuck themselves. They laughed. We always told each other to go fuck ourselves. My money was just about spent, so I started heading back to the ship. What notes and coins I had left when I reached the docks I gave to some scrawny-looking pedicab driver, telling him I had had a nice time on his island. He didn't seem surprised. I went to my bunk; the ship rocked in the shifting tide, and finally, I slept.

Months later, when I went back to Penang, Fatima was gone. Ohsman was still there, and he seemed just as sour as ever. The inky-dark Tamil girl told me that Fatima had been gone for some time. No one knew where she went. Malacca, maybe. Hookers often cover their tracks when they leave a place. They are often in debt to the company store. Sometimes they've been dealing drugs or other contraband. A few may have robbed a client. Sometimes they change their names, and not for the first time. I didn't even know if Fatima was her real name.

I stayed with the Tamil girl that night. I figured it was the closest I could get. She was very pretty in her sari. And she was kind as well—yes, I can tell you that she was a very kind person. She treated me very well, and she said that if she ever saw Fatima again, she would give her my address. A kind person, yes. But I can't remember her name.

I have only been able to find Fatima in one place: at the pushcarts down by the grassy esplanade. I can smell her hair when the cooks press coconuts for oil. I smell her skin when they smoke their clove-laced Krakatoa cigarettes. I cannot inhale the deep aroma of *blacan* without seeing her in my mind's eye and hearing her discourse on the idea that "my country is many places." Her R trills in the bubble of broth. She speaks in the sizzle of woks. And the tastes of lemon grass and tamarind are forever synonymous with her inspiring Malayan kiss. When I dine there beneath the palm by the side of the road, I am once again with the phantom woman from the elegant table at the Eastern & Oriental. I dine lingeringly with her. I feed richly on her memory. And I carry her within me when I go.

CURRY PUFFS

Fatima gave me this recipe. It's the same one she made the day we met. The filling would vary with whatever she had available. As she put it, "Sometimes I make them different, and sometimes I make them the same."

The Filling

2	tablespoons vegetable oil
2	cloves garlic, minced
2	small red chiles, such as jalapeños, stems and seeds removed, minced
4	shallots, minced
1	teaspoon ground turmeric
¼	pound small shrimp, shelled and deveined
¼	pound bean sprouts
2	scallions, minced
1/4	pound tofu, chopped
	Salt to taste

Heat the oil in a wok and stir-fry the garlic, chiles, shallots, and turmeric until fragrant. Add the shrimp and cook for 1 to 2 minutes, then add the bean sprouts and scallions and cook for another 2 minutes. Add the tofu, stir to heat through, add salt to taste, and remove from heat. Set the mixture aside.

The Pastry

1	cup flour
5	tablespoons vegetable oil
¼	cup water mixed with a pinch of salt
	Vegetable oil for deep frying

Combine the flour, oil, and enough water to make a dough and knead for 5 minutes. Roll out the dough and use a cookie cutter to make rounds about 3 inches across. Place a teaspoon of filling on each round, dampen the edges with water, and fold over to make a half-moon shape. Seal tightly with a fork. Deep fry till golden.

Yield: Makes about 12
Heat Scale: Mild

BEE HOON MEE

Mee is the Malayan word for noodle, and *bee hoon* refers to the type: rice vermicelli. This is a very common dish and is one of the few that Malayans do not eat with their hands, but use forks or chopsticks.

4   tablespoons vegetable oil
1   onion, finely chopped or grated
4   cloves garlic, minced
6   dried chiles, such as Thai, stems removed, broken up and soaked
¼   pound fresh shrimp, shelled and deveined
¼   pound tofu
¼   teaspoon salt
¼   teaspoon shrimp paste
½   tablespoon dark soy sauce
3   ripe tomatoes, sliced
2   eggs, beaten
¼   pound mustard greens, chopped coarsely
¼   pound bean sprouts
½   pound rice vermicelli, soaked for 15 minutes and cut into 5-inch lengths

Heat the oil in a wok and stir-fry the onion, garlic, and chiles until fragrant. Add the shrimp and fry for 1 minute. Add the tofu, salt, shrimp paste, soy sauce, and tomatoes, and cook, stirring, for 3 minutes. Push the ingredients to the side of the pan, pour the eggs into the middle, and cook for 1 minute. Add the remaining ingredients, mix all together, and cook for 2 minutes more.

Yield: A meal for two or side dishes for four
Heat Scale: Medium
Serving Suggestion: Serve with cucumber and tomato, lime wedges and sliced chiles.

CHICKEN CURRY FATIMA

This dish makes use of oil-rich candlenuts, the fruit of the candleberry tree. They are quite common in Malayan cookery and take their name from the old-time Malay practice of burning them as candles. The turmeric would be fresh in Malaya, in the form of a rhizome, like ginger.

6   shallots
3   candlenuts (or substitute 3 macadamia nuts or Brazil nuts)
1   teaspoon turmeric
3   fresh red chiles, such as jalapeños, stems and seeds removed
4   tablespoons vegetable oil
½   pound potatoes, peeled and diced
½   pound whole button mushrooms
1½ cups coconut milk
¼   teaspoon salt, or to taste
1   pound chicken, skin and bones removed, cut into bite-sized pieces
10 small whole dried red chiles, such as Thai

In a mortar or blender, grind the shallots, nuts, turmeric, and fresh red chiles to a fine paste. Heat the oil to medium in a wok and stir-fry the paste until fragrant. Add the potatoes and mushrooms and stir-fry for 1 minute. Add the coconut milk and salt and bring to a gentle boil. Add the chicken and small red chiles and cook, stirring often, for 15 to 20 minutes. Serve over rice.

Yield: Serves 6
Heat Scale: Medium Hot

ASAM PEDAS MALACCA (SMOKY HOT MACKEREL)

The chiles called for in this recipe are the small ones we often refer to as "Thai type." In Malaya, they are known as "bird's eyes."

1   tablespoon coriander seeds
½   teaspoon cumin seeds
½   teaspoon fennel seeds
2   tablespoons dry, grated coconut
1   teaspoon ground turmeric
15 dried chiles, such as Thai or chiltepins, stems removed, soaked
1   tablespoon blacan (dried shrimp paste)
3   cloves garlic
1   inch fresh ginger root
1   small Spanish onion
¼   cup vegetable oil

½ teaspoon salt
3 tablespoons tamarind paste
1 pound mackerel or bonito, cut into steaks and rubbed with a little salt
2 cups water, or more to cover
¼ cup sliced scallions

In a pan, dry-roast the coriander, cumin, fennel, and coconut until browned. Let the mixture cool. In a mortar or blender, grind the cooled spice mixture and the turmeric, chiles, blacan, garlic, ginger and onion together. Heat the oil to hot in a wok and stir-fry the ground ingredients until fragrant. Stir in the salt and tamarind, then add the fish steaks, turning to coat with the mixture. Add enough water to cover, sprinkle scallions on top, bring to the boil, then reduce heat and simmer for 10 minutes, turning the steaks once.

Yield: Serves 4
Heat Scale: Very Hot

CHILE PRAWNS

It took me years to get this recipe. The waiter at the See Kong Hooi restaurant had apparently been quite spooked by my dinner with the Sultan, and he would never let me into the kitchen. Through experimentation, I finally got it right.

2 tablespoons peanut oil
1 tablespoon chopped garlic
1 tablespoon minced fresh ginger
2 jalapeño chiles, stems and seeds removed, chopped
1 pound large prawns, shelled and deveined
1 tablespoon fermented black or brown beans
1 ripe tomato, peeled, seeded, and chopped fine (or substitute ¼ cup catsup)
½ cup thinly sliced scallions
1 cup braised bamboo shoots
1 tablespoon soy sauce
2 tablespoons dry sherry or rice wine
1 teaspoon sugar
½ teaspoon sesame oil
1 tablespoon cornstarch mixed with 2 tablespoons water
Fresh cilantro for garnish

Heat the oil in a wok and add the garlic, ginger, and chile. Stir-fry for 1 minute. Add the prawns and stir-fry for 2 minutes. Add the fermented beans, tomato, scallions, bamboo shoots, soy sauce, sherry, sugar, and sesame oil and stir-fry for 2 to 3 minutes. Add the cornstarch mixture to thicken, if desired, and cook one more minute. Garnish with the fresh cilantro.

Yield: A meal for you and a sultan
Heat Scale: Medium
Serving Suggestion: Serve with rice and steamed asparagus with water chestnuts.
Variation: This recipe is also popular as Chile Crab. Have the merchant clean and dismember 2 crabs and divide the bodies into fourths. Omit the bamboo and cornstarch and double the amount of sherry or rice wine. Follow the same procedure, but add the crab last and cook covered, shaking the wok, for 10 minutes.

CHILE PRAWNS IN THE SHELL

The term "chile prawns" is like the term "gumbo." It denotes a style or a broad approach, not a fixed recipe. This one comes from a pushcart cook on Gurney Street. Diners must peel their own prawns.

1	tablespoon cayenne
1	tablespoon ground coriander
1	teaspoon ground turmeric
2	teaspoons black pepper
1	teaspoon ground lemon grass
½	teaspoon salt
1	cup water
1	pound giant prawns in the shell
4	tablespoons vegetable oil
1	small onion, grated or chopped fine

In a bowl, combine the cayenne, coriander, turmeric, pepper, lemon grass, salt, water, and the prawns. Marinate for 10 minutes, then drain, reserving the liquid. Heat the oil to medium high in a wok and stir-fry the onion until fragrant. Add the drained prawns and stir-fry for about 5 to 7 minutes; then remove the prawns from the wok and keep warm. Pour the reserved liquid into the wok and reduce it to a thick sauce. Serve the sauce alongside the prawns as a dipping sauce.

Yield: Dinner for two
Heat Scale: Hot

SATAY MALAYA WITH TWO DIPPING SAUCES

There are many variations on satay, but this one is the most traditional and tastes just like the one served by George at the E&O. Commander Stanbury, with whom I became good friends until his death a few years later, approved this recipe.

Chile-Tomato Sauce:
½   teaspoon salt
1   teaspoon shrimp paste
½   teaspoon sugar
2   jalapeño chiles, stems and seeds removed, chopped
1   large ripe tomato, seeded, peeled, and chopped fine

Combine all the ingredients in a bowl and whisk or beat together until blended. Pour into a small bowl and set aside.

Peanut Sauce:
1   tablespoon peanut oil
1   clove garlic, crushed
1   cup water
1   teaspoon crushed red chile
1   tablespoon tamarind paste
½   teaspoon salt
1½   tablespoons sugar
¼   teaspoon shrimp paste
1   cup crunchy peanut butter

Heat the oil to medium in a wok or pan and stir-fry the garlic for 1 minute. Add the water, chile, tamarind, salt, sugar, and shrimp paste. Stir the mixture until it begins to simmer and then add the peanut butter. Simmer, stirring, for 5 minutes more. Pour the mixture into a bowl and set aside.

The Marinade and Satay:
2   teaspoons ground coriander seed
¼   teaspoon ground cumin
3   cloves garlic, crushed
1   teaspoon salt
1   tablespoon brown or raw sugar
1   tablespoon tamarind paste
1   pound beef, cut into thin, bite-sized pieces

Combine all of the ingredients and marinate for at least 2 hours.

The Baste:
2   tablespoons sweet soy sauce
1   tablespoon water
1   tablespoon vegetable or coconut oil

Combine all of the ingredients. Thread the marinated meat onto skewers and brush each one liberally with the baste. Grill the meat over charcoal to the desired doneness and serve it with the two sauces for dipping.

Yield: 18 Skewers
Heat Scale: Varies according to which sauce is used.

SATAY FOR PORK

The Malays, being Muslims, do not eat pork. But the other peoples of Malaysia do, and they cook it many ways. This one is my favorite version.

The Dipping Sauce:

2	tablespoons sugar
1	tablespoon vinegar
1	teaspoon salt
2	tablespoons hot water
1	cup sliced cucumber
1	tablespoon chopped shallot
1	jalapeño chile, stem removed, sliced

Combine all of the ingredients in a bowl and set aside.

The Marinade and Satay:

1	strip lemon peel
1	red onion, chopped
1	tablespoon soy sauce
2	tablespoons vegetable oil
1	teaspoon coriander seeds
1	tablespoon chopped cilantro stalks
1	teaspoon ground cumin
1	teaspoon ground turmeric
¼	teaspoon cinnamon
1	teaspoon sugar
1	teaspoon salt
2	tablespoons peanuts
1	fresh chile, such as serrano, stem removed
2	cloves garlic
1	pound pork, cut into thin, bite-sized pieces

Combine all ingredients except the pork in a blender and puree to a paste, adding a little water if necessary. Combine the paste with the pork and marinate for at least 1 hour. Thread the meat on skewers and grill over charcoal until the marinade forms a crust. Serve the satay with dipping sauce.

Yield: 3 to 4 Servings
Heat Scale: Medium

SOMERSET SOLE

According to the waiter at the E&O dining room, this was Somerset Maugham's favorite dish. The barman also said that Maugham was fond of Pink Gin. Try both after reading his thoughtful story, "Rain."

3　tablespoons butter
1　cup fresh shrimp, shells and tails removed, reserve the shells
1　tomato, peeled, seeded, and chopped
1　teaspoon tarragon
1　teaspoon chopped chives
1　tablespoon dry sherry
2　sole fillets
　　Salt and white pepper to taste

Melt 2 tablespoons of the butter in a skillet over medium-high heat and saute the shrimp shells to extract their flavor. Remove the shells and discard. Reduce heat to medium and add the shrimp, tomato, tarragon, chives, and sherry, and simmer for 10 minutes. With a fork or potato masher, mash the mixture into a coarse paste and set aside and keep warm. Melt the remaining 1 tablespoon of butter in a pan and saute the sole fillets. Transfer the sole to plates and dress with the sauce. Add salt and white pepper to taste.

Yield: 2 Servings
Heat Scale: none

GREEN BEANS WITH COCONUT

This dish requires a lot of work because it calls for grated fresh coconut. The only way to get that is to buy a fresh coconut and grate it yourself. I promise you it's worth the effort.

2	tablespoons coconut oil or peanut oil
1	small onion, sliced thin
1	green chile, such as serrano, stem and seeds removed, sliced thin
1	teaspoon turmeric
½	teaspoon mustard seeds
½	cup finely grated fresh coconut
1	pound green beans, or Chinese long beans, cut to 1-inch lengths
½	cup water or coconut water (the liquid inside a fresh coconut)
	Salt to taste

Heat the oil to medium in a wok and stir-fry the onion, chile, turmeric, and mustard seeds until slightly browned. Add the coconut and cook until fragrant. Add beans and water and cook, stirring, until tender. Add salt to taste.

Yield: 6 Side Servings
Heat Scale: Mild

CUCUMBER SALAD

This is not a cooling salad, but it is spicy, refreshing, and cleansing for the palate. For a cooling salad to accompany a hot curry, see the recipe for Sambal Salat.

2	cucumbers, peeled, seeded, and sliced
	Salt to taste
	Juice of 2 limes
2	small red chiles, such as serranos, stems and seeds removed, sliced
2	small green chiles, such as serranos, stems and seeds removed, sliced
1	red onion, thinly sliced
¾	cup coconut milk

Sprinkle cucumbers with salt and let set 5 minutes. Rinse and drain them. Combine all ingredients and serve.

Yield: 4 Servings
Heat Scale: Hot

THREE SAMBALS

An important item on the Malay table is a relish called sambal. A simple meal might be just plain rice and a sambal or two to flavor it. Every cook has his or her own recipes. Here are three of my favorites.

SAMBAL BLACAN

6	red chiles, such as jalapeños, stems and seeds removed, chopped
2	tablespoons blacan (dried shrimp paste)
	Juice of two limes

In a mortar, pound the chiles and blacan together into a coarse paste. Mix in lime juice and serve.

Yield: ¾ Cup
Heat Scale: Hot

SAMBAL SALAT

1	tablespoon peanut oil
8	ounces green beans, French cut
2	cloves garlic, chopped
1	red chile, such as jalapeño, stem and seeds removed, sliced
1	tablespoon tamarind paste
	Salt to taste
	Juice of 1 lime
1	onion, sliced thin

Heat the oil in a wok and stir-fry the beans and garlic for 2 minutes. Add the chile, the tamarind, and salt and cook until the beans are tender. Toss in the lime juice and the onion; cool and serve.

Yield: 1 Cup or more
Heat Scale: Mild

SAMBAL SOTONG KERING

2	onions
15	dried chiles, such as Thai, stems and seeds removed, soaked
2	teaspoons blacan
5	tablespoons vegetable oil
1	pinch salt
1	tablespoon sugar
1	dried squid or cuttlefish, soaked in water for 2 hours and coarsely chopped
2	tablespoons tamarind paste

In a mortar or blender, grind together the onions, chiles, and blacan. Heat the oil in a wok and stir-fry the ground ingredients with the salt and sugar until fragrant.

Add the squid and cook 5 minutes. Add the tamarind and simmer until the mixture is reduced to a paste.

Yield: 2 Cups
Heat Scale: Very Hot

PENANG OKRA

Okra is very popular in Southeast Asia, where it is called "lady fingers." This recipe always reminded me of Cajun cooking, so I also like to call it "Gumbo Malaya."

The Spice Paste:
2	red chiles, such as jalapeños, stems and seeds removed
2	green chiles, such as jalapeños, stems and seeds removed
1	teaspoon turmeric
1	inch piece ginger
3	cloves garlic
½	teaspoon salt

Combine all ingredients in a blender and puree to a paste, adding a little water if necessary.

The Vegetables:
4	tablespoons vegetable oil
1	onion, sliced thin
2	large tomatoes, peeled and chopped
1	pound okra
1	tablespoon chopped cilantro

Heat the oil in a wok and brown the onion. Add the spice paste and stir-fry for 2 minutes. Add the tomatoes and stir-fry for 3 minutes. Increase the heat to high, add the okra, and cook 3 minutes. Cover, reduce the heat, and simmer till the okra is tender, about 7 minutes. Garnish with the cilantro.

Yield: 6 servings as a Side Dish
Heat Scale: Medium Hot

CHAPTER 5

MOJO RISING

A ND DRINK YET AGAIN. *Drink to mark the crossroads, and drink to make a beacon in the memory. Not drinks to slake the thirst, but drinks to smooth the way and mark the path to reverie.*

Toby, the silver-haired owner of the bar and a decorated veteran of the battle of Leyte Gulf, set a pair of frothy drinks in front of my shipmate Mike and me. Mike was a golden-haired private-school dropout from New England. He was very fussy about his drinks.

"Okay," Toby said, "this is what I always served to Francis Ford Coppola whenever he came in. Makin' that Apocalypse movie took him so much time, he was in here a lot drinkin' these, so I decided to name the drink after him. I call it the Francis."

"The Francis?" Mike winced. "Couldn't you think up something a little less prosaic? Like the Coppola Cup, or a Double Apocalypse?"

"No. I like callin' it the Francis. It sounds dignified that way." Toby never used nicknames. Even my buddy Fred the Peace Corps guy was Frederick to Toby, with all three syllables pronounced.

Our drinks had the perfumy aroma of mango, the tang of pineapple, and a strong undercurrent of rum. As I sipped, I looked out through the dining room to the waters of Subic Bay, Philippines. The sun was setting amidst the great splashes and swashes and mottled candy colors that are unique to the Philippine Island sky. I once counted fourteen separate hues in the crazy quilt of a Philippine sunset—purple, green, orange, six shades of blue, pink, and some colors I had no name for. They made the sky look like something delicious and fun to eat.

Toby's Beach Club Bar and Restaurant and his four thatched and terraced bungalows sat square on the beach of the eastern shore of the bay, about five miles out of Olongopo City. He was one of those American GIs who fall in love with the East and stay around when their enlistments expire, or when they retire. They marry a local woman, or at least set up housekeeping with one, and go into business as salvage divers, exporters, or innkeepers. Toby and his wife had run the Beach Club for many years. Actually, his wife controlled it, as foreigners couldn't own real estate or a majority share of an enterprise in the Philippines. Legally, Toby was her employee. I was staying in one of the bungalows at $3.00 a night.

"Hey, Toby," Mike said as he downed his Francis, "you've been here forever, you know everything."

"Sure," he said, running his fingers through his white muttonchop sideburns. "Waddaya wanna know?"

Mike looked at me. We both looked around the room to see if anyone might overhear. Then we both leaned over the bar, conspiratorially. Toby leaned outward over the bar, toward us.

"Toby," Mike said in a hush. "Have you ever heard of a place called Marilyn's?"

Toby gave us a blank stare.

"Yeah," I urged, "Marilyn's."

"You know," Mike insisted, "the knobber shop, gobbler's gulch."

Toby still looked blank, so I said, "C'mon. You've heard the Fellatio Alger story. The whorehouse where only oral sex is available, but it's, like, world-class. They say the women even have to go through some kind of special training program!"

"I heard they even have a fellow working there, too!" Mike said. "They say he does more business than any of the girls! Hot damn!"

"Spill it, Toby! Is it in Olongopo City?"

"C'mon! What's the story?"

"Okay, look," he said, holding his hands up as if to stop us. "You guys been hearin' too many crazy sea stories. People tell you that just to pull your chain. That stuff's only fantasy. Besides, hey, if it were true, I'd be there spendin' all my money! Ha ha! Okay? Here, let me get you two turkeys a couple more Francises. And if you ever do find a place like that, you be sure and tell me, okay? Just don't tell the wife, you know?" He smiled at the thought as he peeled another mango.

Mike looked glumly at the setting sun and said, "Well, maybe it isn't true, but it ought to be."

"Yeah."

Toby brought us two more Francises and reminded us that the martial law curfew was still in effect every night at midnight. President Ferdinand Marcos didn't want his enemies skulking about after the witching hour. Toby warned us: "The last thing you want to do is get arrested around here. Could be bad for your health. And it's gettin' hard to bribe your way through after midnight because all the cops are gettin' in on the act. It's gettin' downright expensive. That reminds me, Richard, your girlfriend was here, that cute one with the stand-up bazooms. What's her name?"

"Erlinda."

"Yeah, okay. She said to make sure you meet her in the bungalow by curfew or she's gonna get jealous. And she says not to be a butterfly while you're out drinkin'."

In the Philippines, a butterfly is a man who goes from flower to flower. It's even a verb, "to butterfly." Many of the women carry a switchblade-type weapon known as a butterfly knife. When pressed beyond endurance, they are known to clip the wings of the butterflies in their lives.

"Why is it," I asked, "that when I'm in port, and for as long as I'm in port, I'm the one who supports her, but she's the one who gets jealous? Something's amiss here."

"Don't you like her?" Toby asked.

"Well, yeah. She's the best girlfriend I've ever had here in the P.I.—and the best-dressed, too. A woman of style. But I just don't like having the butterfly knife of Damocles hanging over my head. Or over my privates."

"Well, that's what happens when you stay with 'em more than once or twice," the old sage counseled. "Suddenly you're their rice bowl and that's that. Besides, the women here just get attached easy, okay? Hey, maybe you like this girl more than you say. You think she might be something permanent?"

"It could happen. I'm not saying it will. It might not be worth it. But maybe, you know."

"If you don't piss her off too much. But I know, it's hard when you're a sailor, bein' gone all the time. During the war I was gone so much, my first wife got tired of it. She left me. So, okay. 'Nuff said. You gotta get it when you can."

90

Mike broke in and said, "Well, the night is young, Richard. Let's go bar-hop our way along the bay shore. I'm not spoken for and I can butterfly all I like. You can watch."

We began a gradual progress east and north along the bay. At each noisy, colorful stop there were women who would approach our table and politely say, "Hello. May I sit beside you for a while?" Others were more aggressive and yelled from across the room or the road, "Hey, Joe. Let's go overnight!" In the Philippines, all Americans are called Joe. "Hey, Joe. What do you want? I got it!" Through several miles of shoreline we traversed the sexual carnival that was Subic Bay. Whenever I seemed to be interested in a woman, Mike reminded me of my "knife-wielding darling-true-love."

That's not to say that Erlinda was a hard or a violent woman. She wasn't. She was sophisticated and cultured beyond the norm, having come from a well-educated Manila family. She was warm and charming and carried herself with dignity. An inner strength came through in her every word and movement, and yet, at the same time, she was vulnerable and bruised. I was quite fond of her. My complaint was that she had little control of her passions. I had seen her vent her rage before, in public even, and I didn't care to see it again. I felt sure that if she went unchecked she would do some serious injury to herself or me or to whomever might get caught in the middle.

About ten miles from Olongopo, we came upon a relatively quiet collection of a dozen or so buildings. Half of them were brothels, and the others were bars and restaurants. A few sported colorful signs with splashy names like the Galaxy, the Stardust, and Stumpy & Gimpy's Muffdivers Inn. On the shore side three buildings were wedged tightly together near a small boat dock. The building in the middle looked particularly scrunched and the front was recessed, giving it an even more crowded look. A wooden walk descended from road level down a few feet to a little porch. An unpretentious sign over the door read "Marilyn's." Mike and I saw it at the same time. We stopped, very quietly, and simply gazed, smilingly, upon the sign.

"Do you think it's really...?"

"Shhh. We're in the presence. I feel it. Shhh."

Through the open door a light the color of candleglow shone warmly. A low hum of conversation filled the air. Wordlessly, Mike and I took a single, tentative step forward. Mike reached with his right foot to the wooden walk and tested it. Nodding, he said, "I think it's safe. We won't be walking on an illusion." Shoulder to shoulder we approached, slowly, quietly, indeed reverentially, till we came to the door and peered in. Small, round tables with matching chairs occupied the floor, and a bar took up the far wall. Candles in hurricane globes burned on all the tables. To the left, a stairway led up to the next floor, and to the right was a little alcove for a band. Patrons collected in knots around the small tables. A larger group sat at three tables pushed together in a corner, drinking beer and punch.

Two waiters were working behind the bar, and they were perfectly dressed in starched white shirts, black bow ties, and cummerbunds. When one of them saw us, he immediately put down his work and came forward to greet us.

"Welcome, gentlemen. Welcome to Marilyn's. Please sit down and have something to drink. Do you want beer? Or we have a special drink, a punch. We call it Mojo."

"Uh...beer, yeah, beer. Two beers," one of us muttered as we took it all in.

"Is this, uh...is this...Marilyn's?"

"Of course. Did you not see our sign outside?" The waiter took as much care in enunciating his words as he did with his fastidious appearance.

"I mean, is this, like, the real Marilyn's? You know, the one people talk about?"

"Ha ha," the waiter laughed. "There is only one famous Marilyn in all of Subic, and this is her place."

"You mean there really is a woman named Marilyn? An actual woman? It's not just the name of the place? It's all true? Everything we've heard is true?"

"Well," he said, "I can't know all that you have heard. But I'm sure pretty much everything is true. I have been working for her for many years. I know what I'm talking about. I hope you will like it here and come often."

A middle-aged American man, a civilian by his haircut, came wearily down the stairs, a smile on his flushed face. He lumbered across the room and sat down heavily with the patrons at the corner tables. Then a girl in a ponytail, short skirt, and blouse tied fetchingly beneath her breasts came bouncing down the stairs. As she passed our table she flashed us a white, toothy smile and waved hello. She went out through a door by the bar and called to the civilian, "Goodbye, Doug. See you again." Doug gave her a tired little wave and sighed a sigh of the content of heart.

When the waiter brought our drinks, we told him how we had heard so often about this place but never knew anybody who had actually seen it. We went on to say that it was a real thrill to be sitting in a living legend, or something like that.

"And you look so elegant in your cummerbunds," I said. "Everything about this place is just marvelous."

The waiter seemed immensely pleased with our compliments and enthusiasm. Then I asked, "Is Marilyn still alive? Does she live in town, or in Manila, maybe?"

"Oh, she lives very near," he said. "Would you like to meet her?"

"Pinch me, Mike. I'm dreaming."

Our waiter, whose name was Mando, conferred briefly with his partner, then led us outside where we began walking along the shore. "Marilyn likes to meet new people very often," he explained. "She likes American guys very much. But first we have to stop at the Sari Sari store. If you are going to meet Marilyn, you have to bring her a present."

A Sari Sari store is a Philippine kiosk, or a tiny convenience store. In the towns, every street corner has one. On the highways and byways there's one every mile or so. We stopped at one of two that serviced the collection of a dozen or so buildings and bought Marilyn the finest article available: a bottle of cologne. It was men's cologne, but it was all the Sari Sari store had. And Mando said it would be the thought that counted with his mistress.

We continued down the beach till we came to a well-lighted, walled compound. We stopped at a wrought-iron grille gate where Mando pressed a button and jabbered into a speaker.

"It's a villa!" Mike whispered with admiration. "A demi-palace! A palace for the queen of head!"

The gate buzzed open and Mando led us down a curvy, tile walkway lined with ferns and flowers. An ornate birdbath stood four feet high in the middle of a well-trimmed lawn. Laughter and party voices floated toward us from the main building as we approached it.

"What do you think is going on there?" Mike murmured.

"Whatever it is, I hope we're not too late."

"By the way, don't forget to get home on time tonight. Otherwise, you might turn into a butterflied pumpkin."

"Mike, did I ever tell you you're an asshole?"

"Yes."

"Just checking."

The front door of the main building opened and happy noises, color, and light spilled out. The walls and ceiling of the large room were painted a pale coral. Majestic ferns and elegant potted palms made it lush with jade green. Rattan and wicker furniture with colorful cushions dotted the room and capiz shell lamps bathed it in velvety yellow light. The occupants of the room were certainly not what I expected.

They were society folk—local politicians, high-ranking U.S. naval officers, civilian bigwigs from the nearby U.S. Navy base, businessmen, both Philippine and American, some people I took to be artists of some kind, and musicians I had seen in night clubs. Most of them were accompanied by their wives! One of the naval officers, a full commander (with his wife), was in crisp, dress-white uniform, and I recognized him from a brief encounter in the past. The missus wore blue chiffon and affected an ivory fan with little feathers hanging from it. The civilians schmoozed and the politicians conspired and the businessmen talked business. A man in a corner softly strummed a twelve-string guitar. Servants served drinks and tidbits. Dominating the whole scene was Marilyn.

She sat in an enormous rattan empress chair, or peacock chair, furnished with gaily-colored floral cushions. A girl of about sixteen, dressed casually in faded jeans and a billowy tee shirt, stood leaning lazily against one side of Marilyn's throne. Now and then they whispered. Marilyn was smartly dressed in a finely woven cotton pants suit, expensive looking sandals, and pearls. She looked to be about thirty-five to forty. It is an unfortunate fact that women in the Philippines tend to go to fat very early in life, and very quickly, too. I've seen women on the eve of their thirtieth birthdays go to bed thin and wake up twenty pounds heavier. Or so it seems. I don't know if it's diet, climate, or heredity; I only know that it happens. But Marilyn had beaten the odds. I don't know if she had been slimmer in her youth, but at the time when I looked upon her she was the size and shape of Marilyn Monroe—a luminous Monroe rendered in brunette and brown.

All the talk halted as we were conducted into the room. With the dignified strut of a major domo, Mando approached the throne and announced: "Marilyn, I have the pleasure to introduce these two American gentlemen. They have heard of you all the way from their home, and they would like to be your new friends."

The whole company broke into polite applause, smiles, and remarks.

"New friends, new friends!"

93

"How nice."

"Mabuhay!"

"Heard of Marilyn all the way from stateside."

"Great."

Marilyn smiled at us engagingly and turned her full attention to us. Mando gestured us forward. I was holding our cologne offering, so I approached and said, "Marilyn, I am Richard, and this is Mike. We've heard of you for such a long time. But we thought you were just a dream. Forgive us, and accept this small gift as a token from two of your admirers."

She took it in her finely manicured hands and read from the label, "Ah, Rawhide cologne. You're very nice to bring me this."

Mike found his tongue and said, "Well, that's all there was at the Sari Sari store. But we'd have brought you diamonds if we could. Diamonds!"

"This will be very good for my nephew," she said, handing it to the tee-shirted girl to take charge of. "And now come and sit by me and tell me your stories."

"Yes, yes," the courtiers all urged. "Tell your stories."

Mando, his duty done, slipped quietly away, so Marilyn gestured to another cummerbunded servant, who brought out two low footstools and set them at her feet.

"Sit, sit, sit," she insisted with gestures of offering. "And bring them someting to drink, too, Vincent. Bring them a Mojo."

"Mojo, Mojo," the people chanted.

We sat at Marilyn's feet, our heads on a level with her lap, and were soon served two icy highball glasses filled with a pinkish-orange punch that was rather the same color as the paint on the walls. It smelled of fresh pineapple and other sweet fruits, though I could not identify them. And it tasted just the same: delicious.

"I don't taste any alcohol in this," I said. "Is it a soft drink?"

A ripple of knowing laughter shivered through the crowd.

"Soft drink!"

"Hardly!"

"It has a lot of rum in it," Marilyn warned us. "So you have to be careful when you drink it because it can fool you a lot. I know. I'm the one who always makes it. And now, your stories. Please?"

And so we told Marilyn and her admirers our stories: where we were from, where we were going, places we had visited, and what was important in our lives. Marilyn listened with a very attentive ear and with sympathetic and pleased expressions. She asked lots of questions. Whenever I made a joke, she laughed sincerely and touched me on the shoulder. The Mojo flowed. I felt that I was in the company of someone special, a generous and commanding personality. Very *simpatico*. It must have been something like Othello and Desdemona: he loving her because she loved his stories. Marilyn was a person I wanted to be close to. I wanted to put my head on her lap and let her sing me a lullaby. Or feed me more Mojo.

When we had exhausted our stories, Marilyn's followers gave us polite applause. Marilyn asked us, "Where are you staying now?" Mike named his hotel, and I said, "In a bungalow at a place called the Beach Club, down the road a few miles."

"Oh, then you must know my friend Toby," she said with pleased surprise.

"Toby?"

"Yes, with white hair and big sideburns?"

"Oh yes. Toby. Yes, of course. Uh, we know Toby, don't we, Mike?"

"Toby," he nodded.

"He's a friend of mine a long time," Marilyn smiled. Then she reached down and patted and stroked me gently on the head, like a pet dog, smiling all the while. Noticing my empty glass, she playfully scolded Vincent, charging him to be more attentive, and never again to let her guests hold an empty Mojo glass. Leaning over to me and petting me again, she said, "Would you like to hear my story now?"

"Marilyn's story!" one of the faithful cried out.

"Yes, yes, Marilyn's story," they all gushed, and yet again rendered polite applause.

"I never tire of it," the commander's wife said as she fanned herself coquettishly. The guitarist stopped his soulful strumming for the first time since we had arrived. Vincent topped off my glass and stood back in rapt, respectful silence.

"Well, I was born a very poor girl on the island of Cebu," she began. "And when I was still just young I came to Subic to make my fortune. I tried to be a dancer, but if you know me very well you know I'm not very good. So I worked in the bars, I worked in the clubs. I worked every day and night. And I knew what my customers wanted."

At this all the courtiers nodded and murmured their agreement. "So I practiced. And I became the best."

"The best, the best," the hangers-on added in refrain.

"And soon they were all coming to me. I began to earn a lot of money."

"Lots of money!"

"Ha ha!"

"Bravo!"

"I soon got to have too many customers and boyfriends. And I had money in the bank. So, I opened my own place. The first was in Olongopo. And I hired the girls, and I taught them myself. And I always treated them well and paid them well. And they all became experts like me. I told them the secret to success is to always be the best. So, I have been very successful. And now I have my other place here on the beach. I am a woman with two very successful businesses."

Marilyn was warming to her theme, smiling in satisfaction and making pumping motions with her arm. A giggle wanted to escape from her, but she harnessed it and turned it into words, "I now have money and friends and houses and everything. And I got all this," she said stretching out the word "all," and making a grand sweeping gesture with her arm, "I got all this from sucking dicks."

"Ho ho ho!" her fans laughed with delight at the joke they had doubtless laughed at many times before.

"Bravo, well said!"

"Sucking dicks, ha ha ha!"

"I never tire of it."

"Commander," Marilyn called over the tumult to the Senior Officer Present. "Do you know the big sign on the Navy base that says 'What have you done for the fleet today?'"

95

"Of course, Marilyn. And what I have done is go to work. What have you done for the fleet today?"

"I sucked their dicks!"

And the people went into hysterics yet again. Mike seemed bemused. I couldn't tell how much rum was in the Mojo, but by this time I had copped a mighty buzz and was laughing like a fool along with all the rest of her fans. As the hubbub died down, they all started chatting among themselves, the story over, and Vincent appeared at my side to fill my glass again. He smiled as he slipped away, and I realized that I was resting one arm on Marilyn's lap. She stroked my head like a poodle once more and looked down at me with mirthful eyes. "Did you like my story?"

"Ha, it's a great story. Really good. But, hey. Tell me something, Marilyn. How do you know Toby?"

She considered for a moment, then decided to tell. "Well, he used to be my boyfriend."

"No."

"Yes. But his wife was jealous. So now...he's just...just my friend."

"C'mon. Don't be a tease. Tell me everything."

Cradling my head in the crook of her arm, she leaned down low and whispered in my ear with breath warm and moist, "He helps me when I'm training my new girls. I can't teach them everything with a banana or a squash. They have to know the real thing. I pay him a little bit. His wife keeps him on a short string; she doesn't give him very much. In more ways than one. But you need some more Mojo. Vincent!"

It was now after 11:00 p.m. Those of Marilyn's admirers who were not houseguests began to make ready to leave in order to beat the curfew. Nobody wanted to have to pay a badly inflated bribe to the police or, worse, confront the constabulary troops: the Federales. Mike had accepted an offer of a ride from one of the businessmen and was on his way out. I remembered Erlinda. Erlinda with her perfect bosom, her refined ways, her clever conversation, her high degree of lover's skill, and how delicious it was to awaken in the morning to her and the sound of the lapping baysurf. I had enough time plus ten minutes to make it back to her before midnight. And as I was low on cash, I lacked sufficient funds to bribe my way out of a tight spot.

"Stay," Marilyn said. "Stay."

"Stay?"

"Yes. Stay."

"Here?"

She laughed prettily. "With me."

We were standing now. She was reaching up to tug at my ear, still treating me like her favorite pet. I looked at my watch. It read nine minutes to jail.

"Stay," she repeated, like a mantra, running her fingers through my hair. "Stay." Eight minutes to spare. I had upset Erlinda once already this week. Sometimes when the women are angry they whip out their butterfly knives and say, "I'll give you a Filipino Haircut," with a slashing motion across the throat.

Seven minutes. I really liked Erlinda. I really, really did. I once fought another man over her. And she was worth it. When she was good, she was very very good.

Six minutes. "Stay."

"I'm cutting this awfully close," I thought. "Just think of the story I'll have if I stay. In every bar I go to, and every other night at sea, guys will say 'Richard, tell the story of Marilyn, the queen of head!' They'll buy me drinks all night. I'll be famous in maritime circles. They'll all say, 'Oh, that's Dickie Sterling, what a salty guy he is. Get him to tell you a story.' On top of all that, I'll bet Marilyn can be brutally satisfying. Furthermore, I like her, I really like her. But I like Erlinda, too. And she's waiting for me. And so is Marilyn."

Five minutes.

MOJO

Marilyn was an amazing woman. And so, in her way, was Erlinda. Sipping this drink on a quiet evening alone brings me back to both of them. I find that particularly satisfying, considering that in the past I had to choose either one of them or the other. I won't tell you which one it was, but there was no best choice.

1½   **cups pineapple juice**
1½   **cups orange juice**
1½   **cups 7-Up**
½   **cup rum (preferably Manila light)**
½   **cup vodka**
1   **tablespoon grenadine**

Pour all ingredients over ice and mix well. This drink will sneak up on you, so be careful. Sip slowly and ponder the road not taken.

Yield: 4 Powerful Mojos

THE FRANCIS

Toby said that the reason Coppola spent so much time at his place was that Francis had to do several takes of a special scene. The famous helicopter assault, with Wagner's "Ride of the Valkyries" for background music, was filmed just down the road from the Beach Club Bar and Restaurant. According to Toby, "They had to build that whole village from nothin'. Then they flew in all those helicopters and blew it to hell. Burned it to the ground. But Francis came into my place at the end of the day and said he didn't like it. 'We gotta rebuild the village and wreck it again,' he says. He ended up sayin' that *eight* times. He drank a lotta Francises."

½   **cup ripe mango flesh**
¼   **cup crushed pineapple**
1   **tablespoon lime juice**
1   **teaspoon sugar**
2   **tablespoons cream or half-and-half**
1½ **ounces rum**
½   **cup party ice**
    A few drops of Triple Sec or Grand Marnier

Combine all ingredients in a blender and whip them into a froth. Pour into a chilled glass and sprinkle with the Triple Sec or Grand Marnier.

Yield: 1 Francis

CHAPTER 6

A FEAST OF SORROWS:
THE FALL OF SAIGON

*F*OOD FOR LIFE AND FOOD FOR LOVE. *Drink for joy and drink for contemplation. Food and drink for all aspects of life. And so for death as well.*

*"A*ND THE AFFLICTED SHALL EAT, AND BE SATISFIED." —Psalms

DAWN, APRIL 30, 1975

At the mouth of the Mekong River, I stood on the foredeck and watched the sun come up on the last day of the long conflict the Vietnamese have come to call "the American War." It was the most beautiful dawn I had ever seen before or since. Still air hung warm and moist and soft. A thick, creamy quilt of cloud lay along the coast, and the rising sun painted it red, orange, and yellow. The colors blazed and constantly changed their patterns: mixing and moving and dancing majestically as though they were heaven's own fire. To the east of the clouds the sea lay quietly glassy and blue. The jungled hills that stood to the west were the greenest of green, and they formed a dam that held back the fluid cloak of clouds, so that we could watch the sun paint them for a while longer. It was gloriously beautiful—and deceptively peaceful.

By degrees, the painting vaporized, and the last story of the war began. The scene opened when a lone helicopter streaked in at low altitude from the direction of Saigon. Coming over water, it circled the command ship, the USS Blueridge, steaming just offshore. Orbiting the ship, the chopper climbed and fell several times, and its tail wagged back and forth as though the pilot were in a dither. Crossing the ship's bow a second time, it ran out of gas and fell into the sea. It sank quickly, and if its passengers were not drowned, they were crushed by the Blueridge's fat prow.

Soon another helicopter appeared. Then six, then a dozen. Then I couldn't count them all. They were everywhere, and their roar filled my ears; out on the weather decks, we couldn't even hear alarms or commands, and we had to communicate with hand signals. All the choppers were low on gas. Those that ran out stopped in midair, wobbled for a moment as though they were wounded birds struggling for flight, then went down. Left and right they fell out of the sky, crashing into the water, their rotors beating it into a froth as the sea swallowed them. They sank astonishingly fast, taking their occupants to the bottom as often as not. We launched boats to rescue those we could. They were few, and the coxswains reported sharks and pink water. The choppers that stayed aloft were lining up one behind the other to land on any vessel large enough. They began to land on our deck, and to my surprise they were carrying mostly women, children, and old people.

During the chaos of the day, we went ashore to pick up people. Again they were mostly women, children, and old folks. Some were deserters, and by now there were a few "spooks": CIA men wearing dark glasses and clutching briefcases, some people from the CIA's front company, Air America, and even the families of Vietnamese president Thieu's bodyguard. But mostly they were civilians—non-combatants—the people who pay the greatest price of war.

We took the people to the ships, any ships: fighting ships, cargo ships, support ships, any kind of ship that had room for them. Some of them were wounded and still bleeding, and a number had died. Many were alone, while some were with families, or pieces of families. They stood at the lifelines, clutching all that they now owned, and stared mutely landward as they embarked on lives of exile. Some wept. Some were too tired. Others were too scared. On that day, we gathered up more than one hundred thousand fleeing people. They huddled on the weather decks of every vessel in the fleet; exposed to the sun, the rain, the wind, and their enemies whom they still feared would pursue them. And they were all hungry.

I would have thought that the loss of homeland, family, and future had killed their appetites, but they hungered deeply. Maybe it was a hunger that expressed another kind of emptiness. Maybe their stomachs were in sympathy with their souls. I don't know, but they begged wearily for food.

Navy cooks are trained to expect sudden increases in the number of mouths they must feed. Ships will sink and their crews and passengers need rescue; soldiers and Marines might need to be picked up from the beach; natural disasters call for relief efforts. In all such cases, people need to be fed.

Toward the end of the long day, I noticed the smell of a rich stew from the galley. The Navy recipe book calls it "El Rancho Beef Stew." It's common for GIs to bitch about the chow they get, but the U.S. Navy feeds fairly well; its beef stew wasn't bad. We liked to call it "El Rauncho Beef Stew," but it wasn't bad. When they took their care with it, it reminded me of something my own grandmother would have made. I've heard other men say similar things about it.

Two by two the cooks came up from the mess deck carrying great pots of stew, and the thick aroma hung about the ship like a cloud. They ladled it onto trays and passed it to the hungry people. The spooks took theirs quickly and ate with gusto and were restored. They even asked for more. But the Vietnamese refugees merely picked at it, hungry as they were.

I watched a pretty lady, tall and slim and fashionably dressed, take her tray and sit down on a bollard next to the lifelines. She took tiny bites and drew deep sighs in between. Now and then, she glanced to landward for last glimpses of home. Then she looked back at the stew, and I thought she would weep. Bravely, she always took another tiny bite and repeated her longing glances. All the Vietnamese seemed to catch the same mood. The more they ate, the bluer they became.

Somebody, I don't know who, hollered to the cooks, "Hey, these people don't eat beef stew. In fact I bet they don't even eat beef. They eat rice. Why don't you give 'em some rice?"

After a while, two beefy cooks hauled a stewpot full of steaming white rice up to the weather deck. When the people saw it, they quickly lined up for it in good order and reverential silence. The cooks gave them each heaping mounds, and the people smiled with relief and bowed slightly as they received their portions. I saw a man in a torn, dirty flight suit put a fat spoonful into his mouth and just hold it there, as though it were a kind of communion. An old man ate with his hands, running his fingers through the rice like a farmer testing good soil. And the pretty lady sat down on her bollard again and eagerly mixed the stew and the rice together, and she fed well. A very simple meal she had—but it gave her solace and was enough. The cooks served the people rice with every meal for the next several days that they were in our charge.

On that last day of the war, I ate a great deal of El Rancho Beef Stew. If the refugees' stomachs were in sympathy with their souls, so was mine. I felt sharp sympathetic pangs of homesickness for them. Pangs that made me feel the need to reach out for something from home, something elemental, something primal, something that would connect my body and soul with all that I am and have been. I needed the food from home.

I think that for every eater there is a food from home. There are some foods that are of and from the place we call home that our bodies have long assimilated and our souls have anchored themselves to, and they will always help to restore us when we are far away and feeling lost or alone. To feed on them is to suckle at the breast of one's homeland and be one with her again, if only for a while.

After days or weeks at sea or in the field, sailors and soldiers begin to talk about memorable meals at home, about what their wives and mothers cook best, and what they will have as their first meal upon returning. Through countless such conversations, I have never heard anybody long for Duck a l'Orange or Tournedos Rossini. There were no requests for "made dishes," elaborate concoctions, or elegant entrees. The food from home is simple, prepared with the easy grace of untold repetitions. At home it is always offered up with love, assurance, promises of continuity, faith, and reaffirmation. It makes strong again the bonds with family, history, and culture and the soil from whence they all come. The Indians of the American Southwest attach religious significance to their food from home, corn, and they believe that to eat it plain is to commune with God. The peoples of Asia have long had similar attitudes towards rice, and the Egyptians have revered their unbuttered loaves of wheat bread for four thousand years. The Jewish Passover feast, the Seder, takes its participants to an ancient spiritual home with simple dishes set around the plain, unleavened matzo.

For most of us, the food from home is heavy and stays long as a presence in the belly and the mind. I know of no one who can take comfort in lettuces, bean sprouts, or watercress. It has to be substantial and offer something to the teeth and be big in the mouth and warm going down. It is often a carbohydrate; heavy starches have a sedative effect on most people and help promote a sense of well-being.

For some people it is something sweet: layer cakes, made by mothers on Sundays or holidays; cookies warm from the oven and heavy with the orchidian scent of real vanilla; dark and chewy brownies, or something else very chocolate. The sweetness helps to chase away the bitterness of the moment. It awakens the child in us, takes one back to another place and time; takes one home for just a little while. And the magic work of chocolate, whether it works upon your own self or not, is a phenomenon we have all observed. Its Latin name is apt: *Theobroma*, God's food.

For me, the food from home can be a simple stew made the way my grandmother would make it. Or fried potatoes and the venison chops that speak to me of the

Pacific Northwest timberland where I grew up. Being from California, I take great solace in the deep red wines of my native state and always carry two small bottles when I travel. Their bouquets carry their home address, enabling me to identify the individual counties where they were grown. The distinctive aromas of the California soils billow up from the liquid, and I am instantly transported to Sonoma, Napa, Monterey, or my own Mendocino. On the ship or plane that brings me home, I plan my first meal after arrival, the same one every time: a cheeseburger, french fries, and a draft beer served in a sawdust bar and grill where the juke box plays Elvis, Chuck Berry, or Hank Williams, Sr.

Mark Twain speaks to us all in A Tramp Abroad, longing for the food from home. Throughout Europe, he hungered for the taste of America. The grandest cuisines of France and Italy—at first interesting—became ordeals, and every mealtime he thought of yet another dish he might have if he were home:

> "Imagine a poor exile...and imagine an angel suddenly sweeping down out of a better land and setting before him a mighty porterhouse steak an inch and a half thick, hot and sputtering from the griddle; dusted with fragrant pepper; enriched with little melting bits of butter of the most unimpeachable freshness and genuineness; the precious juices of the meat trickling out and joining the gravy, archipelagoed with mushrooms; a township or two of tender yellow fat gracing an outlying district of this ample county of beefsteak; the long white bone which divides the sirloin from the tenderloin still in its place; and imagine that the angel also adds a cup of American homemade coffee, with the cream afroth on top, some real butter, firm and yellow and fresh, some smoking-hot biscuits, a plate of hot buckwheat cakes, with transparent syrup. Could words describe the gratitude of this exile?"

Yes, Mr. Clemens, I think so. And I know a hundred thousand Vietnamese who think so, too.

VIETNAMESE HOME RICE

Every country that uses rice as a staple has its own variety of the grain and its own unique way of preparing it—just as no two European countries have quite the same bread or beer. The method for Vietnamese rice is very exact and produces a unique, pleasing texture: Put the rice into a pot and spread it out evenly. Place the tip of your index finger on top of the rice and hold it there. Pour water into the pot until it reaches the first knuckle of your finger. If that is flying too much by the seat of your pants, try these proportions.

2   cups long-grain white rice
3¼ cups water

Put the rice and water in a pot together and bring to a boil over high heat. Boil for 3 or 4 minutes until you begin to see small holes or indentations in the water's surface, indicating that the water is being absorbed by the rice. Cover the pan tightly, then reduce heat to very low. Cook for 20 minutes. Remove from the heat and without lifting the cover, let the rice rest for 20 minutes. It will keep hot for an hour with the lid on. Fluff it before serving.

Yield: 6 Servings

EL RANCHO BEEF STEW, NAVY RECIPE CARD NO. 23 (1)

This recipe was graciously provided by Chief Warrant Officer Gary Young, U.S.N., Ship's Secretary of the helicopter assault ship *USS Tarawa*. I have not changed it.

30   pounds beef, diced, thawed
1   pound flour
3   ounces salt
½   ounce pepper, black
1   gallon water, hot
6   pounds, 8 ounces carrots, quartered
2   gallons water, boiling
10   pounds potatoes, quartered
4   pounds onions, peeled and coarsely chopped
2   pounds peas, frozen

1. Dredge beef in mixture of flour, salt and pepper. Shake off excess.
2. Place equal quantity of beef in each of several roasting pans. Cook in the oven for an hour or until browned.
3. Add 2 quarts water to each pan. Cover. Cook 2 hours or until tender.
4. Cook carrots in water for 15 minutes. Add potatoes and onions. Cook 20 minutes.
5. Add peas. Cook 20 minutes or until tender. Drain.
6. Add vegetables to beef in each pan, Stir. Heat to serving temperature.

Yield: 100 Portions

UNITED STEAKS OF AMERICA

Taking my inspiration from Mark Twain, I created this as the ultimate American food from home.

Arizona mesquite charcoal
1   cup Tennesee hickory chips, soaked
1   thick New York steak
1   Washington (Walla Walla) onion, peeled and quartered
1½ tablespoons Minnesota sweet butter
12 cloves California (Gilroy) garlic, minced
¼   pound Oregon button mushrooms, sliced
2   New Mexico green chiles, roasted, peeled, stems and seeds removed, chopped
4   tablespoons grated Wisconsin cheddar cheese
    Melted butter
    A-1 steak sauce

Prepare a fire with the mesquite charcoal and add the hickory chips. With a thin, sharp knife, pierce the lean edge of the steak and drive the blade as far as the fat edge, but not clean through. Using short sawing motions, cut a wide pocket into the meat, so that you will essentially have two steaks united along three sides.

Chop one of the onion quarters. Heat the butter in a skillet and saute the garlic, chopped onion, mushrooms, and chiles until the mushrooms have given of their liquid. Stuff the cheese into the pocket of the meat, making sure that it goes all the way to the inward edge. Fill the remainder of the pocket with the sauteed mixture and secure the open edge with toothpicks.

Grill the steak and the remaining 3 onion quarters over the charcoal and hickory chips, basting them all with melted butter and A-1. As the cheese melts inside the steak, it will mingle with the garlic and mushrooms and appear at the open edge just about the time the meat is medium rare.

Yield: 1 Serving
Heat Scale: Mild
Serving Suggestion: Serve with a baked Idaho potato, Kansas corn on the cob, a Hawaiian fruit salad, and a California wine.

PART II

PILGRIMAGES

I COULD SAY THAT I CAME OF AGE IN SOUTHEAST ASIA. *It was there that I first learned to love, acknowledged death, embraced philosophy and thought deeply of God, and received my culinary education. For the rest of my life, no matter how far or how much I wander, the lands of the South China Sea will always beckon, and I will always respond.*

I bought my first cookbook in a Keelung, Taiwan bookstore. Taiwan does not subscribe to copyright treaties, so a book's price is the sum of its manufacturing and distribution. The latest novel by Stephen King or Pat Conroy might cost less than a tawdry romance if the romance is heavier. I often bought my books by weight. One day I purchased a few pounds of Shakespeare and Kipling and several ounces of collected essays. I had some change to spare, so I put Pei Mei's Chinese Cookery *on the scales and a lifetime of collecting began.*

I took my first cooking lessons from pushcart cooks on Orchard Road in Singapore. I paid for them with cigarettes. In those days, American cigarettes were still nearly as good as currency. They were hard for most people to find and were expensive as well. Now, of course, they are so heavily taxed in the U.S. that it's cheaper to buy them abroad. And they are so widely distributed that the Marlboro man can be found in Hanoi. But in the seventies, they purchased me much knowledge.

With that body of knowledge and a grounding in the culinary arts, I was better equipped to explore the world. I had made many happy discoveries previously, but so many of them I had merely blundered into. Now, the world came into perspective and its depth was revealed. I knew where to travel and what questions to ask. I knew how to search for the meaning in what I found.

CHAPTER 7

TO DINE WITH GHOSTS

I was alone in the club car on the night train from Singapore. I was heading north for Ipoh, where I would stay at the Station Hotel and meet my friend Stan the next day when he came up from Malacca. From there we would travel to Penang, and then on up through the Isthmus of Kra to Sattahip, Thailand, where we would meet the rest of our trekking party. I was hungry and in the mood for some lively Malayan chile-fare, but the dining car was closed. I would have to wait until I reached my destination, where once again I would have to sup in the old Imperial dining room.

I was not really all that keen on going to the Ipoh Station Hotel again. I had a Malaysian Railway pass and could have stayed on the train in a cozy compartment all the way to Penang. Stan, however, was eager to see this bit of British Imperial history and wanted me to show it to him. He wanted to have kippers in the dining room or gin and tonic in the bar and pretend that we were British empire-builders in white linen suits and pith helmets. "Okay," I had told him, "if it means that much to you. I guess everybody should visit the Hotel of the Living Dead at least once."

The Ipoh Station Hotel had been a place of some renown. But although it still stood and still operated, it was a ruin. It had been one of the farthest outposts of the British Raj, where empire-builders and hangers-on met on the road to riches or rags. When it was occupied, though, by the soldiers of General Yamashita, the Tiger of Malaya, during the Pacific war, it went into the same irreversible decline as the Empire. The adventurers stayed away. The Imperial administrators no longer came; the mercenaries, the planters and miners, and the hustlers and the whores had all gone elsewhere. As the Empire receded like the tide, the hotel was left high and dry. The staff remained. The service (more or less) remained. Everything was as the Empire left it, but in a slumping, twilight world of decay.

The train arrived well after dark and the hotel stood big, white, imperial, and incongruous at the edge of the moonlit Malayan jungle. When I stepped off the train, I noticed that I was the only one on the platform. Nobody else had gotten off. As the train fled into the night, I asked myself, only half-jokingly, if the other passengers knew something I didn't.

I walked into the lobby. The old electric lights produced a dim, yellow, hazy glow. The wallpaper had turned a tasteless gray, and the place felt airless. I could see into the dining room, large and gloomy, yet somehow claustrophobic. The tables were all set with the old Empire ware and heavy, starched napery. One cadaverous old waiter stared blankly in my direction.

That dining room had been full of people once. It had hosted sultans, colonial governors, mysterious ladies, tin magnates, mining engineers, and fortune hunters. A lot of big deals had been consummated in there. Now it seemed to yawn wide and tired, exhaling ghosts.

I went to the registration desk and signed my name in the book. Every full registration book in the hotel's history was on a dusty shelf behind the desk. The earlier volumes bore many illustrious names; the volume I was signing carried only the names of occasional wayfarers, like myself, and the pen names of local adulterers. It seemed like the vultures were feeding on the corpse. I noticed that there were only two other people registered for that night. They were a Mr. and Mrs. Patel, the local equivalent of Mr. and Mrs. Smith. I wondered if they had already trysted and gone.

After checking in, I went to the lounge to have a drink. I needed fortitude if I was going to go into the dining room for any length of time. Like the rest of the hotel, the lounge was dim and close. A fat Malay barman in shirtsleeves was behind the bar. He was conversing very softly with a waiter in a red jacket. All Malays converse softly. When they saw me come in, they broke off their talk and looked at me with mildly glazed eyes. I moved toward the bar, but the waiter gestured me to a table and kept nodding his head, saying, "Please, please." I thought maybe he wanted something to do, so I sat where he directed. I ordered gin and tonic, and it came true to British style, just tonic and gin—no ice, no lime. I finished the drink quickly and moved on.

In the sepulchral dining room, I took a seat near the entry. As I waited in the thick, dim gloom, I wondered what its ghosts might look like. I could almost hear the echoes of tinkling crystal, the clatter of china, the hum and buzz of conversation as deals were struck, information was exchanged, and successes and failures were recounted. I suddenly became aware of the old waiter standing beside me. The menu he brought me was English to the bone: meat, fish, and boiled potatoes. At the waiter's suggestion, I ordered steamed sole.

As I waited to be served, I realized that there were others in the room. On the far side were an Indian man and a Chinese woman. (Mr. and Mrs. Patel?) I couldn't figure how they got there without my noticing. I had taken the table near the entry, so I would be aware of anyone coming or going. They were sitting shoulder to shoulder and were in a whispered and animated—but deliberately subdued—argument.

When the sole arrived, I found it bland, insipid, and uninspired—food fit only for ghosts. "This is like eating death," I thought. "I need food for the living!" I caught the waiter's attention, and the old bag of bones shuffled over my way.

"This is...very nice," I said, referring to the meal. "But isn't there anything on the menu with a little bit of...spice?"

"Pickled eggs, sir?" he suggested.

"I was thinking of something spicy hot."

He excused himself and disappeared into the kitchen. He soon returned to say, rather apologetically, that "Cook is fixing himself and staff a bit of Malay curry if..."

"I'll take it!"

He returned with a blue Chinese porcelain bowl filled with cubes of snowy white potato and toasty brown peanuts swimming in a thick, red-flecked yellow sauce. A sheen of red chile-scented oil floated on top, and a sprig of green cilantro graced it at the edge. He set it in front of me, ceremoniously turned the bowl ninety degrees, then shuffled quietly away.

The vapors rose up and stung my nostrils with delight. The sharp scents of chile, garlic, and ginger were powerful. The buttery smell of peanuts and the mellowness of turmeric combined with them as they formed an almost visible wreath of aroma around my head. I ignored the spoon and picked up the bowl with both hands. I sucked at the creamy sauce. Savory spice-fire rushed through my mouth, tiny beads of sweat popped from my brow and and my palate sang, "Alive!" I had sucked in a small piece of chile, so I bit into it, and it burst into an explosion of flavor-heat. I swallowed, and the glow went down to my gut and my body screamed again, "Alive, alive, alive!" I took up the spoon and scooped the curry into my mouth and chewed. The capsaicin struck my taste buds and they resonated like tiny tuning forks, each one a different tone, but all together in harmony, keeping the ghosts at bay.

As I reached the bottom of the bowl, I tipped it up and let the last tasty, searing bits slide into my mouth. Had the bowl been shallower, I'd have licked it. The curry was so hot my mouth throbbed with a burning, life-affirming pleasure-pain. I felt like the only man of flesh in a cold charnel house.

I sat back for a few moments to bank the fires. Savoring the now slow burn, I thought I might sustain it with a glass of whiskey. I signed the check, rose from the table, and noticed that the Indian man and Chinese woman had vanished. Or had they ever been there?

I ambled over to the bar, but when I got there the lights were out, and it was deserted. I turned back toward the dining room and found that it was suddenly dark and deserted too. Outside, even the platform lights were off. I could find nobody, anywhere. Even the ghosts were gone.

The only light still burning was the single bulb leading upstairs to the rooms. I creaked up the steps to the narrow hallway, and it was dark, too. Not finding any light switches, I felt the numbers on the doors till I found mine. I felt for the keyhole beneath the porcelain doorknob and guided in the antique steel key. Entering, I found the old light switch and turned it, breathing a sigh of relief when a small bulb glowed faintly in the corner.

The room had a nightstand, a bureau with a pitcher and basin on it, a lumpy-looking bed, and shadows. It had the same gray wallpaper as the lobby. I wished the bar were open or that I had some valium or a bottle of gin so I could knock myself out and wake up when the witching hour was over.

I turned down the bed and was glad, at least, to see that it had a heavy comforter; the jungle can get as cold as a tomb at night. As I lay down, the bed creaked, the mattress sagged, and the musty-smelling pillow wrapped itself around my head. The entire hotel was bound fast in silence. A shaft of moonlight pierced the room and illuminated a small rectangle on the floor. All else was darkness. With the tip of my tongue I probed my lips for any remnants of hot oil that might still cling to them. I found a lively, stinging deposit at each corner. I licked them off slowly, clinging to that burning essence like a child at unwelcome nap time, eyelids heavy, clinging to wakefulness. "If I could see taste," I thought, "this would be pure light."

IPOH STATION POTATO CURRY

Most Asian cuisines have embraced such New World crops as chiles and peanuts, but potatoes and tomatoes are rarely used in the Orient. Malaya is an exception. At this writing, the Station Hotel does not include this dish on its menu. You have to ask for it, and it may or may not be available at the time. But it can always be available at home. If you're alone, and it's a damp, drizzly November or 3:00 a.m. in your soul; if the dead seem to walk in your parlor and life tastes gray, make this curry. Make it hot and make it extra saucy. Wash it down with beer and follow it with whiskey. The sun will shine within you.

3	cups coconut milk
2	jalapeño chiles, stems and seeds removed, finely chopped
3	cloves garlic, minced
1	tablespoon ginger, minced
2	teaspoons ground turmeric
4	fat scallions, minced
1	pound potatoes, peeled and diced
2	teaspoons salt
1	teaspoon ground cardamom, or substitute nutmeg
1	cup peanuts
1	tablespoon red chile oil
	Cilantro or mint for garnish

In a wok, bring the coconut milk to a simmer. Add the chiles, garlic, ginger, turmeric, and scallions, and stir and cook for about 5 minutes. Add the remaining ingredients except the garnish and cook, stirring occasionally, until the potatoes are tender, about 20 minutes. Serve over white rice and garnish with cilantro or mint.

Yield: 4 Servings
Heat Scale: Medium Hot

TOMATO CURRY

If you overcook this dish, the tomatoes will disintegrate and you will be left not with an elegant curry fit for a connoisseur, but a thick pinkish sauce with bits of tomato floating in it. If that happens, tell no one. Pour it over fish or poultry and call it Sauce Malaise. Tell your guests you made it special, just for them. Do as Julia Child who says, "Be a fearless cook, and never apologize!"

The Paste:

2	inches fresh ginger, peeled
6	cloves garlic
2	onions, coarsely chopped
4	tablespoons coriander seeds
5	dried red chiles, such as Thai, stems removed and soaked
1	teaspoon turmeric
1	inch-long piece of lemon grass stalk
4	tablespoons plain yogurt
	Salt to taste

In a blender or mortar, grind all ingredients into a paste.

The Curry:

4	tablespoons vegetable oil
1	onion, sliced thin
1	teaspoon ground cardamom
¼	teaspoon ground cloves
1	stick cinnamon
1	pound ripe tomatoes, peeled and quartered

Heat the oil in a wok and stir-fry the onion, cardamom, cloves, and cinnamon till fragrant. Add the paste and continue to stir-fry for about 5 minutes. Add some water if the mixture begins to dry out. Add the tomatoes and turn them in the sauce to coat thoroughly. Reduce the heat to a simmer and cook 5 minutes, shaking gently now and then.

Yield: 6 Side Dishes
Heat Scale: Medium

CHAPTER 8

TRAIN FARE

*E*RNEST HEMINGWAY CALLED PARIS *"A MOVEABLE FEAST," but for me the phrase always brings to mind a train. I've ridden in them and dined in them all over the world, from first class compartments to boxcars. I've feasted with hoboes on dry bread and bad wine and called it good. I've shared tea and cakes with a mob of Sikhs who took over an entire car, bringing their own traveling kitchen (sink included). I've rolled through the downs sharing sausage rolls with Englishmen and crossed France eating Dutch cheese with vacationing Spaniards. But no trains ever provided more memorable dining than this Far Eastern pair.*

This is a story of two of the great railway journeys of the world. They are the International Express from Penang to Bangkok, operated by Thai National Railways, and the Rangoon to Mandalay Express-Mail of Burma State Railways.

Both of these trains run overnight from south to north. They both run through the stunning scenery of low, tropical plains, jungle-covered mountains, monsoon skies, and outlying provinces swarming with bandits and rebels who occasionally waylay the train. They both depart from former centers of British colonial administration and arrive at ancient royal capitals. They both run on time. What makes them both memorable railway journeys, however, is not how they are alike, but how they are different.

What makes a train journey great? Maybe not what you would think. It isn't comfort. The Southern Pacific Commuter from San Francisco to San Jose is "comfortable." It isn't speed. The Japanese Bullet train runs at 100 miles per hour, and it's fun, but it isn't great. Surprisingly, it isn't a great dining car, although that helps a lot. It isn't any one thing. It isn't even any two or three things that you could cite as constant criteria for railway greatness. Rather, it's the unique combination of factors that make the journey unforgettable.

The Thai train is the one I rode first. To board it bound for Bangkok, you take the first ferry of the morning from the island of Penang to the Malayan mainland where the station is. It's always very quiet and peaceful at that time, and the only people on the boat are those who will be traveling with you on the train. The morning air is always still and the slanting sun highlights the place to the west where the jade-green water of the Pacific Ocean meets the inky blue of the Indian. At the station, orderly baggage handlers and ticket agents go about their work. A Thai conductor in crisp khaki uniform, like a friendly Boy Scout leading you across the street, shows you to your compartment.

On the other hand, the first time I caught the Burmese train, I had to come from Tazi on the top of a truck. The back of the vehicle was already jammed to capacity with humanity, and the only place left was on top of the canopy with the baggage. I spent six hours roaring over dusty, bumpy dirt roads at top speed with nothing to hang on to but a suitcase, but it was better than being pressed into the sweaty mass below.

When I arrived at the station that afternoon, I was plunged into a scene of pandemonium, crowding, and dirt. The place looked like it hadn't been cleaned since the

British departed in 1946. Brown, scaly crud grew on the bare concrete walls and pillars. Roaches big enough to barbecue lounged where they pleased, undisturbed. There were no attendants, orderly or otherwise, no bulletins or schedules in sight. A tattered poster exhorted the masses to continue on the "Burmese road to socialism."

Worse still, the train had no dining car. Travelers had to buy supplies for the journey at a kiosk in the station. They had for sale such things as deep-fried beetles, broiled chicken feet, rice cakes, and assorted bottles of a mysterious opaque liquid, each filled to a different level. I bought some quinine water and prepared to fast on the road to Mandalay.

But on the Thai train, if you book first class non-air-conditioned, one steps through the portals of time into a bygone era. The cars are handcrafted and paneled with tropical hardwoods. The compartments are spacious and cozy and your name, in three languages, is posted on the door. The porter arrives to ask what time to wake you from your afternoon nap or in the morning and whether he should bring you coffee or tea. This train is one that belongs to colonial times. It should be carrying rich planters, European adventurers, governors general, and mysterious ladies.

In the dining car, starched white linen graces the tables, fresh flowers sit in silver vases, lacy curtains hang from the windows and wonderful, spicy smells fill the car whenever the kitchen door opens. This place is where I like to lounge when I'm tired of reading or napping or watching the scenery go by.

It's a good place to meet and chat with fellow passengers, sip tea or Thai beer, or have a friendly game of cards with a traveling Chinese businessman who looks like he might be a spy or a smuggler. One time I stayed up all night in the dining car with five fellow travelers, each from a different country. We drank Mekong whiskey and taught each other songs from our separate homelands till the conductor, very politely, suggested that since it was nearly dawn we might want to sleep a few hours before arriving in Bangkok.

On the Rangoon train, the transportational pride of the Socialist Republic of the Union of Burma, there is not only no dining car, there are no compartments. The first time I rode the beast, I was at least able to get a seat on the only first-class car. At any rate, they called it first class. It looked like the interior of a bus. I guess I wouldn't have minded crossing town in it.

Its most memorable feature was its suspension. It was bad. It was very bad. Coupled with the poor condition of the tracks, it made for a ride so bumpy that every now and then I was lifted bodily from my seat and then dropped back down with a thud. I suppose you might eventually get used to the steady beat of the small bumps that merely shake your fillings loose, but to actually "catch air" every five minutes is more than the spine can bear. Even the sturdy Burmese travelers find it so. They come prepared with pieces of rope with which they make seat belts. The uninitiated have to make do with whatever they have. I had to remove the belt from my trousers and jury-rig my own arresting gear.

Of course, it's impossible to sleep under those conditions. The Burmese close their eyes and make a show of it. I, however, was prepared, at least, for this. Being a veteran of many a military flight and many arduous overland journeys, I usually travel with a pocketful of Valium. I can make long, overnight trips short when I take one or two Valium tablets, quickly fall asleep, and then wake up at my destination. Over the years, I have worked out a scale of difficulty for such trips and rate them in milligrams of Valium. The Rangoon-Mandalay Mail weighs in at a whopping fifteen milligrams and a half-pint of potent Burmese whiskey; a record unmatched by any other form of transportation in the known world.

As I said earlier, that was the first time I rode the Burmese "Iron Maiden." The second time was worse. I had to ride third class. That means they put you on a second-class car but give you no seat. You are expected to sit on the floor. Knowing that the seats were like park benches, made of hard, wooden slats with spaces between the slats, I figured it didn't really make any difference. Besides, I'd be able to roll out a blanket and stretch out on the floor. Not so. Most of the people in the second-class car were traveling third class. Not only were there no seats, there was no place on the floor in that, or any other car. The aisles were jammed. The ends of the cars were jammed. Even the toilets had passengers. They would vacate long enough to let others use the facility but would insist on returning to their bunks afterward.

The only places left were underneath the slat benches, and they were filling up fast. I dove for one. I squeezed beneath it in such a way that my upper body was under a bench on the left side of the car, my hips lay in the aisle, and my legs were stuffed under a bench on the right side of the car. After I had ensconced myself I took stock of the situation. The floor was filthy, and I would probably come down with some dread disease. It was cramped, and I couldn't roll over. My midsection, exposed in the aisle, would surely get stepped on. Looking up through the slats of the left-side bench, I could see that a large woman with a small baby and a huge behind was sitting over my face. I took my Valium. I had the prescribed fifteen milligrams, but if I'd had more, I would have taken it.

As I lay there in the suffocating, cramped, filthy space, waiting to be carried off to drugged oblivion, it became clear to me that the lady above me suffered from gas. Not stomach gas, no. The woman was farting. Long, windy farts, the kind that go "whoosh." I was not a happy camper. Somehow I was able to wriggle out of the noxious fume trap and reverse my position. The drug then took its merciful effect and whatever other harsh winds may have blown, passed without my knowing.

When I awoke the next morning, still under the seats, I could feel some warm liquid drizzling onto my bare feet beneath the left bench. I then remembered what was above them. Thinking that the woman had lost control of her bladder, I swore that I would never again come to Burma. However, I had been hasty. It was not the woman passing water, but her motion-sick baby vomiting.

On this last leg of the trip to Mandalay, you can buy food on the train for breakfast. Teen-age boys hop the train as it rolls by their villages. The conductor will not allow them in the cars, so they climb up on the roof. When the conductor goes in some other car, they climb down with their barbecued chicken thighs, legs and feet, and sell them to the hungry passengers. Then they climb back up to the roof, clamber over to the next car, and let themselves down again.

The chicken is very tasty and succulent. It's marinated in soy sauce and ginger. As it turns over the coals, the cooks baste it with pineapple juice, brown sugar, and soy.

It makes a shiny brown glaze with little bits of toasted pineapple clinging to it. Sometimes the cooks sprinkle it with sesame seeds and drizzle it with honey.

Unfortunately I have never been quite hungry when the boys came aboard. Arriving at Mandalay, or Rangoon, I stagger off the train thinking only of clean water, plain food, and undrugged sleep. But on one occasion I ate the chicken. Bruce Harmon and I were coming south from Mandalay. In the morning after a particularly frightful night under the benches, we met a very friendly sarong-clad Burmese man who wanted to talk to foreigners and practice his English. We stood at one end of the crowded car and spoke over the morning hubbub. The man was explaining that he was a graduate of his nation's agricultural institute, when the chicken boys dropped down into the car. Eagerly taking the role of host, he bought a skewered leg and thigh for each of us. I was in no mood to put anything in my stomach, but I accepted it gratefully and began nibbling at it. He went on with his tale.

"I'm just doing my part to help the people," he said. "Just doing my part." And he bit deeply into the meat. He went on to tell us that he had been up in the mountains in the north of the country teaching the hill people animal husbandry. Specifically, he was teaching the techniques of artificial insemination.

"It's a good way to help the people," he explained. "They need to have more stock, more swine," and he shook a nearly bare chicken bone for emphasis.

As I bit into my chicken leg, he began telling us how to inseminate a pig. "It's very easy," he assured us, "I've done thousands. I'll show you." I chewed slowly as he went through the motions, using his chicken bone as a prop. He successfully put a reluctant imaginary sow into the family way and then said, "I'm going to Rangoon now. I have almost a full liter of swine semen in my luggage. It's frozen, of course. I intend now to improve the stock in this part of the country. This is helping the people." I thought it might be safe to swallow, when he waved his bone at me and said, "You know, it's a very interesting thing, how to get the semen from the boar...."

Waking on the Thai train is quite different. Having spent the night in privacy, on clean sheets and being gently rocked by the slowly swaying train, I rise feeling rested, refreshed, and good about the world. I always have the porter bring me coffee. Then I go to the bath compartment where I can take either a western shower, or if I prefer, a Thai bath using a dipper and a large urn full of water. Feeling eminently civilized, I can then repair to the dining car where both western and Thai breakfasts await. It's the one place where I eat fried rice. I'm not usually fond of fried rice. I tend to find it bland and full of uninspired leftovers, an Asian's answer to the Englishman's Bubble & Squeak. But the chef on the Thai train makes it ambrosial.

He will make it from chicken, pork or prawns, as you wish. He serves it with an egg, barely fried, sitting atop the mound of aromatic rice, dressed with slices of crisp cucumber and sweet red onion. The dish is simply seasoned with scallion and pungent with garlic. Black pepper nips at your tongue like a puppy dog's playful small teeth. Bits of cilantro release their cool freshness as you chew them. A condiment is served alongside, usually a cup of thinly sliced red and green chiles in a consomme-rich fish sauce.

The last few hours of the journey I might spend swapping addresses with new-found friends, finishing a book, or just being glad I'm not on the railroad to Mandalay.

Now you may think that one of these two railway journeys is not quite what you'd call great. But remember what makes the journey great. It's that unique combination of things that makes it so unforgettable. And believe me, I'll never forget either one.

MANDALAY MAIL CHICKEN

Although I confess I never really enjoyed this very much on the train, at home it is delightful. It conjures up happier memories of Burma and makes me glad I'm not on the train.

The Marinade:
1   cup soy sauce
1   cup strained pineapple juice
1   tablespoon lime juice
1   tablespoon ginger, minced
1   whole chicken, cut up into parts

Combine all the ingredients and marinate the chicken for at least 2 hours.

The Baste:
½   cup soy sauce
½   cup chopped pineapple
1   tablespoon brown sugar
1   tablespoon sesame seeds

Combine all ingredients and mash the mixture to reduce the pineapple flesh to an uneven pulp. Grill the chicken over hot coals, turning and basting once or twice.

Yield: 6 Servings

INTERNATIONAL EXPRESS FRIED RICE

Here is a humble dish, but one worthy to be set on any table. I like to place a small vase of flowers next to it and imagine the jungle scene from the window of the dining car rushing by.

2	tablespoons vegetable oil
½	onion, diced
½	green bell pepper, sliced thin lengthwise
3	cloves garlic, chopped
1	red chile, such as jalapeño, stem and seeds removed, chopped
½	cup fresh chicken or pork, sliced thin
1	tablespoon oyster sauce
1	tablespoon soy sauce
1	tablespoon fish sauce
½	teaspoon black pepper
2	cups cooked long-grain rice, refrigerated overnight
1	cup bean sprouts
2	scallions, sliced thin
1	egg, broken into a bowl and allowed to come up to room temperature
2	tablespoons pickled, sliced jalapeños with their liquid
2	tablespoons fish sauce
2	tablespoons cilantro, chopped

Heat the oil in a wok until very hot. Add the onion, bell pepper, garlic, and chile and stir-fry for 2 minutes. Add the sliced meat and cook another 3 minutes. Add the oyster sauce, soy sauce, fish sauce, and black pepper and cook for 1 minute. Add the rice and continue cooking while mixing all the ingredients in the wok for 3 minutes. Use more oil if necessary.

With a spatula, lift up the mixture from the bottom of the wok and slip in the bean sprouts and scallions. Cook, shaking the pan, for 1 minute. Again lifting the mixture up, slide the egg underneath and cook for 1 to 2 minutes. Remove from the heat and turn onto a serving platter so that the egg is sitting on top. Combine the pickled jalapeños, fish sauce, and cilantro and spoon over the top.

Yield: 2 Servings
Heat Scale: Medium

DOM YOM KUNG

This soup is found in every kitchen in Thailand, including the kitchen of the train. The words, in order, mean: soup, sour, prawn. It is very simple to make and is addictively delicious.

1	pint fish or shrimp stock
1	cup prawns, shelled, shells reserved
3	inch-long stalks lemon grass, bruised
2	kaffir lime leaves, or peel of 2 limes
1	cup button mushrooms
½	teaspoon black pepper
2	tablespoons fish sauce
1	teaspoon chile paste
1	tablespoon chopped cilantro

In a saucepan, simmer the stock and the prawn shells to extract their flavor, then discard the shells. Stir in the lemon grass and lime leaves and cook until aromatic. Add the prawns, cover, and simmer for 3 minutes. Add the mushrooms and pepper and simmer for a few more minutes. Remove from the heat and stir in the remaining ingredients.

Yield: 3 Servings
Heat Scale: Mild

PAD THAI

Like Dom Yom Kung, Pad Thai is as common in Thailand as hamburgers are in the U.S. The International Express' kitchen would be incomplete without it.

2	eggs
1	tablespoon fish sauce
1	tablespoon ketchup
1	tablespoon chile paste
1	tablespoon sugar
2	tablespoons vegetable oil
4	cloves garlic, chopped
10	medium shrimps, shelled and cleaned
½	pound rice noodles, soaked and drained per package instructions

2   teaspoons shrimp paste
8   ounces bean sprouts
2   scallions, sliced
3   tablespoons chopped peanuts
    Basil leaves and lime wedges

Beat together the eggs, fish sauce, ketchup, chile paste, and sugar and set aside.

Heat the oil in a wok or skillet to high and stir-fry the garlic for 1 minute. Add the shrimp and the egg mixture and cook, stirring, for 1 minute. Add the noodles and shrimp paste and mix well to heat through. With a spatula, lift up the mixture from the bottom of the wok and slip in the bean sprouts and scallions. Cook, shaking the pan, for 1 minute. Garnish with the peanuts, basil, and lime wedges and serve.

Yield: 2 Servings
Heat Scale: Medium

COCOCHILENUT SOUP

This is another very popular Thai soup, a constant in every kitchen.

1   tablespoon vegetable oil
4   cloves garlic, chopped
1   teaspoon minced galangal (or substitute ginger)
6   small dried chiles, Thai type, stems removed, split lengthwise and soaked
½   pound chicken meat, chopped
4   cups chicken stock
2   lime kaffir leaves or the peel of one lime
     Juice of one lime
1½   cups coconut milk
     Whole cilantro sprigs

Heat the oil in a stock pot and fry the garlic, galangal, and chiles for 2 minutes. Add the chicken and cook for 2 minutes more. Add the stock, lime leaves, and lime juice, and bring to a boil. Cover, reduce the heat, and simmer for 10 minutes. Stir in the coconut milk, garnish with the cilantro, and serve.

Yield: 6 Servings
Heat Scale: Medium

CHAPTER 9

A PARTY ON THE IRRAWADDY

*T*HE LANDS OF SOUTHEAST ASIA CALL ME TO THE TABLE, *sometimes through the voice of the poet.*

Ship me somewheres east of Suez,
Where the best is like the worst,
Where there ain't no Ten Commandments
And a man can raise a thirst.
For the temple bells are callin'
And it's there that I would be,
By the old Moulmein pagoda,
Lookin' lazy at the sea.

—Rudyard Kipling

Bruce Harmon, myself, and our fifteen-year-old pedicab driver/guide, Din Tun, lingered in the small amphitheater near the grand market of Mandalay, in the heart of Burma. Attendants were snuffing the red and gold paper lanterns one by one, and the women of the classical dance troupe were gathering up bits of costume jewelry and swaths of silk. The audience had melted away into the night, leaving behind a faint scent of the sandalwood paste that all the women wear on their cheeks as sunscreen, makeup, and perfume. All else was open starry sky and stillness.

"Go now?" Din Tun asked. "Time...late."

"Yes," I said. "Time to leave Mandalay. It was a long time journey getting here, Din. But now it's time to go."

"Go," he nodded. "Come back Mandalay? Sometime?"

"Ha. That's what Kipling says in his poem, you know."

"Kipling, yes," he nodded and smiled indulgently, knowing and caring nothing of the Imperial poet, but he knew that Kipling held something special for me. Din had taken me to Mandalay Hill, the great temple complex with its "thousand steps" heavenward. We had taken off our shoes at the bottom of the hill and mounted the steps that go straight up the steep slope like a causeway. Reaching the top of the stairway and the uppermost temple that crowned the hill, I paused to catch my breath and mop my brow. Then, while Din watched in bemusement, I shinnied up a drainpipe, clambered onto the roof, and mounted the peak of the highest gable. Far below me lay the green and abundant Mandalay Valley, rich with the season's planting. Surrounded by abrupt hills, it called to mind a huge serving vessel, for such it is. Looking down into it and into the town, I had recited aloud Kipling's poem, "The Road to Mandalay," for it was the poet as much as Din who had brought me to that high point. "For the wind is in the palm trees, and the temple bells they say, 'Come ye back, ye British soldier, come ye back to Mandalay.'" Din had watched and had concluded that I was on a pilgrimage of some kind.

Many of my travels in the East have been inspired by the writers who preceded me. Kipling is high among them. Although he wrote from another century and another land, the experience of the soldier or sailor in the Orient is universal. He speaks to me as clearly and as currently as though he were reporting directly to me about his most recent voyage or patrol or an evening in a tavern. Kipling's poems have always been a compelling call echoing through time and space, through mind and imagination. My early sailings had never taken me to Burma. As a Navy man I had never called at the ports of Rangoon or Moulmein. Yet the power of poetry is such that Kipling made it my destiny to see the land of Burma and the city of Mandalay.

But it was not an easy destiny to fulfill because in the late twentieth century, a clique of generals, led by Ne Win, with xenophobic and hermitic leanings and a vaguely leftist vocabulary, took over the gentle land of Burma. They closed the borders, shut out the world, and embarked upon an ill-defined and very slow journey down "the Burmese path to socialism." It was a unique enterprise, whose successes have never been tabulated. Had they been, few would have had the interest to read the slim record. Burma became a place where nothing ever happened. No news was ever issued from the capital of Rangoon because no news occurred. The nation's once lively trade dropped off to the barest trickle. Journalists, travelers, and geographers showed no interest. The generals liked it that way.

Burma is now a land of echoes of things past. So many things and places are not what they seem to be, but are mere shadows and provocative suggestions of what they once were. The generals have held the land in stasis for so long it seems that time stopped when the British Empire departed. Auto manufacturing is nonexistent and the imports are so few that the most common motor vehicles on the roads are 1940s-vintage Willys Jeeps. A native parts industry, scrap metal, and brilliant mechanics keep them going. The mechanics make house calls—and even road calls. A team of them will travel for two days by boat, train, or bullock cart to reach a broken-down Jeep or truck. Arriving on the scene, these consummate masters of their trade can effect a complete overhaul using only the tools they carry and parts they cannibalize or fashion from tin cans and old tires. For such a job they might receive $25.00.

The trains in Burma are slow, and as I've told you, nearly impossible to ride. The airplanes rarely fly. The warehouses, offices, and houses of trade the British built are all in a general state of disrepair and peeling paint. Nothing happens to make it better. Nothing seems to happen to make it worse. Nothing happens. The generals like it that way.

However, even generals can become desperate for cash. When nothing happens in the economy, nothing comes to the tax man, and tourist dollars are needed to make up the loss. Visas can still be difficult to get, and they might not last long. But we got ours, and I finally arrived in Mandalay. Bruce and I landed in Rangoon from Bangkok and immediately departed for the old royal capital on the Irrawaddy River. And nearly all that I hoped to find, I found: the beauty, the ease, the history, the culture. It is a dusty town of memories. Everywhere are tantalizing hints of what was—and what might be again on that near day when the last general dies.

I found everything I wanted with one exception: the food. Nowhere were we able to find a complete, well-made Burmese meal! The restaurants in the city were all either Chinese or Indian. They might offer the odd Burmese dish, but seemingly only as a nod to the dominant culture. The occasional market food stall offered things vile and unfit for healthy palates, and while they called it Burmese food, I felt sure it was slander. Nowhere in this place of my pilgrimage, nowhere in this cultural capital, was I able to find a decent repast in the national style. I had read about Burmese cookery. I had spoken to knowledgeable people about it. I had yet to encounter it. I had been warned: "There aren't many Burmese restaurants in Burma. If you want real Burmese food, it's best to get yourself invited home to dinner."

I believe we cannot know a people, or claim to have truly visited any land, without experiencing some of its arts. But painting and sculpture can be confusing; literature needs translating and explicating; and most of the other arts need some kind of introduction. But cookery is approachable by all. Even the most untutored wanderer, with a willing palate and a passionate curiosity, can acquire at the table an intimate knowledge of any land and its people. "Tell me what you eat, and I will tell you what you are," wrote Brillat-Savarin.

From Mandalay we planned to travel by riverboat to the ancient city of Pagahn. Somewhere along the river, somehow, I vowed, I would get myself invited home to dinner.

We climbed into Din's pedicab with all our gear that starry night and rolled across town to the booking office to pick up our boat tickets. Taking our leave of Din, he asked, "You give me a present?" Everybody we met in Burma wanted a "present." Not anything of value necessarily, but a souvenir, something of that outside world that was forbidden to them by the generals. Anything manufactured, anything of cultural significance, anything personal was a rich gift to the Burmese. In the market, we found that our property was more valuable than our Burmese money. We each bought beautiful handwoven cotton blankets. Bruce paid for his with a Daffy Duck tee shirt; I got mine for a collapsible umbrella. The merchant seemed to be afraid he had cheated us.

On departing Mandalay, we gave our guide a brass belt buckle. His eyes shone like the metal itself. Din Tun took his treasure, mounted his pedicab, and rode away into the night.

"I still wish his name were Din Gunga," I said. "It would have been perfect on government forms."

Bruce and I turned towards the river. High clouds had rolled in, and the resulting darkness was so profound and thick that it seemed to have texture. It swirled and engulfed us like a black tar fog. I half expected it to feel gooey. As we approached the docks, the road narrowed to a sinuously snaking alley with dark, somber shapes of decrepit buildings squatting on either side. I said to Bruce, "Keep your eyes and ears open. If there's one thing I learned in all my years as a sailor, it's that a darkened waterfront is not a very salubrious place."

"Huh?"

"You wouldn't want to take a date there."

"Oh. Dangerous?"

"Could be. Why don't you go first."

Neither of us considered my comment to be remarkable. Bruce is a good man with his fists. We originally met in the boxing ring when we were both amateur pugilists with a California athletic association. Our first meeting was attended by flurries of lefts and rights, one small shiner (his), two headaches and one very bloody nose (mine). We became instant friends. Neither of us competes any more, but Bruce continues to work out, spar regularly, and keep his fighting weight. I think about it a lot.

Bruce's keeping in top form has come in handy. He once bounced a troublesome Iranian fellow from the kick boxing ring in a nightclub in Pattaya Beach, Thailand. The crowd went delirious and started chanting "USA, USA!" The manager was grateful enough for Bruce's excellent service to pay him a fighter's purse and offer him a job. During a trip to China, Bruce coldcocked an armed mugger with a one-two combination worthy of the great champions. The bad guy hit the pavement like a sack of bricks. "Let's boogie," Bruce said afterward. And we did.

And so in Mandalay I told Bruce, "You walk ahead. I'll see that no one comes up on you from behind."

"Thanks. I guess."

We came to a point where we could smell the river and hear it lapping against the pilings of the wharves. A large, dark shape loomed ahead, but I couldn't tell if it was a building or a riverboat. I remembered my seaman's training: when you're on look-out duty on a dark night, objects are difficult to see if you look directly at them. If you look at them askance, observe them obliquely, they come into better view. So I shifted my gaze first to port, then to starboard, and the shape revealed itself as a flat-bottomed, two-decked, screw-driven Mississippi-type riverboat.

"Is it ours?" Bruce asked.

"Dunno," I said, slipping off my pack. "You watch the stuff and I'll go see." I felt around gingerly with hands and feet for a gangway. Finding it, I went aboard and ascertained that it was our vessel. Returning to Bruce, I said, "You're going to love this boat."

"Why?"

"Because of the story you'll have when it's all over."

"Is it that bad?"

"Yes. But only hard times are interesting. Come on."

The two open decks of the boat were crisscrossed with painted lines that marked out spaces six feet by four feet. Each space was occupied by a family: parents, children, baggage and all. In that space they would eat, sleep, and wile away the time for the next two to four days, depending on their destinations.

We found that there were no spaces left. Both decks were thickly carpeted with humans. Arms, legs, and torsos seemed all tangled together into a single, massive, quivering, unevenly woven blanket of flesh and clothing. Smells of fuel oil, sweat, babies, and onions drifted about the deck in currents. Snores, murmurs, grunts, and mumbling floated up from the blanket of flesh. There was no place for us even to set foot, let alone lie down.

Out of the gloom on the far side of the deck, a piercing female voice rang out with a shocking Irish brogue, "Piss off or I'll chuck ye into the Irrawaddy!" A thumping sound and a masculine groan followed.

At almost the same moment, a harried-looking Burmese man in a formerly white

132

shirt and a tattered seaman's cap appeared out of the blackness. He gestured impatiently for us to follow him. We complied, and he led us up a spiral ladder to the upper deck where another fold of the human carpet lay wriggling and yawning. Just forward of the ladder head was a cabin door. Our conductor opened it and gestured us in, grumbling something about "Farangs." Apparently the boat's captain, or the generals, didn't want us pressing the flesh too closely with a discontented populace. Forbidden thoughts might be exchanged, untoward criticisms offered.

The door closed behind us, and we were in complete and fathomless dark. Somewhere in the inky space we heard a shuffle, followed by the click of a cigarette lighter. Behind its cheery flame grinned the man we came to know as "Mad Max the Aussie."

"Hello, mates," he said. "Yanks?"

"Yeah. How'd you know?"

"It's a gift."

Other voices spoke up, although their faces were still obscured. "Hello!"

"Allo!"

"Good evening!"

Accents from New Zealand, France, and England. But no native tongue sounded. We had been billeted in a foreign ghetto. We were in the only passenger cabin on board.

"Pull up a bit of deck, mates," Max said as he let the light go out. "There's only two bunks, and the sick girls have 'em."

We felt around among the other western bodies for open deck space and let down our packs. Then the door opened again and two Irish women and a man joined our exiled group. Max repeated his welcome ceremony, and we all chimed in.

"Seems we've all been shunned," the Irishman said with something combining relief and bewilderment. He told us that the three of them had ensconced themselves among a pile of rice bags on the stern of the lower deck and had been looking forward to a night of relative comfort. "But it seems we were situated directly below the spot on the upper deck where the Burmese gentlemen relieve themselves. Why at first I thought it was raining a wee bit. But no, not at all!" I could hear sniffing sounds in the dark as he inspected his clothes and bag.

"That ain't the worst of it all!" I recognized the female voice of several moments before. "One o' those Burman lads was lyin' right beside me an' 'e kept tryin' to touch me tits! An' 'e kept grinnin' at me an' sayin' 'Boom Boom'! Boom Boom 'e wants now, is it? I gave 'im Boom Boom with me right foot. 'Piss off,' I told 'im. Boom Boom indeed!"

We all went resolutely to sleep, and before dawn, the boatmen cast off their lines and quietly headed the craft downstream. We awoke sometime after daybreak, and Mandalay was miles behind us.

The Irrawaddy was in flood, and the river's vast expanse stretched out in all directions. The green and distant shoreline, roiling with tropical growth, lay flat throughout the morning. In the afternoon, it rose into wavy hills. From time to time we saw little army posts that were keeping an eye open on behalf of the generals. The two sick girls whom the wildly bearded Max had mentioned the night before were sisters from New Zealand. They were slim and pretty, dressed in Burmese sarongs and blouses. They were unfailingly polite and proper and suffered their traveler's ailments with Victorian stoicism and propriety. Fortunately, our cabin had a private toilet, such as it was—a closet with a hole cut in the floor overhanging the water. When the bellyache flared, they were able to reach "the lavat'ry" without unladylike haste or display. In their times of gastrointestinal calm, they sat up with correct posture and wrote demurely in their journals bound with creamy white paper. Any of us who spoke to them, even during the worst of their suffering, received a genuinely friendly and courteous reply. I wanted to tell them that if ever I had to spend days and nights huddled in a bomb shelter and suffering illness, danger, and deprivation, I hoped that they would be there with me. Somehow that just didn't sound like what I meant to convey, so I didn't say it.

The rest of our cabin mates were a quiet lot. The Frenchwoman kept to herself and a novel. The young Englishwoman, who looked like a basketball player, would chat as long as anyone spoke to her but never said anything first. Max contemplated the river with a special intensity. A cigarette always hung from his mouth, but he tended to forget about it, and the ash would drop onto his beard. Periodically he brushed it away, like a bothersome fly. The Irish played cards.

Around midday, as the sick girls politely voided their guts yet again, I realized that mine was empty. A breeze from astern told me someone was cooking. Bruce stepped out the door to reconnoiter. In a few minutes he returned to say, "There's a galley on the stern, and they're serving food."

"Can we get across the populated deck?" I asked.

"No. But I think I know a way. Follow me."

Bruce led me through a dim passageway along the cabin wall to the starboardside railing. Directly below, the brown Irrawaddy frothed in the boat's wake. Stretching aft from where we stood, the dense human tapestry that carpeted the deck had come to life and was even more impenetrable, if such a thing could be.

"Are you ready?" Bruce asked.

"For what?"

He swung first one leg and then the other over the rail. With his feet on the deck's outer edge and his hands gripping the rail, he began crabbing his way aft. When the tapestry people saw him, they began to laugh and wave and cheer him on. He grinned hugely and waved back, once even letting go and saying, "Look, no hands! Ha ha!" I wiped my sweaty palms on my trousers and followed. We reached the little open-air galley to general applause.

The cook was dressed in a frayed and faded loincloth and a tattered undershirt that was a lot less of its original self than more. He had dark stains on his teeth, thick black dirt under his nails (all ten of them), and his galley matched him in all the important details. We sat at his greasy plywood counter and he greeted us in passable English.

"Good afternoon! You want food? You want drink?"

"Do you have tea?"

"Oh, yes, yes, yes. Tea." He picked up a pot from the stove and reached for two empty cups on the counter. Seeing that they had not been emptied by his previous patrons, he casually dumped their contents over the side and refilled them.

"Do you have soda?"

"Soda, yes, yes, yes." He opened two bottles of greenish froth and set them before us. They smelled like a wet cow pasture. The bottle mouths were surrounded by a brown encrustation.

"Do you have straws?"

"Yes, yes, yes." He stuck a straw into each bottle. They had teeth marks on them.

"Do you have beer?"

"Beer no. No, no, no. Nowhere on boat. Captain say no beer. Too bad, eh?"

The coming days looked to be very long and dim. Deciding to make the best of it, we asked the man what he had in the way of food. He removed the covers from a pot of rice and three pots of things we could not recognize. One of them looked like curried dirt, but I could not be sure. The others were anyone's guess. I pride myself on being able to eat anything. I might even eat dirt. But it has to be clean dirt.

"I'll have rice," I said.

"I'll try the green one," Bruce said, pointing to one of the pots. "And rice, too."

The rice was clean and smelled wholesome. The cook served it with his stained smile and a small dish of condiment. "In Burma we eat rice every time," he explained. "Sometimes only rice. It's okay when you have something for taste. This one is good."

His offering was simply peanut oil infused with garlic and sesame. But drizzling small amounts of it over the rice, or forming the rice into balls and dipping them into the oil, made it as good as pasta with a simple sauce of olive oil and Parmesan cheese.

As we ate, I repeated to Bruce, "Somewhere between here and Rangoon we've got to get invited home to dinner. It's the only way I'm going to taste enough of Burmese cooking."

"So what have you learned about it so far?"

"I know that their hospitality is extravagant. I've heard that they'll even get up from the table to fan guests who are overheated. And they like to have dinner together at sunset. They have a saying that goes, 'Eating together is a buttress against night's approach.' And, of course, they eat curries and a lot of different salads and greens. Like the Chinese, they connect food and pharmacology and rather than use medicine for an ailment, they might prescribe a change of diet. Although, unlike the Chinese, who have the concept of the Five Flavors, the Burmese have thirteen! One of the most interesting things I've learned is that they are connoisseurs of water. H-two-O is never simply *agua*. They divide it into numerous categories: rainwater, hailwater, pondwater, water from a creek, water from a ravine, water from a well; it goes on and on."

Sipping through his chewed-up straw and sniffing at the bottle, Bruce said, "You think they do the same for soda? You know, soda from a swamp, soda from a ditch, soda from a puddle?"

We finished our meal and returned to the cabin the way we had come, amusing the deck passengers yet again. We told the others what we had done, and the Irish followed our example. After they reached the galley, the woman with the shocking brogue leaned over the stern and located Mr. Boom Boom on the lower deck. When she caught his eye, she gave him the finger. She returned to the cabin exhilarated, although somewhat put off by the bill of fare. All the other cabin mates, except the sick girls, eventually crabwalked to the galley and got something to eat.

Except for our brief trips to the galley, the day was long, uneventful, and quiet. Because of the heat in the river valley, we all became lethargic and sleepy. The sun was just touching the horizon when the boat slowed, and her pilot guided her to a sand spit where a huge banyan tree had overturned. Crewmen leapt ashore and wrapped two hawsers around the tree, securing the boat for the night. The deck passengers began arranging themselves for sleep, gathering up their children and rolling out their cotton blankets. The two sick girls were relieved that the vibrations from the boat's engines had ceased, and they lay peacefully with no angry rumblings from their tired tummies. The others in our exile lay down too. Even the river seemed to still itself. In the gathering dusk, I saw lights winking on through the jungle foliage a short distance downstream.

"Bruce," I said, "there are people down there. And I'll bet they're about to have dinner. Do you think they'd like some company?"

We headed for the door and the English basketball woman spoke first at last. "May I go with you? I'm frightfully hungry. Couldn't eat a thing at the galley."

"Of course. Glad to have you."

"If you see soldiers after dark," Max warned, "give 'em a wide berth. They won't take any cheek."

No gangway had been laid out when the boat was tied up, so to get to shore we had to climb over the rail and shinny down one of the poles that support the upper deck. From there we swung down the hawser to the banyan tree and jumped down to the beach. We followed the shoreline downstream in the last of the light, through the jungle by the edge of the Irrawaddy, and by the time dark had fallen, we were able to follow the happy sounds of feasting.

We arrived at a thatch and bamboo village of about a dozen families who were just sitting down to a communal dinner. At their first sight of us, a shout went up as though both the circus and the Wells Fargo stagecoach had just arrived. The children instantly ran to us and took us by the hands, laughing and squealing. At the lantern-lit tables set up in the village quad, the fattest and most prosperous-looking man present gazed up in happy amazement and immediately set aside his dinner, knocked back a swallow of some beverage, and came waddling up to greet us. He pressed his hands together in a prayerful attitude and made what must have been a speech of welcome, to which all the villagers applauded in approval. Somebody said something humorous, and the whole populace broke into waves of laughter, the kids jumping up and down in a kind of ecstatic dance. Nobody spoke a word of English.

I began to wonder if we had been expected and that I had slept for many days and forgotten about it. Had Din Tun told us to look up his people downriver? Had he sent word ahead to treat us like heroes? Did one of us resemble somebody's prodigal son? Or were we being mistaken for someone else who would soon arrive? Or fail to arrive? Would we end up hogging someone else's glory? Were we, in reality, in a Hope and Crosby road movie, the English woman really being Dorothy Lamour?

One of the men approached us with a red two-and-a-half-gallon gasoline can, all the people making way for him. As he got near he began to screw on the nozzle. Was the movie turning into a nightmare? Were we about to become a roaring sacrifice which would guarantee this year's crops? Had we trespassed? "Maybe they'll just kill the girl," I thought. "Maybe they need somebody for a suttee, and being a head taller than us, she'll make a better blaze." Reaching into a shoulder bag, the man produced three small glasses and filled them with the clear contents of the gasoline can. It was rice wine, and powerful rice wine, too.

My companions sipped theirs, but I knocked mine back neat, and the people cheered. I came to wish they hadn't done that, as it inspired me to further acts of alcoholic bravado which culminated in a huge headache.

The village children seemed to lay particular claim to us, and soon we each had our own retinue, if not rival factions. They clung to us, led us around the village, never took their eyes off us, even petted us. I began to feel like a show horse they had just purchased. But then they took us to the tables, and I felt like a king. The portly speechmaker spoke again. He seemed to be offering a toast or a grace, some prologue to dinner to which everyone nodded agreement. Then it was time to feast.

The women laid out a great variety of meats, vegetables, rice, and condiments. And the variety of salads was amazing. Anything that grew in the ground seemed to be chopped up raw or cooked and tossed with oil and herbs. Many varieties of greens arrived, each cooked in a different spice bouquet or aromatic oil. A flurry of cutlery sounded from the nearby open communal kitchen as still more food was prepared and sent to the table. The gas can bearer stood by, never allowing an empty glass. The kids all schooled around their chosen ones, and the men all beamed with pride and amusement. It struck me that we three were the only ones eating, but the people didn't seem to mind a bit. We were nightclub entertainment, and they weren't going to miss a thing.

The jewel in the crown of this night's feast was braised pork. Its color was like a burnished copper. It swam in a decadent thick sauce of ginger, garlic, soy sauce, and light sesame oil, and undercurrents of chile and black pepper swirled through it. It was cloaked with rings of translucent golden onions and sat enthroned in a silver server, all the lesser dishes paying it humble homage. One of the girls in my troupe of young followers dished it up for me. She kept speaking to me and seemed to be saying, "This is my mother's dish. It's the best you'll ever taste." It had been cooked slowly and the meat fell apart on my tongue, resolving itself into a saucy, rich and heavy dew that coated the mouth with tasty pleasure. The rice wine was its perfect foil as it cleansed the palate of the not-quite-cloying richness and made it ready for more.

We ate our fill. After dinner, we were led around the village again, presumably to shake it down. We returned to the tables and more rice wine flowed. We tried to converse with our hosts in sign language, but it proved a poor second to the language of the table with its unambiguous messages of welcome and cheer. Then, some of the kids began to sing. At first it was two girls and a boy. And it was clear they were singing to us. Soon all the village children were singing, with their parents clapping time, a few even swaying to the music. At the end of their song we all applauded. Then two men took the stage. They sang what I thought must have been a working song because of the lifting and hauling gestures. They were followed by more applause and more wine.

Then Bruce said, "Richard, do 'Gunga Din' for 'em!"

"But they won't know what I'm saying."

"It won't matter. Just be dramatic and rhythmic."

So I stood up, and lifted up my hands to ask for their attention. "You may talk of gin and beer, when you're quartered safe out here," I began, stressing rhythm and rhyme. "And you're sent to penny fights and Aldershot it." They were immediately rapt. They had no idea what I was about to do, but they were going to savor every bit of it. I acted out the story. I hammed it up. Kipling would have been aghast, but they loved it. With very little coaxing, I got the kids to join in at the refrains with "Din, Din, Din!" They had no idea what the poem was about. They might have thought it was "Little Red Riding Hood" or the *Ramayana*. But they loved it. I ended with a dramatic flourish as I portrayed Gunga Din dying. They went bananas. Another song followed.

By this time I could see that Bruce was up to something he loves: arm wrestling. He is very good at it and often wrestles for beers in taverns. He taught me the trick of leveraging yourself from the foot up in order to gain maximum advantage of an opponent. If the other guy doesn't know how to do that just right, a smaller man can often take a bigger one.

Bruce was gesturing to a man whose arms suggested he lived behind a plow and had some good-natured pride in his strength. Everybody else saw it at the same time and a cheer went up because they suddenly realized that the entertainment program included not only performing arts, but sport as well! Amidst shouting and wagers on the conqueror, the two men were led to where the whole village could see: the terrace of a thatch and bamboo house raised on stilts that put the floor at eye level. A perfect stage.

I mounted the steps with Bruce to act as his second. A friend of the plowman did the same, and we were accompanied by the portly greeter whose house it turned out to be. He addressed the people like a Las Vegas ringside announcer, and the whole population whooped and hollered. The two contestants nodded to each other, went to the floor, and took each other's measure. I looked carefully at the Burmese man's body language and could see that he didn't know how to play this game.

"He doesn't know the trick, Bruce. Play it out. Give the folks a good show." I knelt down and put their hands together. Out in the crowd I saw the Englishwoman, who looked worried. I gave her a wink, counted loudly to three and hollered, "Go!"

Bruce gave the man a couple of inches to start, then played him like a fish on a line for a good two minutes. The crowd went delirious. Then, pretending it was a huge effort, Bruce brought his foe to an honorable defeat. All cheered, and Bruce's child groupies gloated. Money changed hands.

As Bruce congratulated his opponent for fighting the good fight, I noticed a line of strong men form at the bottom of the terrace steps, happily awaiting their chance to wrestle. Bruce took on two of them, not drawing it out this time, so as not to lose his strength too soon. For his fourth combat he had to switch to his left arm, which necessitated finding southpaws among the challengers. He dispatched two more.

But by now he was beginning to tire, although the crowd was lustily yelling for more. As I massaged his arms while his child pages brought him drinks, I felt someone tap me on the shoulder. I turned to see a walking collection of cord-like muscles topped by a shaggy head with a gap-tooth grin. One of his tree-trunk arms was making wrestling motions, the other was pointing at me. And the whole village was screaming their approval. I began massaging Bruce's arms more quickly. "Come on, Brooster. Let's get those arms ready!"

But he insisted that I take the challenge. "Go ahead," he said. "You can do it."

"What if he falls on me? I'll be crushed!"

"You can take him. Remember, it's like boxing, where the jab begins at the foot and works its way up through the body like a whip. It's just like that."

I looked at my would-be opponent. At least he didn't seem hostile. I looked at the Englishwoman, who was now enjoying the show. The village folk who had feasted us were chanting. Then I looked at my child faction, the kids who had fed me, sang to me and Gunga Dinned with me. They were hopping up and down in transports of ecstasy at the thought that their knight was about to do battle. If I were to turn such a tide of enthusiasm by refusing the challenge, I would regret it forever. Better I should suffer whatever injuries might befall me. I dropped down to the floor and held up my hand to be crushed, twisted, or deformed in whatever way fate might feel disposed. The tree-trunk man lowered himself in sections, settling his mass onto the floor one joint at a time. My arms felt like matchsticks. I wanted to ask the crowd to pray for me, but I didn't know how. The portly householder, Bruce, three other guys, and a couple of kids now occupied the terrace with the man-mountain and me.

A relative calm came over the crowd as Bruce knelt down and placed my hand into the other's. "You're in perfect position," he said. "And he's got both feet together. He'll have no leverage. All you need to do is work against his weight."

"Well there's enough of that, I'll tell you!"

"Go!"

I felt a sudden twisting in my shoulder joint accompanied by electric-like shocks and an enormous pressure running laterally through my forearm as though the guy were trying to drive my elbow through the floor like a knife. It hurt, too. But Bruce was right. The man didn't know how to direct his strength in this kind of contest. If I could hold out and throw him off-balance by feints, I might beat the big S.O.B. At the least, I'd make him work for it.

Sweat streamed down our faces. Our bodies shook with effort. The crowd screamed. It seemed to go on forever. The people on the terrace with us were jumping up and down, causing the thin floor to undulate and making it difficult to stay positioned. And then it broke. With a loud snapping sound, two of the bamboo poles that held up one side of the terrace broke. The floor came out from under us and fell to an angle of thirty degrees before hitting the ground. Of the jumpers-up-and-down, some slid down the incline as though on a waterslide, some tumbled end-over-end, and the owner fell off completely and went straight to the ground with a splat. My opponent and I rolled like a drum, hands still locked in the struggle, all the way down. I didn't even realize what had happened till we were halfway to the ground. We were still wrestling when we hit bottom. The entire village, even the ones who had been on the terrace, the owner included, were beside themselves with laughter. The tree-trunk man suddenly became confused. I took advantage of his momentary distraction, and, with the mightiest heave of my life, put his arm to the ground. I stood up the victor.

I offered congratulations to the defeated, who was a good sport about it, and calm returned to the crowd. The excitement had peaked with the breaking of the terrace, and we all needed to catch our breath. But the night was still young. Or so we thought.

"What you doing?" a voice at the rim of the crowd demanded in broken English. "What you doing?" Before we could even realize what was happening, the crowd had melted away just as quickly as breath into the wind, leaving behind only the scent of sandalwood paste. All else was open starry sky and stillness. We three Farangs stood alone facing one of the generals' watchers. A soldier, in army-issue underwear, stood there panting, an old submachine gun leveled at us. We had apparently disturbed his rest.

"What you doing?" he shouted again. It must have been the only English he knew. We began backing off slowly.

"Well...uh," the Englishwoman said.

"Yeah...uh," I followed.

"We're getting the hell out of here!" Bruce yelled. And we all turned and ran in a frenzy back up river. I remembered to weave as I went, just in case he tried to draw a bead on me. As we approached the boat, still running like bats out of hell, I could hear him, although faintly, still repeating his demand. Then he fired a burst into the air for good measure. When we reached the boat, we leapt up onto the banyan, hauled ourselves up the hawser and shinnied up the deck support. We found the passageway blocked by cargo, so we crab-walked along the railing forward to a cabin window. Our cabin mates were waiting for us as we crawled through, breathless.

"What happened?" they all asked, seemingly in unison.

"Cross a soldier?" Max wanted to know.

"Are you all right?"

"Are any of you hurt? We heard shouting and shooting. Was it a riot of some kind? A revolt? Whatever happened?"

I braced myself against the cabin wall and slid down to sit on the deck. "Nothing at all to be upset about," I said between gasps. "Nothing to worry about at all. We just got invited home to dinner."

BALACHAUNG

Side dishes, tidbits, and condiments are common on the Burmese table, regardless of the meal's abundance or complexity. And for simple meals, as the riverboat's cook demonstrated, a little bit of strongly-flavored accompaniment can go a long way to stretch a bowl of plain rice. It fills the bill.

1	serrano chile, stem removed, chopped
2	teaspoons salt
1	teaspoon dry shrimp paste (or Malayan blacan)
½	cup vinegar
20	cloves garlic
2	cups peanut oil
4	onions, sliced thin
8	ounces coarse shrimp powder (dried shrimp coarsely ground in a mortar)

Combine the chile, salt, shrimp paste, and vinegar and set aside.

Place the garlic cloves on a cutting board and strike them firmly with the side of a knife blade to loosen their skins. Peel and slice the cloves.

Heat the oil to medium and fry the onions and garlic separately, then remove them with a slotted spoon and set aside to cool. Pour off all but 1 cup of the oil and fry the shrimp powder for 5 minutes. Add the onion and garlic mixture and stir-fry until crisp. Remove from the heat and let cool completely.

Combine the two mixtures and serve over rice.

Yield: About 3 cups
Heat Scale: Mild

RED-GOLD PORK

Because of our abrupt departure from the river village, I was unable to get that particular cook's recipe for the pork we enjoyed so much. However, I learned that it represents a common approach to pork in Burma. Every cook has his or her variation of it. This recipe was demonstrated to me by a cook in Rangoon, and it is close enough to the village cook's to conjure up memories of Gunga Din and fill me with an urge to arm wrestle.

2	pounds pork, cut into 1½-inch cubes
1½	tablespoons dark soy sauce

1	teaspoon black pepper
½	cup light sesame oil (or mix dark sesame oil to taste with peanut oil)
1	tablespoon minced ginger
4	cloves garlic, minced
1	cup water
1½	tablespoons light soy sauce
1	teaspoon cayenne
3	small onions, sliced
	Salt to taste

Rub the pork well with the dark soy sauce and pepper and marinate for 30 minutes.

Heat the oil in a wok and stir in the ginger for 30 seconds. Add the meat and stir-fry for 5 minutes. Add the garlic and ½ cup water, cover and simmer until the water is absorbed. Add the light soy sauce, cayenne, and ½ cup water, cover and simmer till the meat is tender. Add the onions and cook until the water is absorbed again, and the pork is well browned. Salt to taste.

Yield: 6 to 8 Servings
Heat Scale: Medium

BURMESE WATER GREENS

A common vegetable in Burma is kazun, or Ipomea aquatica. It grows abundantly along the riverbanks and lake shores. Tender young collards or even Romaine lettuce make adequate substitutes.

1	pound greens, leaves and stems separated, chopped
2	tablespoons vegetable oil
1	onion, sliced
2	tablespoons shrimp powder
2	tablespoons soy sauce
2	cloves garlic, crushed
	Salt to taste

Wash the greens well and leave them in water. Heat the oil to medium and fry the onion until translucent. Add the shrimp powder and stir-fry for 1 minute. Stir in the stems and the water that clings to them. Cover and cook for 2 minutes. Stir in the leaves and the soy sauce, cover and cook for 2 minutes. Stir in the garlic and stir-fry for 1 minute. Add salt to taste.

Yield: 6 Side Servings

CABBAGE WITH PORK

Cabbage is probably the most common vegetable seen in the Burmese market, and every cook has several recipes for it. Pork is the most popular meat. Chinese butchers provide it as they do not have the Burmese proscription against killing animals. As I was told by Rangoon restaurateur Aung Tun, "All kinds of meat are allowed to us. But we must make a very nice distinction between the killing and the eating. In our religion, it is a sin to kill the pig. It is also a sin to order the pig to be killed, but less so. But if you buy a chop or a leg from a nice fat pig that has already been killed without your asking, why, that is no sin at all!"

1	head cabbage, shredded
1½	tablespoons vegetable oil
1	onion, sliced
¼	pound pork, sliced thin or julienned
¾	cup chicken stock
2	tablespoons soy sauce
1	teaspoon mashed or pressed fresh garlic

Soak the cabbage in a bowl of cool water.

Heat the oil in a wok and stir-fry the onion until translucent. Add the pork and stir-fry for 2 minutes, then add the stock and half of the soy sauce. Cover and simmer for 3 minutes. Remove the cover and raise the heat. Take a large handful of cabbage and squeeze out most of the water, but allow some to cling. Add it to the wok and stir-fry for 30 seconds. Repeat the process until all the cabbage is in the pan. Add the remaining soy sauce, toss, cover, and simmer until done. The total cooking time for the cabbage should be 5 to 6 minutes. Remove from the heat and mix in the garlic.

Yield: 6 Side Servings

EGGPLANT WITH EGG

Try serving this as an appetizer with lettuce leaves and prawn crackers. It also makes a good lunch with bread or tortillas.

2	large eggplants
½	teaspoon salt
1	pinch turmeric

2	tablespoons vegetable oil
1	large egg, lightly beaten
2	New Mexican green chiles, stems and seeds removed, sliced thin
2	scallions, sliced thin

Roast the eggplants in a very hot oven or over coals until the skins char and the flesh is pulpy. Remove the skins, place eggplants in a large bowl, and mash them with the salt and turmeric.

Heat the oil to high in a wok and stir-fry the eggplant mixture for 2 or 3 minutes. Add the egg and stir-fry well. When the egg is cooked, sprinkle the mixture with the chile and scallion strips.

Yield: 6 Side Servings
Heat Scale: Mild

GREEN BEAN SALAD

Salads are essential to a true Burmese menu. It is not uncommon to serve several at a single meal, or even to make them the centerpiece of a meal.

2	tablespoons vegetable oil
1	onion, sliced
1	pound green beans, cut in 2-inch pieces
	Salted, boiling water
1	large red fresh New Mexican chile, roasted, peeled, stem and seeds removed, minced
2	tablespoons shrimp powder
1	tablespoon fish sauce
1	tablespoon toasted sesame seeds
1	tablespoon light sesame oil
	Juice of one lime

Fry the onion in the vegetable oil until brown, drain on paper towels and set aside. Cook the beans till fork-tender in boiling, salted water. Drain and cool. Combine with the remaining ingredients and toss well.

Yield: 6 Side Servings
Heat Scale: Mild

CABBAGE SALAD

I call this "Burmese Cole Slaw," but it's lighter, healthier, and much more flavorful.

3   cups finely shredded cabbage
1   onion, sliced
3   green chiles, such as serrano, stems and seeds removed, chopped
2   tablespoons shrimp powder
1   tablespoon light sesame oil
     Salt to taste
     Juice of 1 lime

Soak the cabbage in cool water for 2 hours, then drain well. Combine all ingredients and toss well. Using the back of a spoon, crush the cabbage slightly while tossing it to release some of its juice.

Yield: 6 Side Servings
Heat Scale: Medium

BURMESE RADISH SALAD

This salad is very refreshing and cleansing to the palate. It goes well with any fried food or heavily-sauced dish.

3   small red chiles, such as serranos, stems and seeds removed, sliced thin
3   small green chiles, such as serranos, stems and seeds removed, sliced thin
3   tablespoons cider vinegar
2   daikon radishes, peeled and sliced thin
½   teaspoon sugar
½   teaspoon salt
1   tablespoon light sesame oil
1   tablespoon toasted sesame seeds
1   tablespoon shrimp powder
1   small onion, sliced and fried brown

Place the chiles in the vinegar to marinate. Toss the radish slices in a colander and set in a well-ventilated place to dry for 2 hours. After 2 hours, combine all ingredients and toss well.

Yield: 6 Side Servings
Heat Scale: Medium

CHAPTER 10

THE FEAST OF THE
NECROPOLIS

*A*ND CALL THROUGH THE VOICE OF THE POET YET AGAIN.

"No you won't 'eed nothin' else
But those spicy, garlic smells,
And the sunshine and the palm trees
And the tinkly temple-bells..."
—Rudyard Kipling

In the heart of the ancient Burmese necropolis of Bagan, a bush bearing small red chile peppers grows wild in a temple ruin. This lively spice, thriving amid tombs, is a metaphor—one for all of Indochina. This vast land is one of necropolises. Ghost cities, both lost and found, nestle in the vital, living, jungle landscape of the present day. Remnants of golden ages and dusty ruin are so common that they go unseen by the people who live among them. But the traveler, the stranger, and the sojourner can feel their ghostly presence at every turn.

Side by side with the ghosts of days dead are the vivacious cuisines of Indochina, mirroring the pulsating life of the present day. And those cuisines are symbolized by the firespices used by every cook in Burma, Thailand, Cambodia, Laos, and Vietnam. Thoreau said that the difference between the quick and the dead was simply a matter of "animal heat." Whether that heat comes from Promethean fire or spice fire, it's all the same to those who love the Lively Spice. And Burmese cookery provides it in judicious abundance.

The chile pepper, of the *Capsicum* genus, was introduced to Indochina in the sixteenth century, probably by the Spanish or Portuguese. The most commonly used chiles in the region are local varieties which resemble jalapeños and serranos. As the name indicates, Indochina is a blend of Indian and Chinese cultures. Burmese cookery leans closer to the Indian, and so the Lively Spice plays its role most often in curries.

The Burmese cook approaches curry in a way as constant as the ancient past or the monsoon cycle. Using a grinding stone, the cook pulverizes together onion, garlic, ginger, turmeric, and chile, making a thick paste. Many recipes will contain other ingredients as well, but this one is the basic mixture for all true Burmese curries.

The process is particular as well. The oil, usually light sesame, is heated to smoking and then the curry paste is stirred in. The cook reduces the heat to low, covers the pan, and simmers, stirring often, for ten or fifteen minutes. This method mellows the ingredients by slow frying and cooks off the water content. When it is done, the oil appears at the edges or on top of the paste. This stage is what the Burmese call *see-byan*, the return of the oil. Meat or vegetables can be added to simmer, releasing their own liquid to form a smooth curry sauce. The result is somewhat oilier than many cuisines, in the way that salad dressings and many Mediterranean cuisines are oily. It produces a silky-smooth, tasty sensation in the

149

mouth that not only satisfies, but soothes as well. The best meal I ever ate in Burma was prepared in this fashion, one starry night in the midst of the ruins of Bagan.

Today the sleepy little village of Bagan exists on the outskirts of the ghost city. A laquerware school operates there, as well as a small Buddhist seminary. But a thousand years ago, Bagan was a young and eager city. She grew up from a level plain on the right bank of the Irrawaddy River, about one hundred miles downstream from Mandalay. Her buildings were wood, thatch, and bamboo; her hardy people were devout and industrious.

In the year 1057, Anawratha, king of Bagan, led his army south against the rival city of Thaton. Thaton fell, was sacked, and the victors bore the spoils back to Bagan in processions rivaling Roman triumphs. The booty included whole libraries, living scholars, religious texts, and gold. Their sudden abundance sparked an explosion of religious, artistic, and cultural enterprise that brought about a two-hundred-year golden age in Bagan. Temples and temple complexes, on a scale previously unseen in Indochina and greater even than Angkor Wat, clogged the twenty-square-mile plain. Houses and palaces were still made of wood, but the temples were all of heavy masonry.

In 1287, Kublai Khan led his army south against Bagan and razed the city. All the wooden buildings were burned, and the people were driven away. But the innumerable temples remained, gravestones to the dead metropolis. In time, nature reclaimed the land. Jungle foliage hid the temples and the world passed by. Bagan would not come to light again for centuries. The whole of Indochina is strewn with such ghost cities; Bagan is simply one of the grandest.

To reach Bagan, Bruce Harmon and I flew from Bangkok to the Burmese capital of Rangoon. From there we took the regularly scheduled overnight train to Mandalay. At the Mandalay docks, we booked passage to Bagan on a leaky, creaky old flat-bottom riverboat that took two days and nights to reach our destination. On board we met a small group of other likeminded palefaces with whom we traveled the next few days.

I ate very little on the boat. The food from its galley was filthy and fly-specked, and the dishes were washed with plain water of a dubious source. Had I known, I could have brought my own rations. We tied up the second night near a village where the people were kind enough to feed three of us, but the only thing I had consumed on the boat was rice, four cans of warm beer I had brought from Mandalay in the event of drought, and several pots of bad tea that dyed my mouth a bright orange. Bruce, unaffected by the boat's hygienics, ate his fill and laughed at my "tangerine smile." I got off the boat at Bagan feeling like a starving refugee.

Visitors to Bagan can stay at a pleasant thatch and tin-roof guest house for a few dollars or in a neat bungalow at the government-owned Thiripyitsaya Hotel for a few dollars more. Most of the ruins have been relieved of their jungle shroud and are only a short walk away.

Trudging to the guest house, we passed a merchant selling one of the Lively Spice's kin: the melon-like durian fruit. Durian grows wild all over tropical Asia. Wild pigs and orangutans feed on it voraciously. I call the durian kin to the Lively Spice not because of heat—it has none—but because of the sheer gastronomic power, a lot of it in its smell. Anyone who has ever sniffed a durian will tell you that it smells like pig's manure and turpentine whipped in a blender and garnished with a dirty gym sock. But if you hold your breath, the taste is sweet and delicious and leaves a pleasant tingling on the palate. Durian is high in complex and simple carbohydrates, vitamins, and many other nutrients. It is as nourishing and wholesome as a potato and leaves the belly feeling satisfied. Just remember to hold your breath when you eat it.

The Bagan merchant knew how to make the durian hold its own breath. He dried it, which reduced the horrible stink to a sweet and pungent aroma. It was still recognizable as durian, but no longer unpleasant. The man cut the yellow flesh into squares and sold them on bamboo skewers for about a penny each. I ate several, which not only banished my hunger, but also cleansed some of the orange tea stain from my mouth. Revived, I was ready to visit the ruins.

The sun was near zenith and dust hung in the still air. There were no guides in Bagan, so we half-dozen foreigners started out in a loose group for the ruins. As we passed a row of trees, huge squat temples with bulbous domes rose up from the ground—large temples and tiny chapels, temples with walled courtyards and a hundred spires, temples sprouting demons and sprites, temples covered with carved stone flames representing the fire of enlightenment. They stretched out across the plain as far as the distant hills—all of them empty and breathing the breath of echoes, like seashells held to the ears.

As our little group explored the monuments, we began to spread out till we were ones and twos and out of each other's sight. Bruce and I stopped to peer into the dark recess of what seemed to be a tomb. We were standing in what must have been a broad avenue, a processional route. A silence so profound it almost moaned lay upon the plain, but in my mind bells and trumpets of sacred and festive processions rang out. Saffron robes and prayer beads and god-kings on litters glimmered fleetingly in the mind's eye. A hot wind blew up from the south, shaking the palm and the banyan trees, rattling their leaves and fronds.

All afternoon we plodded through the ghost city while the light lasted. Bruce and I returned to the village as the sun set in a sky of blood. In ones and twos we all regrouped in front of the Thiripyitsaya Hotel, in sight of a great cluster of now-darkening temples. We were two Americans, two New Zealanders, one Australian, one Brit, and three Irish, all quite subdued as we greeted each other. Wordlessly, the hotel manager appeared with lawn chairs, and we sat in a close circle, saying little. We were served tea. The light waned. Dour silhouettes of the ancient temples stood against the sky in their ranks and brooded, threatening to let slip their ghosts. We huddled more closely, and spoke of home. Night fell. The Milky Way shimmered, casting kaleidoscope shadows that flickered among the ruins. The day's awesome silence returned as a heavy cloak muffling the scene.

Suddenly, a tinkling little kitchen clatter broke the silence as though it were crystal, its shards breaking off and fluttering to the earth like leaves. A pungent, pleasantly stinging aroma found its way to our nostrils. The Lively Spice was afloat upon the air. A sputtering, sizzling sound gave it voice: "I'm here, I'm here. Let the ghosts walk if they will." The cook began to hum a tune and chopped and pounded and

151

clattered some more. Sniffing hungrily and smacking our lips, we began to speak again.

"Wonder what the old sod's got for us?" the Aussie pondered. "Chiles," Bruce said with satisfaction.

Scurrying workers set a table with a clean white cloth in full view of the starlit monuments. Upon it they set pots of glutinous rice, plates of tidbits, and bottles of the coldest Mandalay beer. Then they brought curries, eight or nine of them—meat, fish, and vegetables, red, green, orange, and yellow, a vibrant chromatic display that glowed alive. Steam billowed from the porcelain bowls, swirling about and caressing us with warm, savory tendrils of vapor. We fell upon the good fare. The spirited firespices awoke our palates, glowed down to our gullets and filled us with Mr. Thoreau's animal heat. As beads of sweat appeared on our foreheads, perhaps the lowering monsters of Bagan issued forth their legions and ghosts howled, but vainly; the Lively Spice hummed on our palates and sang in our bellies. We ate, drank, talked, and laughed, and then ate more in the midst of old Bagan. At dinner's end, we sat with pepper-full bellies and slow-burning mouths.

We paid our bill, then ambled off in a warm and friendly gaggle to the guest house, about a mile away. The only light was starlight, and we passed many an empty tomb and temple as we blithely wove our way, our Aussie sucking on a chile. The monuments held no spooks for us, for we were too much aglow. I could have slept in a tomb that night and called it warm and cozy. I thought of the chile bush I had seen that day growing in the ruin. It had sparkled red and alive against the dead gray of the walls. Indeed, the quick and the dead are side by side in Indochina; but when we are filled with spice fire and animal heat, there is no room in us for ghosts.

SWIMMING CHICKEN CURRY

This is a wet curry, or curry with gravy; it cries out for rice, or even mashed potatoes, to sop up the delicious sauce.

6	tablespoons light sesame or peanut oil
4	Japanese eggplants, peeled and diced
2	serrano or jalapeño chiles, stems and seeds removed, chopped
2	onions, coarsely chopped
4	cloves garlic
2	teaspoons chopped fresh ginger
1	teaspoon turmeric

½	teaspoon lemon zest or 2 inches of sliced lemon grass
1	chicken, cut up
1	cup beer or water
¼	cup dry white wine or juice of ½ lemon
1	tablespoon fish sauce or light soy sauce
2	tablespoons chopped cilantro
¼	teaspoon ground cardamom

In the oil, quickly brown the eggplants, turning often. Remove the eggplants and set them aside.

Whirl the chiles, onions, garlic, ginger, turmeric, and lemon peel in a blender or food processor until they make a thick paste, adding a little water if necessary.

Cook the paste in the oil for 10 to 15 minutes as described in the story. If it cooks too quickly and begins to stick to the pan, add a little water and stir often. When the paste is done and the "oil has returned," and the color is a deep reddish brown, add the chicken pieces. Turn them over in the sauce to coat them, cover, and simmer for 20 minutes, when the chicken will be half done.

Add the beer, wine, eggplants, and fish sauce. Stir and cook 20 minutes more until done. Before serving, stir in the cilantro and cardamom. Cover, and let it sit for a minute or two.

Yield: 4 Servings
Heat Scale: Medium

MANDALAY LIVER CURRY

I know the idea of liver curry sounds strange, but we encountered it all over Burma. In the small restaurants and food stalls, you are served a complete meal of rice, vegetables, tea and tidbits and your choice of curry. If you don't speak Burmese, you just point to the curry that looks most appealing. Somehow Bruce always ended up with liver. This recipe works equally well with hearts or gizzards.

1	serrano or jalapeño chile, stem and seeds removed, chopped
2	onions, coarsely chopped
½	bulb garlic, peeled
2	teaspoons chopped ginger

1	teaspoon turmeric
3	tablespoons light sesame, corn, or peanut oil
	Water as needed
1	pound chicken livers
¼	teaspoon ground cumin
¼	cup chopped cilantro
	Salt to taste

Whirl the chile, onion, garlic, ginger, and turmeric in a blender or food processor until they make a thick paste, adding a little water if necessary. Cook the paste in the oil for 10 to 15 minutes as described in the story. If it cooks too quickly and begins to stick to the pan, add a little water and stir often. When the paste is done, the "oil has returned," and the color is a deep reddish brown, add the livers. Turn them over in the sauce to coat them, cover, and simmer for 20 to 30 minutes, adding water to prevent the curry from thickening and burning.

Just before serving, add the cumin and cilantro, and salt to taste.

Yield: 4 Servings
Heat Scale: Mild

GHOSTBANE CHICKEN CURRY

Dry curries, like this one, are usually served with a thin soup of vegetables, prawns, or tamarind to moisten the rice. A wet vegetable curry would do as well. This curry is good accompanied by steamed rice, but is equally tasty with boiled new potatoes and grilled tomatoes.

1	serrano or jalapeño chile, stem and seeds removed, chopped
2	onions, coarsely chopped
4	cloves garlic
2	teaspoons chopped ginger
1	teaspoon turmeric
½	teaspoon lemon zest or 2 inches sliced lemon grass
¼	cup light sesame or peanut oil
1	chicken, cut up
¼	teaspoon ground cardamom
⅛	cup chopped cilantro
	Salt to taste

Whirl the chile, onion, garlic, ginger, turmeric, and lemon zest in a blender or food processor until they make a thick paste, adding water if necessary. Cook the paste in the oil for 10 to 15 minutes as described in the story. If it cooks too quickly and begins to stick to the pan, add a little water and stir often. When the paste is done, the "oil has returned," and the color is a deep reddish brown, add the chicken pieces. Turn them over in the sauce to coat them, cover and simmer for 20 minutes. Stir in the cardamom and cilantro, add salt to taste, let sit 5 minutes, and serve.

Yield: 4 to 6 Servings
Heat Scale: Medium

SWEET POTATO AND COCONUT CURRY BAGAN

This recipe departs a bit from the norm, but it is a lot simpler to prepare. This dish is very liquid. It goes well with rice and dry chicken curry, accompanied by fried onions, plain yogurt, and toasted nuts. Iced melon makes a good dessert.

2 serrano chiles, stems and seeds removed, sliced thin
1 onion, sliced or diced
1 tablespoon minced garlic
1 teaspoon turmeric
1 teaspoon minced ginger
½ teaspoon ground black pepper
½ teaspoon cayenne
1 tablespoon fish sauce or soy sauce
⅛ cup coconut cream or 1/2 cup rich coconut milk
1½ cups water
   Salt and lemon juice to taste
1 pound sweet potatoes or yams, peeled and sliced thinly

Combine all the ingredients except the sweet potato in a saucepan, bring to a boil, then reduce the heat and simmer for 5 minutes. Add the sweet potato and simmer until done, about 20 minutes.

Yield: 4 Servings
Heat Scale: Medium Hot

PRAWN AND MANGO CURRY

The Burmese cook would shell and devein the prawns, but leave the heads on. They contain a very flavorful essence that oozes out during cooking. There is no substitute for it. This is a very elegant-looking dish, though fairly simple to prepare. It will elicit many oohs and ahs from your guests when you bring it to the table. If mangoes are not available, substitute papaya, star fruit, or pineapple. Or go wild and use them all.

1/2	cup vegetable oil
1	teaspoon turmeric
3	cloves garlic, chopped
1	onion, grated
1	teaspoon ginger, minced
3	pounds fresh prawns, shelled and deveined, heads left on
1	teaspoon cayenne
12	small dried red chiles, such as piquin
1	tablespoon soy sauce
1	ripe mango, peeled and cut into small, bite-sized pieces
	Salt to taste
	Sliced toasted almonds and a sprig of fresh basil for garnish

Heat the oil to high in a wok and add the turmeric, garlic, onion, and ginger. Reduce the heat and cook, stirring, for 15 minutes. Raise the heat slightly and add the prawns and cayenne and stir-fry for 3 minutes. Add the dried chiles and soy sauce, and stir-fry for 3 minutes more. Add the mango and salt to taste and stir-fry for 1 minute. Remove the whole chiles and serve garnished with the almonds and basil.

Yield: 6 to 8 Servings
Heat Scale: Medium

BEEF SLOW-COOK

In Burma this would be cooked in a clay or cast-iron pot. An electric crockpot would work well, too. Water buffalo meat is difficult to find in supermarkets, so I've substituted beef.

2½ pounds beef, cut into 2-inch cubes

1½	tablespoons fish sauce
1	teaspoon turmeric
1	tablespoon vinegar
1	tablespoon garlic powder
2	onions, grated
1	teaspoon cayenne
2	teaspoons ground ginger
¾	cup oil
2	teaspoons salt
3	bay leaves
2	cinnamon sticks
5	cloves
5	peppercorns

Rub the meat well with the fish sauce, turmeric, and vinegar. Cover and refrigerate for at least 2 hours or preferably overnight. Combine the meat with the garlic powder, onions, cayenne, ginger, and oil, and massage it all together. Place the mixture in a tightly covered vessel and cook over the lowest possible heat till the meat is tender. If it becomes dry in the process, add enough water to keep it moist. When tender, add the salt, bay leaves, cinnamon sticks, cloves, and peppercorns. Cook slowly, stirring, until the oil rises clear to the top.

Yield: 6 to 8 Servings
Heat Scale: Medium

FISH CURRY

Any kind of white fish is good in this recipe, from salt water or fresh. Just as the Burmese are proscribed from killing the animals that roam the land, fish are off-limits too. And yet, fish is their chief source of animal protein. How do they get around this dilemma? In the hierarchy of animals, fish are at the bottom. It is a lesser sin to kill one of them than a cow or pig, so the Burmese fisherman takes some comfort. Furthermore, he is a revered person in the community, unselfishly risking his next incarnation as a lower species for the good of his fellows by killing fish for their tables. Then there is the explanation I heard from a fisherman. Speaking through a translator, he said: "I don't kill the fish. I simply take them out of the water. They die of their own accord."

2½   pounds fish, cut into bite-sized pieces
1   teaspoon turmeric
2   teaspoons salt
⅔   cup vegetable oil
6   cloves garlic, chopped
1   onion, grated
1   teaspoon powdered ginger
1   teaspoon cayenne
2   tomatoes, peeled, seeded, and chopped
1   tablespoon fish sauce
⅓   cup water
8   scallions

Rub the fish with the turmeric and salt. Heat the oil to high and fry the fish, turning it after 3 minutes per side. Remove from the pan and drain on paper towels. To the pan add the garlic, onion, ginger, and cayenne and stir. Add the tomatoes and fish sauce and cook 3 minutes. Return the fish to the pan and add the water. Cover, reduce heat to very low and simmer for 20 minutes, shaking the pan from time to time. Add the scallions and cook 3 minutes more.

Yield: 6 to 8 Servings
Heat Scale: Medium

MOHINGA

This is a variation on fish curry, one of many.

¼   cup rice flour
1   pound fresh catfish, coarsely chopped
2   stalks lemon grass, crushed
¼   cup fish sauce
2   red serrano chiles, stems and seeds removed, chopped
½   teaspoon turmeric
     Water to cover
2   onions, sliced thin
4   cloves garlic
1   small piece ginger
½   stalk lemon grass
2   green serrano chiles, stems and seeds removed
2   tablespoons vegetable oil
1½   cups coconut milk

1   pint water
½   cup chopped bamboo shoots
2   onions, quartered
6   cups cooked rice noodles
    Lime wedges, crushed chile pepper, fried cloves of garlic, and fried onion
    rings for garnishes

Toast the rice flour in an ungreased frying pan over high heat for 2-3 minutes or until very light brown. In a stock pot, combine the catfish, lemon grass, fish sauce, serranos, and turmeric with just enough water to cover. Bring to a boil and cook five minutes. Remove the lemon grass and remove the fish mixture from the heat.

In a blender or food processor, process the onions, garlic, ginger, ½ stalk lemon grass, and serranos to a paste. Fry the paste in the oil in a skillet or wok for about 5 minutes. Stir in the fish mixture and remove from the heat. Put the coconut milk in a saucepan and bring to a boil. Mix the flour and water and stir into the coconut milk. Add the bamboo shoots, onions, and the fish mixture. Simmer for 10 minutes. Ladle over rice noodles and garnish with lime wedges, crushed chile, garlic, and onion rings.

Yield: 6 Servings
Heat Scale: Medium

BURMESE-STYLE RICE

Although the Burmese prepare plain rice also, I prefer this method. It gives the rice a richer taste and a texture that is almost velvety. Serve it with any curry.

2   cups glutinous rice
3   onions
1½   teaspoons turmeric
¼   cup vegetable oil
4   cups water
2   teaspoons salt

Wash the rice and drain it until dry. Slice the onions and sprinkle them with the turmeric. Heat the oil in a saucepan and fry the onions until they are brown (cook them till crisp if you prefer, but don't let them burn). Remove the onions and serve them as a tidbit alongside the rice. Add the rice to the pan and stir well to mix it with the oil, browning slightly. Add the water and the salt and bring to a boil. Reduce the heat, cover, and simmer for twenty minutes.

Yield: 6 Servings

CHAPTER 11

THOUGH IT BE STRANGE

*H*AVING DINED IN GHOSTLY HALLS AND FOUND IT GOOD, *it seemed fitting to explore the farthest reaches of jungle gastronomy.*

"Strange things on my plate, both the bitter and the sweet,
And unknown things I've ate of the things that people eat."
—R.S.

*A*man from Sybaris was visiting Sparta, where a local nobleman invited him home to dine. After the meal, the Sybarite remarked that he had always been astounded to hear of the Spartans' courage; but now he did not think they were in any way superior to other peoples for, he concluded, "Even the most cowardly man in the world would choose death rather than share the Spartans' supper." —Athenaeus

By now you should be getting the idea that no matter what part of the world you come from, if you travel widely, you are going to encounter food that to you is unusual, strange—maybe even immoral—or just plain weird. Of course, "strange" depends upon your point of view. To the Eskimo, a vegetarian diet is strange indeed, for he needs raw meat and blubber. A native of the Himalayas would recoil at the sight of a lobster or crab. The Chinese turn up their noses at cheese, thinking it barbarous food for barbarous people. Long ago I adopted a rule for strange encounters, and it has become my motto: wherever I go, whatever people I visit, I bow to their kings, respect their gods, and eat their viands no matter what. There is nothing I will not eat or drink at least once. And if I don't eat it a second time, it will only be because I don't like the taste; aesthetics be damned. I am a culinary pagan, and I worship at every altar.

In this I am not alone, but in no teeming company. I find it curious that we define ourselves, to a greater or lesser degree, by the foods we eat. When we say that "we are what we eat," we mean it literally, figuratively, spiritually, and even political- ly. And by the same token, we define ourselves by what we do not eat. "Real men don't eat quiche," we insist. And no man believes that women like chili con carne, especially with lots of Tabasco and ketchup.

We use food prejudices to disparage others and prove their lack of moral fiber or other depraved status. I have heard American matrons in New England huff that they weren't going to go out and eat "starchy old Italian food!" Gringos will sneer that the tacos at Tijuana food stalls are made with dog meat (although I can tell you that's slander, it wouldn't bother me if it were true). Even the otherwise progressive legislature of the state of California has made it a crime to eat an animal commonly considered a pet. And the English, a people certainly not celebrated for gastronomy, criticize almost every kitchen practice to be found outside their island. Religious proscriptions are too numerous to mention. The foods we eat are right up there with the gods we pray to and the candidates we vote for. And just as we denounce the devil and the candidates we vote against, we seem to have a need to denounce the next man's diet. Especially if what he eats is too close to home.

While I was in the Navy, I was traveling to Manila and stopped on my way at the small Philippine town of Pampanga. I was hungry and had walked into a hole-in-the-wall restaurant, the kind that has a counter for about three and seats for two. The proprietor spoke no English, but I spoke enough Tagalog to say something like, "Give me your best."

He brought me a steaming bowl of something that looked like river bottom mud, the kind that gooshes up between your toes when you walk barefoot in it. Now, I had heard that people who live along the Nile and the Amazon sometimes eat the silt from their river bottoms in times of famine. It is said to have a lot of nutrients. I had no problem with that, *per se*, but I happened to know that the only river for miles around was an open sewer. I asked the man what the dish was, and he said, "Dinuguan," but it meant nothing to me. "If it's river silt," I thought, "I hope it's well cooked. Very well cooked."

I took a bite, and it was delicious. Even though it had the look and texture of mud, it tasted somewhat like a rich beef stew cooked with a lot of red Bordeaux wine. In the mush, there were also what seemed like little dumplings or big gravy lumps that stuck to the roof of my mouth like peanut butter, but were even more tasty than the surrounding goosh. I had two bowls of it, some rice, and a San Miguel beer, and called that a good meal, whatever it was.

A week later I was on board ship and out on a tossing sea. It was the kind of sea that makes shave-tail junior officers and lubberly recruits hang over the rails or wrap themselves around the toilets and "pray to John." Shouting above the wind, I described the strange, delicious dish to Ricardo Paglinawan, a Filipino shipmate, and asked him if he knew what it was.

"Oh, sure," he said as the ship tossed in the heaving sea, "that's blood."

"Blood!?"

"Yeah, blood."

"Blood?"

"Sure. They make it from duck's blood or pig's blood. It's like a blood soup. So you liked it, eh?"

"Blood? You mean they flavor the soup with blood?"

"No, they just cook some blood. Maybe they put some salt in it, but mainly, it's just blood."

"But...but...what about the little...the little lumps? What were the lumps?"

"Oh, sometimes they cook it too fast and it clots. So you liked it?"

On another occasion, I was served a variation on this simple dish. The blood of a pig was cooked with chopped bits of the animal's flesh and entrails added to it. It was then seasoned with vinegar and salt. Years later, while reading Plutarch's *Life of Lycurgus*, I realized how similar that was to the recipe for the infamous Black Broth of the Spartans: pork cooked in its own blood, seasoned with vinegar and salt.

The feast of blood was not my only venture into Filipino dining-on-the-edge. On the main Philippine island of Luzon, in the province of Zambales, is the small port city of Olongopo. Just outside the former U.S. Naval Base at Subic Bay, now a commercial port, it is a camptown gone wild. It is a place of glorious, outrageous, and sinful excess. The U.S. Navy Medical Corps once estimated that there were fifteen to twenty thousand prostitutes in that city. I wish I knew who had the job of counting the noses of twenty thousand hookers. I'd like to know his scientific methods. I wonder if he counted twice for accuracy?

A place like Olongopo, naturally, spawns legends. I'll just mention two of them to give you an idea of the kind of place we're talking about. The first you've already heard of—it served the notorious drink, Mojo. The other legend is that someplace (only the locals know where), is a restaurant that specializes in, and serves only, dog flesh. Most of the Americans think it's just a quaint local fiction.

Well, I found the restaurant. Rather, I should say, I was led to it. True to the legend, only the local people know where it is. The Filipinos know that when Americans think of dogs, we think of Lassie. Not wanting to have to explain their different point of view about a collie on a plate or put up with any insults or sanctimony, the owners located the place, called "The Three Roses," far from Yankee haunts.

Though I always enjoyed running riot with American and Australian pals in the sinful center of town, I also had Filipino friends and often stayed in their home in the local neighborhood. Thirsting for culinary adventure, I asked them about the restaurant. At first they smiled nervously and mumbled and changed the subject. So I dropped it. I asked on another occasion, and they told me quietly but earnestly that dog was delicious and that they believed it prevented tuberculosis. The third time I asked, they agreed to take me there on the condition that I not bring anyone else along.

I dressed for the occasion in the Philippine formal shirt, the Barong Tagalog. We left the house in the evening, me in giddy excitement. We walked for many minutes through a nighttime maze of close and dusty streets lined with dimly lit shops, food stalls, ladies fanning themselves, and people milling about. My friends led me "this way, now this way," to a hidden bend in the wicked city's guts. Colored lights at the end of a short alley announced the place.

As we walked into the yellow lantern light of the dining room, people looked up in surprise to see a Gringo but then returned to their dinners. "To their plates full of pooch," I thought. Chuckling to myself, I wondered if anyone was having hot dogs. A giddy urge came over me to cry out, "I'm from the American Kennel Club! This is a raid! Up against the wall!" But I restrained myself.

We sat down and, without warning, the gravity of the step I was about to take stole upon me and dulled the ardor of my adventurous palate. I was about to eat man's best friend, true companion of my own childhood! It suddenly seemed like cannibalism. I began to think of excuses. Maybe I could say I wasn't hungry. Yeah. Or that I had a touch of the Asian flu. Sure. But it was too late to repent now. The die was cast when the waitress set the dish in front of me. My hosts were looking at me with expectation in their eyes and the words "We trusted you" hanging on their lips, ready to be spoken.

Outside, in the back of the restaurant, a dog yipped as it met the knife.

I tried to be flippant. "Oh look," I said. "A spot of Spot, ha ha."

"Ha ha," said my hosts, still waiting for me to begin. The light dimmed perceptibly.

I looked into the dish. It was a stew and I could see that it had been a small dog. The meat had been left on the bones, and the carcass had been broken apart by hand rather than carved. They say that the bones have a lot of flavor and breaking them releases it better than carving.

I looked up from my plate to see that every dog I had ever owned was sitting where my hosts had been. My white collie, Sad Sack, looked sad and shook his head. My mongrel stock dog, Bullhead, growled and called me an ingrate. My little spaniel, Penny, who died young, sat with tears welling up in her warm, brown eyes.

"I...I'm sorry, guys," I whispered to my ghostly canines, "but this is a different country, and you've got to go home now."

With grim determination, I thrust my spoon into the chunks of meat, splintered bone, and pieces of vegetable. I sampled the broth, but the reproachful phantoms were still eyeing me, dulling my sense of taste. But I was resolved. Ignoring the ghosts, I picked up a bone. Vigorously, I chewed the meat off it, daring every canine on earth, in hell and in Dog Heaven to protest. My guts churned. A thousand huskies howled. I chewed fourteen times and swallowed, defiantly. I looked up in triumph to see that my hosts had returned to the table and were smiling broadly, and the room brightened.

I must tell you that it was tasty. The flavor was somewhere between beef and pork, and it was very tender. It was, after all, a puppy. The broth was seasoned with garlic and vinegar and the vegetables were fresh and not overly cooked. My hosts sucked the bones with satisfaction, but I didn't join them in that. Afterwards, I bade them goodnight, thanked them for a truly pleasant evening, then went out and got drunk.

Vegetarians are not more disposed to food prejudice than others, but they are often more ready to voice it. As I sat beside a vegetarian in a restaurant once, I was eating an omelet, and she tried to upset my appetite. She described eggs in graphic terms of menstruation and asked if that didn't bother me. Ha! Little did she know that seven years as a sailor had made me immune to being grossed out. On another occasion, I was dining in an Indian restaurant with a vegetarian; I had curried chicken, and he kept referring to it as pieces of dead bird. "How is your dead bird?" he asked me. I asked him how was his rabbit food and did it make him feel like Alan Alda? Even I can succumb to these little prejudices from time to time, but at least I repent of it.

We properly ascribe vast powers to food, but many of them are inappropriate. Eschewing the evil foods and consuming the virtuous ones, we seek to make ourselves healthier, more politically correct, more masculine or feminine, more civilized and closer to God. Renaissance physicians held that melancholy could be brought on by eating too many beans. Cannibals partake of a bold man's courage when they eat his flesh. Modern prize-fighters swear by beef (you know, "real food for real people") and are hard put to explain the championship of Marvin Hagler, a vegetarian. I'll confess another lapse of my own. When given a roast of bear meat one time, I invited five friends to share it. Without realizing it, I invited only men. Go figure. I guess I might also fail to invite women to a dinner of anything that might be considered "icky."

I guess that's why I was with Bruce when we made a pilgrimage back to Indochina to sup again on strange fare.

"What do you think about the story that guy in Malaysia told us, about how they eat gross things in this country?" Bruce asked as we wandered Thailand's Cholburi provincial bazaar.

"Bah!" I scoffed. "That's just a horror story to scare inexperienced tourists. Seasoned travelers like us shouldn't be alarmed."

At that moment, we heard a friendly sizzle and smelled two of our favorite smells: chile and garlic. We followed our noses to a food stall where a well-fed merchant smiled a greeting. Before him lay two huge woks filled with dancing hot oil, one redolent of garlic, the other breathing ginger. On a table, bowls of minced garlic, crushed red chile, sliced green serranos, and whole, flaming orange peppers were scattered about. Bottles of smoky sauces stood by.

A large basket covered with a green cloth mesh held the merchant's meat: giant locusts—live ones.

We stared open-mouthed at the basket. "Horror stories for tourists, huh?" Bruce sneered.

"Well...don't be such a culinary sissy," I retorted. "Different people, different food. So what?"

"Then eat one."

"Er...uh."

"Don't be such a culinary sissy, Richard. Betcha can't eat one."

"I could if I wanted to."

"Then do it."

"You first."

"Why, seasoned travelers like us shouldn't be alarmed," Bruce mocked.

"I'll flip you for first," I said.

I reached into my watch pocket for a small Malaysian coin I had kept and handed it to Bruce, saying "Toss."

"Call it."

"Tails," I said appropriately.

The coin came down showing a tropical bird. "You lose," I said, taking back the curious little coin with the bird on one side and script on the other and quickly tucked it back into my pocket.

Bruce braced himself and accepted a free sample from the merchant. Grimacing, he bit into the curled, two-inch tail.

I watched through narrowed eyes as he slowly chewed and finally spoke: "The texture is like layers of parchment. Not bad, either. It's sort of like a croissant, but not as elastic, a little crisp."

"Croissant, eh?" I wonder if they'd sell locusts at La Petite Boulangerie? I watched closely to see if he made any faces. "How come you're only eating the tail?" I asked.

Bruce thought for a moment. "I'm afraid the guts will gush in my mouth."

I took the remnants from him. Wings and tail were gone by now. The head looked like one of those roasted, salted soybeans sold as a snack food. I broke it off, popped it into my mouth and chewed. It even tasted a little like a soybean, but it was not as dense. I pulled off a leg for Bruce and one for me, and we nibbled them while looking at the creature's insect brothers, wriggling in the basket.

I regarded the thorax that remained in my hand, high in protein, no cholesterol. I told Bruce, "The Bible says that John the Baptist ate these often."

"And Nero, too," he added.

"Nero ain't in the Bible."

"But he ate 'em."

I broke the body into halves, gave one to Bruce, and in unspoken agreement we ate them simultaneously. No guts gushed.

"You know," Bruce said, "I've eaten jumbo prawns smaller than these things."

"Let's get the garlic flavor."

"With chile!"

"Yeah!"

The merchant reached under the mesh and grabbed a large handful of the squirming giants and dropped them into the hot, garlic-scented oil. They sizzled and hissed and turned from green to golden brown. The merchant put them in a brown paper bag and sprinkled them with fish sauce and chile powder. Then we strolled about the bazaar, chatting with vendors, joking with children and eating the food of Nero and John the Baptist.

"You know, these are like chips and salsa," I said.

"Or nachos, ha. But do you think they'll believe us at home when we tell them we ate locusts?"

Taking another one from the bag and sniffing its garlicky-chile goodness, I said, "Why not? People eat stranger things."

I say that all notions that keep us from eating what we like are balderdash! Real men don't eat quiche you say? Bah! Real men eat what they damn please! A food is nutritious and wholesome or it isn't; it's tasty or it isn't; and that's all we need to worry about. And furthermore, food is a great adventure. In a big city you can explore half the world without leaving town. Through taste and smell you can partake of Humanity's and Nature's infinite variety. A willing palate and an open mind will bring a world of discovery to you. It's scads of fun to eat your way around the world. I confess I didn't always have such an enlightened attitude. Though I was never a culinary bigot, I am still the product of a meat-and-potatoes tradition. My family was never squeamish or prudish about food. They enjoyed it but never pondered it and never considered that there might be other things to eat in the world. They took their food like they took their whiskey: straight and straightforwardly, unadorned, uncomplicated, undemanding of their imaginations and in quantity. It was an always pleasing but never challenging business of consumption. At Christmastime it might be made warm, sweet and frothy; in summer, lighter and cooler. But never anything "strange." So when I left home, eager as I was for new culinary experiences, I did have to overcome an initial queasiness or cultural objection to certain foods. But the efforts were small and the rewards were great: fun, adventure, good eating and warm memories, and the useful wisdom that there are no gross foods, only gross feeders.

So, with apologies to Rudyard Kipling:

I have eaten your bread and salt,
I have drunk your water and wine.
I've eaten your dogs and the blood of your hogs
And anything on which ye dine.

Was there aught that I did not share,
At table, or taking our ease,
One singular snack that I ever did lack,
Dear hearts across the seas?

Now I've written our culin'ry tale,
For a sheltered people's mirth,
In jesting guise, but ye are wise,
And ye know what the jest is worth.

DINUGUAN

Dinuguan refers to anything cooked in animal blood. If you are a huntin'-fishin'-shootin' sort of person, you can save the blood of freshly killed game. Mix a tablespoon of vinegar in it to prevent clotting and keep it on ice till you get home in a day or two. Strain it before using. You can also get blood from the butcher. It is very nutritious and almost a complete food. The Masai of East Africa subsist on cow's blood and little else. I have only eaten pig and deer blood so I am no authority, but people in the know tell me that duck blood is the tastiest.

4   **cups blood**
¼   **pound pork, chopped fairly fine**
¼   **pound chitterlings, chopped**
2   **tablespoons vinegar, any kind**
1   **teaspoon salt**
1   **teaspoon pepper**
1   **tablespoon pork fat, chopped**

Combine the blood, pork, chitterlings, vinegar, salt and pepper in a saucepan (preferably a double boiler) over low heat. Cook, constantly stirring, about 30

169

minutes. Never let it boil. When done, the gravy should be thick, almost black, and silky looking. Remove from heat, transfer to a serving dish, and set aside. In another pan (or in the microwave) heat the fat till it just begins to melt. Sprinkle on top of the dinuguan.

Yield: A vampire's feast for 4

Serving Suggestion: This dish is so rich that it's almost cloying. It screams for something palate cleansing. I recommend a crisp green salad with a lemon juice dressing, crusty French bread, and a sturdy red Italian wine.

AZUCENA

The Philippine word for dog on the hoof (paw?) is Aso. When it's on the table, it's azucena. In certain mountainous areas, people like to eat it raw. They gut it, singe the hair, and then cut it up into small pieces. They serve it with a sawsawan of raw liver mashed with onion and garlic and take it with a few tots of gin. Cooked pooch is taken with a cold San Miguel beer.

A word of warning: In the state of California, it is a misdemeanor to eat a dog. About ten years ago, the state began to receive a lot of Southeast Asian refugees who had no compunctions about dining on dog or cat. When their sanctimonious new neighbors found out about it, they suddenly feared for their pets, imagining that cannibalistic savages were lying in wait for Spot and Puff (certainly, a few hill tribe families were following their age-old dietary habits, but I am confident they came by their dinners legitimately). Other upstanding citizens felt indignant at what they took to be a descent into culinary barbarism, and some decided it was an animal rights issue. A hasty coalition of panicked pet owners, animal activists and struggle junkies prevailed upon the state legislature to ban the practice.

THREE ROSES AZUCENA

To use this recipe in California, substitute rabbit. It's close enough.

1   **pound dog meat (if it's a small dog, cut or break it into parts like rabbit or chicken; otherwise cut the meat into 1½-inch cubes)**
½   **cup apple cider vinegar**
1   **bulb garlic, papery covering removed**
1   **teaspoon black pepper**
2   **tablespoons vegetable oil**
1   **cup water**
1   **tablespoon soy sauce**
½   **pound leafy greens, chopped**

Combine the meat, vinegar, garlic, and pepper in a saucepan and simmer, covered, for 20 minutes, turning the meat once. Remove the garlic, separate the cloves, peel them, and fry them in the oil, then remove and set aside. Brown the meat in the same oil. Put the garlic and all other ingredients in the pan with the meat and simmer till the meat is very tender and the liquid is reduced to a gravy.

Yield: 4 Servings, or if in California, a ticket.

THE MEAT OF SAINT JOHN

It's hard to find giant locusts in North America, but many bait shops sell live grasshoppers. Crickets are available, too, and they taste just as good. Like their marine cousins, lobsters and shrimp, insects are best when they are cooked live or freshly frozen. Freezing has the added benefit of keeping them from hopping out of the pan. If you have live insects and can't wait to freeze them, simply putting them in the refrigerator for 10 minutes will slow them down considerably.

It's a good idea to purge insects as you would with snails, either by withholding food or by feeding them something clean, like bran or fruit, for 2 or 3 days.

Once they are immobilized by cooling or freezing, toss them in a colander to remove any foreign matter, then rinse them under running water.

To cook, you can simmer them in water, stock or wine for 30 minutes and serve them as a side dish; dry roast them with salt at 200 degrees for 90 minutes and eat them like peanuts; saute them in butter and garlic for 12 minutes and toss them with steamed vegetables; or do as our Thai merchant, and make Nero's Nachos by simply deep-frying them in very hot, flavored oil till they turn golden, about 3 minutes. Try the following insectuous recipes, too.

HOPPERS ON HORSEBACK

12   very large grasshoppers, or substitute crickets
6   strips of bacon, partially cooked and cut in half
½   cup grated Parmesan cheese

Saute the, hoppers in butter for 3 minutes. Don't let them get too well done. Wrap each critter in a half strip of bacon and secure with a toothpick. Broil them for five minutes, then dust with the Parmesan cheese.

Serving Suggestion: As an hors d'ouvre, with baby cornichons and iced vodka.

Variation: Replace the bacon with leaves of fresh spinach. The result is "Locusts Rockefeller."

PHILIPPINE KAMARO

¼   **pound crickets or grasshoppers**
½   **cup vinegar**
1   **cup water**
1   **tablespoon oil**
1   **onion, chopped**
4   **cloves garlic, mashed**
1   **tomato, peeled and chopped, or 2 tablespoons tomato paste**
     Salt and pepper to taste

Remove the legs and wings from the bugs. When they have been thus abbreviated, combine them with the vinegar and enough water to cover. Simmer for 15 minutes. Drain. Heat the oil and saute the onion, garlic, and tomato for 5 minutes. Add the crickets and continue cooking 10 minutes. Correct seasonings.

Yield: 2 Side Dishes

CHAPTER 12

SECRETS SHARED:
A CAMBODIAN JOURNEY

THE SIREN AND THE MUSE COMBINE TO GIVE VOICE TO THE LAND, and to call the China Coaster once again to the table.

In Joseph Conrad's short story, "The Secret Sharer," a tall ship eases her way through the warm night, towards the coast of an exotic tropical kingdom. The captain secretly assists a mysterious man over the side, and he swims to the leeward shore of "The Cambogee." Nowadays we call that land Cambodia.

Twenty years ago, as a sailor plying the "China Coast," I often slipped past that spot where Conrad's hero bade farewell to his secret other self. Every time I saw that blue-green, palm-lined shore, the Cambogee—a land of lost temples, colorful ceremonies and beautiful women—beckoned. Many a time I had planned to drop anchor there and attend the magnificent feast of the Water Festival. Old shipmates reported that some of their fondest memories were of Phnom Penh and Sihanoukville, where they had tasted a unique style of spicy cookery that might well have been the best in the East.

I was too late; in April of 1975, the long night of Pol Pot and his Khmer Rouge fell upon the land I would always call The Cambogee. In the years that followed, I read what little news trickled out of the country. I listened to secondhand tales of refugees and sorrowed for them. I still passed the Secret Sharer's landing, gazing longingly at the now-forbidden shore. I greatly missed the country I had never visited, as though I had known her well, as though I, too, had shared her secrets.

Cambodia's nightmare was ending as the '90s began, and the veil had just begun to lift. There was still no regular air service to the country then, all roads but the one leading to Vietnam were closed, and there was no U.S. diplomatic presence. Yet, her tropic siren song still reached my heart. In early 1992, I was conferring with Paul and Bruce Harmon, two companions I have traveled with over much of the world. As we recounted past adventures and plotted new ones, we heard the news that Cambodia's Prince Sihanouk had just returned home from his sixteen-year exile. We decided Cambodia was "now or never."

We flew to Thailand, trusting our luck. At Bangkok's airport, a Soviet-built charter plane from the Cambodian capital of Phnom Penh was on the tarmac, revving up its engines for its return flight. Fast action and Bruce's credit card got us on board. In less than an hour, we landed at Phnom Penh's Pochentong airport. We had arrived without visas, and many days of wrangling with the foreign ministry ensued—but I was in The Cambogee at last!

The first Khmer, or Cambodian, king was Kambu, and the kingdom he established, in the ninth century, was known as Kambujadesa: the Sons of Kambu, or Kambuja for short. The land of the lower Mekong River valley became a confluence and focus of immigration, trade, religion, and culture. From the Sri Vijaya empire of Indonesia came Hindu conquerors, missionaries, and scholars. Although the country has been Buddhist now for over four hundred years, the modern Khmer system of writing is still based on Sanskrit. From the east, by way of Annam, came the Chinese; from the north came the Thai and the Lao; from the west, the Malay; and finally, from afar, the Europeans. Each culture brought its influence in literature, science, the arts—and in the kitchen.

Curry from the Hindu, noodles from the Chinese, basil and other aromatic leaves from the Thai. And from the Europeans? Bread, of course, attributed to the French, as well as wine and beer. But the most common, most important, and most pleasing contribution of the Europeans to Khmer cookery is the chile pepper.

We don't know precisely when or by whom the chile was introduced to this part of the world, but it is logical that the credit belongs to the Spanish or Portuguese in the late sixteenth century. The first documented official contact between The Cambogee and the West took place in 1596. The king of Angkor, Barom Reachea, feared an attack by his neighbors. He sent an embassy, which included a Portuguese adventurer, to the Spanish governor-general at Manila to request the assistance of his musket-armed soldiers. Seeing an opportunity to extend Spanish influence, the governor sent two small expeditions. They presented themselves to the king in 1596 and 1598. We don't know what the expeditions' supplies, provisions, and gifts for the king included, but one hundred years after Columbus, the Spaniards were well-supplied with *Capsicums* from the New World. It is delicious to speculate that, although the military missions came to naught, a culinary mission enjoyed great success. However it happened, chiles are ubiquitous in Cambodia. Every grand market and merchant's corner of Phnom Penh offers them in baskets, piles, and bags.

Today the capital is a once-gracious and beautiful city, emerging from under the rubble of two decades of strife and horror. Broad, tree-lined streets, designed by French colonial planners, ring with the sounds of construction and recovery. So new is The Cambogee's return to the world that Paul, Bruce, and I often seemed to be the only Westerners in the land except for some U.N. soldiers, who tended to keep to their barracks. Outside the city the sight of a paleface was so rare that Cambodians eagerly took pictures of us! Because of my blue baseball cap and military boots, some people mistook me for a U.N. soldier and rendered me salutes. I crisply rendered back. On city streets, we were often followed for blocks by giggling children, the product of Asia's highest birth rate, who wanted nothing but to tag along. But the most common signs of life and recovery were the innumerable restaurants, cafes, food stalls, and snack sellers on every sidewalk, street corner, and dusty country crossroad.

One of Phnom Penh's most memorable eating establishments can be reached by following the main boulevard, Achar Mien, as it leads north out of town. Near the outskirts, as it passes tattered Vietnamese political posters and the still-empty remains of the national university, it narrows to a rutted asphalt track not quite two lanes wide. From here it turns straight for a mile and a half, bordered on both sides by closely spaced houses big and small. Cambodian and Vietnamese women lounge on the porches and verandas and wave languidly to passers-by. The Cambodian women are taller, brandy-brown, and lack the Asiatic eye fold. The Vietnamese women are delicately boned, the color of tea with milk, and more assertive, more apt to step into the street to stop a man as he heads north following an even more primal hunger. As the road leaves the "woman walk" behind, it curves westward past a great heap of field guns, old tanks, and armored vehicles and other warstuffs being reduced to plowshares by busy men with cutting torches. Snaking through a clump of leafy trees, it arrives at a meadow where it intersects with half a dozen other roads and pathways. In the daytime this confluence is deserted, but by sunset, it is a bustling carnival of portable restaurants.

Little bakeries on wheels, butchers on trucks, produce sellers bearing baskets on yokes, and whole kitchens set up on wooden tables clogged the gathering of roads. Glowing paper lanterns hung from posted wires that zig-zagged and crisscrossed throughout the field. Families, packs of young men, gaggles of girls, day laborers, soldiers, beggars, and farmers came there to dine in community.

On several nights, we three travelers took the walk north to the festive "eating meadow." From each of several sellers we ordered food, then sat down on wooden divans covered with grass mats. As each dish was readied, cook's assistants brought them to us, weaving their way through the visiting crowd. They brought us tangy salads of julienned green mango, tossed with shallots, ground peanuts, chile paste, and lime juice. The seafood kitchen sent steaming dishes of giant prawns in the shell. The girls who delivered them stood by and patiently peeled each one, taking the opportunity to joke and flirt with the three exotic "Farangs." Beef, marinated in chile, galangal, and garlic teased our appetites as it sizzled on skewers over hot coals. Little sheaves of asparagus bound up with collars of fish paste, deep-fried and drizzled with a piquant sauce, made us ooh and ahh at their cleverness. Runners kept us well supplied with beer.

The Cambodians are great eaters. Their calendar is full of feasts, and any gaps are filled by weddings, births, funerals, and auspicious alignments of the stars. Theirs is a land of abundance. They enjoy regular harvests of rice, wild and cultivated fruits, fresh and saltwater fish, domesticated animals, fowl, and game. They love to eat meat. Pork is the most popular, and it is excellent, as are all the meats. An English journalist we dined with said of her beefsteak that it was the best she ever had. We didn't tell her it was *luc lac*, water buffalo.

As with so much of Cambodian life and arts, we found its cuisine to be a synthesis of styles in which the whole is greater than the sum of its parts. Though many influences are recognizable, the result is unique and distinctive.

Curries have been popular since the days of the Hindu-inspired Angkor Wat. But, whereas the original Indian blend is based on onions and turmeric, we learned that the "sons of Kambu" base theirs on lemon grass. The Chinese introduced the wok, but the Cambodian cook could not use it fully without such New World ingredients as chiles, peanuts, and squash.

One of the most important aspects of Cambogee fare is the use of delicate aromatics, such as basil and mint, to provide a subtle counterpoint to the robust flavors and heavy meats. And rather than cooking them into the dish, as others might do, the Cambodian cooks often served us a plate of the sweet-smelling leaves alongside the dish. We then used them according to our liking, just as we would use condiments.

Herb and spice combinations are frequently balanced by sweetness. Honey is used extensively, both as a sweetener and as a marinade. The Cambodians were bemused when they learned that we use sugar in tea but not on meats, where it is "appropriate."

Finally, a Cambodian meal includes a small dish of fish sauce, or a hot and sweet sauce, for dipping. The Cambodian cooks strive for a balanced composition, judiciously mixing the delicate flavors and strong spices, the sweet and the sour and the bland and the bitter. They try to satisfy the eater's full range of gustatory experience, not just a narrow sample. In the Cambogee, despite its recent violent history, dinner is still a shared ritual, one that must please both the flesh and the spirit. It reaffirms the ties of family and friendship, and of us humans to the natural world.

Everywhere we went in the The Cambogee I observed people cooking, took notes, and visited restaurants and domestic kitchens. When I made my sad and sweet goodbye, I came away not only with a long-cherished desire fulfilled, but also with a trove of recipes. Upon returning home to California, to my astonishment, I discovered a Cambodian restaurant in the city of Berkeley, across the bay from San Francisco. I rushed to the phone to call there and say hello, that I had just returned from Cambodia, that things were well in the land, and to ask where I could buy the best ingredients for my recipes. The phone at the Mermaid Restaurant was fortuitously answered by Father Narzarin, a Nestorian Christian monk who is the motive force behind virtually every Cambodian restaurant in northern California.

Father N has been working with Cambodian refugees since they began arriving in San Francisco in the late 1970s. While I was plying the waters of the South China Sea, longing to enter Cambodia, he was helping to settle her castaway people, see them through culture shock and, where possible, set them up in business. As he has a flair for the restaurant trade, and is a gourmet himself, there are now about a half-dozen Cambodian restaurants in the San Francisco Bay area.

He had a peculiar difficulty in getting Cambodians to start restaurants, and it explained what I thought an odd situation in Cambodia: most of the indoor restaurants there are Chinese. The Cambodians regard Chinese cookery as the finest expression of the culinary art, much as many Americans so consider French cuisine. When they go out to dinner, they to where they will find what they think of as special. The best of Cambodian cooking is found in the home.

Father N's refugees protested that Americans wouldn't eat Cambodian food. After all, they argued, they can have Chinese or French, and maybe they would even scorn and laugh at what the refugees regarded as their humble native fare. Somehow he prevailed, and Californians are taking Cambodian food to their hearts and stomachs.

Composing all the menus presented a problem too. As the people fled Cambodia, they were able to bring out only what they could carry; some only what they could wear. Cookbooks were not on anybody's list of survival gear. All the recipes, therefore, come from the chefs' own domestic kitchens. The secret recipes of generations and the loving care of the home fires are what diners are served in California's Little Cambodia.

The weary refugees arrived here feeling very small in a very big country. They were dispossessed of goods and homeland, having nothing to call their own. Nevertheless, they found that in their cuisine, they still had something worthy, something worth sharing with the world. As for me, I found a piece of The Cambogee, the land of the Secret Sharer, in my own back yard.

ASPARAGUS SHEAVES KAMBU

Use slender, tender spears, with the lower third removed. If you don't want to make your own fish paste, you can buy it from any Chinese supermarket or fishmonger. It is important that the chile paste have enough sugar content to taste. Thai-style paste is good.

Fish Paste:

1	**pound ling cod or other firm white fish**
1	**tablespoon light soy sauce**
1	**tablespoon dry sherry**
1	**teaspoon fresh ginger**
½	**cup sliced scallions**
2	**egg whites**
4	**tablespoons cornstarch**

Place all ingredients in a blender or food processor and reduce to a paste. It should have the consistency of cookie dough. If it is not dry enough, add more cornstarch.

The Asparagus:

2	**cups vegetable oil**
1	**pound asparagus**
1	**cup fish paste**
4	**teaspoons Thai-style chile paste**

Heat the oil in a wok or other deep, heavy vessel to medium. Take 3 or 4 asparagus spears in one hand and about 2 or 3 tablespoons of fish paste in the other. Wrap the fish paste around the middle of the sheaf to bind it together. Drop it into the hot oil and deep-fry for about 3 minutes, or until the fish paste is set and just beginning to brown. Remove and drain. Repeat, cooking three or four sheaves at a time. Combine the remaining fish sauce and chile paste and drizzle over the cooked sheaves.

Yield: About 8 sheaves

Heat scale: Mild

Variation: To reduce calories, cook the sheaves in boiling clarified chicken or fish stock. You could also use green beans, or bell peppers cut into thin strips lengthwise.

GREEN MANGO SALAD

For reasons I cannot fathom, green mangoes are more expensive than ripe ones. Maybe they're produced by the same people who bring us unleaded gas. If you can't find green mangoes, adequate substitutes are green papaya or white Chinese cabbage. The Cambodians use any number of dried or smoked fish products in this recipe: Thai fish powder, smoked whitefish, dried shrimp, and so on. If you don't have access to any of these, try dark meat tuna. This dish is a staple in Cambodia and is a most excellent accompaniment to a hot, meaty curry.

1   tablespoon chile paste
1   tablespoon chunky peanut butter
1   teaspoon fish sauce
    Juice of 1 lime
1   tablespoon fish powder, or to taste
1   green mango, peeled and julienned very fine
1   green tomato, sliced thin
2   shallots, sliced thin
1   pickling cucumber, sliced thin
    Salt and pepper to taste
1   green onion, chopped
    Red Bell peppers, stems and seeds removed, sliced
    Chopped fresh basil or mint

Combine the chile paste, peanut butter, fish sauce, lime juice, and fish powder. Toss with the mango, tomato, shallots, and cucumbers. Add salt and pepper to taste. Garnish with the green onion, peppers, and basil and serve.

Serves: 6
Heat Scale: Mild

ANGKOR VEGETABLE SOUP

On nearly all the streets of all the towns in Cambodia, there are sidewalk soup restaurants. People stop at any time of day for a bowl of vegetable soup or noodle soup called pho. Although originally from Vietnam, it has become, like pizza in the U.S.A., a national dish. To be authentic, the soup stock should be clarified, so it's best to make "skeleton soup" from last night's roast chicken or "fish bone soup" from your fish fry, or good old marrow bone soup.

8   cups clear broth
4   cups chopped vegetables, any number, any kind

In a large pot bring the stock to a boil. Add the vegetables and cook to desired degree of firmness and serve immediately. In several small dishes, serve any or all of the following for diners to add to their soup:

—*Chopped fresh chiles (serranos or jalapeños work fine)*
—*Paper-thin slices of raw beef (the broth will cook them)*
—*Minced raw shrimp or fish*
—*Crabmeat*
—*Lime wedges*
—*Fish sauce*
—*Cilantro, basil, and mint leaves*
—*Dried shrimp*
—*Cracked black pepper*
—*Chopped scallions*
—*Bean sprouts*
—*Roasted garlic*

Serves: 6
Heat Scale: Varies
Variation: Omit the vegetables and pour the broth over cooked rice noodles that have been dressed with the desired garnishes.

CAMBOGEE BEEF

When the aroma of this dish rises up from the cooking fire, it tantalizes the nostrils. For the best results, use a mortar and pestle to combine the ingredients, or if you lack one, use a blender.

2	red jalapeños, stems removed
¼	cup lemon grass, sliced thin
6	kaffir lime leaves or the peel of 1 lime
4	cloves garlic
1	slice or teaspoon galangal
½	cup oyster sauce
2	tablespoons sugar
1	pinch salt
½	cup water
1	pound beef, cut into thin slices and threaded onto skewers

Mash or blend the jalapeños, lemon grass, lime leaves, garlic, and galangal together into a paste. Combine the mixture with the remaining ingredients, except the beef, in a saucepan. Bring to a boil, and boil for 1 minute. Remove from the heat and let cool. Taste for sweetness—it should be present but not dominant.

Marinate the beef in this mixture in the refrigerator for at least one hour.

Grill the skewers over hot coals, keeping the beef at least four inches from the heat, lest the sugar burn, until desired doneness.

Yield: Eight skewers
Heat Scale: Medium
Serving Suggestion: Before cooking, stick a chunk of fresh pineapple on the end of each skewer. Serve with Green Mango Salad and steamed rice.

BASIC LEMON GRASS CURRY

In Cambodia, as in India, there are as many curries as there are cooks; however all true Khmer curries have five constants: lemon grass, garlic, galangal, and coconut milk are four. The fifth constant is the cooking technique, dictated by the texture of lemon grass and the consistency of coconut milk. This recipe is my personal, all-purpose, four-cup curry which is based on extensive observation and many trials.

To prepare one portion, pour ½ cup of this curry sauce into a shallow vessel or wok. Add ½ cup of meat or vegetables, bring to a medium boil and cook to the desired degree. Try it with frog legs, as the Cambodians do.

⅓ **cup sliced lemon grass**
4 **cloves garlic**
1 **teaspoon dried galangal**
1 **teaspoon ground turmeric**
1 **jalapeño chile, stem and seeds removed**
3 **shallots**
3½ **cups coconut milk (made by soaking 4 cups coconut in a quart of water for an hour, then straining it)**
3 **kaffir lime leaves**
   Pinch of salt or shrimp paste

Puree together the lemon grass, garlic, galangal, turmeric, jalapeño, and shallots.

Bring the coconut milk to a boil and add the pureed ingredients, lime leaves, and salt and boil gently, stirring constantly, for about 5 minutes. Reduce the heat to low and simmer, stirring often, for about 30 minutes, or until the lime leaves are tender and the sauce is creamy. Remove the leaves.

Yield: 1 quart
Heat Scale: Mild

RED CURRY CAMBOGEE

Here is a variation on Cambodian curries.

4   dried red New Mexican chiles, stems and seeds removed
1   cup boiling water
4   tablespoons paprika
2-3 tablespoons vegetable oil
4   cups Lemon Grass Curry (see recipe)

Break the chiles into small pieces. Pour boiling water over them to cover and let steep until they are soft, about 15 minutes. Combine the chiles, chile water, and the paprika in a blender to make a paste.

Heat the oil in a wok or skillet, add the chile paste, and stir-fry until it begins to darken. Reduce the heat, if necessary, to prevent burning.

Stir enough of the paste into the Lemon Grass Curry to give it a good red color and to suit your taste. Bring to a boil, reduce the heat, and simmer for 5 minutes.

Yield: 5 cups
Heat Scale: Medium

RED CURRY CAMBOGEE WITH MEAT AND PEANUTS

5	cups Red Curry Cambogee (see recipe)
¾	pound diced beef
2	potatoes, peeled and diced
½	cup chopped peanuts
2	cups bean sprouts

Heat the curry sauce and add the meat and potatoes. Simmer for 20 to 30 minutes or until the meat and potatoes are done.

Garnish with the peanuts and serve over the bean sprouts.

Serves: 4
Heat Scale: Medium

MERMAID PRAWNS

Sim My is the chef de cuisine at the Mermaid restaurant in Berkeley, California. This recipe is one of her favorites.

1	cup Red Curry Cambogee (see recipe)
6	giant prawns in the shell
1-2	tablespoons tomato paste
1	tablespoon chopped peanuts
1	cup cooked fresh spinach
12	fresh basil leaves
1	tablespoon chile paste or to taste
1	teaspoon finely minced fresh ginger

Combine the curry sauce, prawns, tomato paste, and peanuts. Bring to a boil, reduce the heat, and simmer about 5 to 7 minutes.

Cover the bottom of a heated plate with the spinach in an even layer.

Remove the prawns from the sauce and shell them. Arrange them on the spinach.

Stir the basil and chile paste into the sauce and pour over the prawns. Sprinkle with fresh ginger and serve.

Yield: 1 to 2 servings
Heat Scale: Hot

SIM MY'S VEGETABLE CURRY

Try this with fried catfish and Lover Sauce (see recipe). With rice, it is also a good meal unto itself.

2 red serrano chiles, stems and seeds removed, sliced thin
3 cups Basic Lemon Grass Curry (see recipe)
1 tablespoon sugar or 1/2 cup diced sweet potato
1 pinch salt
¼ cup fish sauce
2 lemon leaves, crushed
½ pound green beans
½ pound eggplant, cut into 2-inch fingers
12 basil or mint leaves

Combine all ingredients except basil or mint leaves in a saucepan or wok. If vegetables are not covered, add a little water or stock. Bring to a boil and cook about 5 minutes. Stir in the basil or mint leaves and serve.

Yield: 6 Servings
Heat Scale: Medium

A-MOK

This is a very popular dish in Cambodia. It is usually cooked in a wrapping of banana leaf, but parchment or aluminum foil will suffice.

¼ cup sliced lemon grass
4 shallots
2 dried chiles, such as Thai or piquin, stems removed
1 teaspoon ground turmeric
1 teaspoon fresh ginger
4 kaffir lime leaves
  Salt and white pepper
1½ cups coconut milk
1 pound of whitefish, cut up into small bites, or use fish paste
4 banana leaves or pieces of parchment or aluminum foil
4-8 leaves romaine or red-leaf lettuce

In a mortar or blender, reduce the lemon grass, shallots, chiles, turmeric, ginger, lime leaves, and salt and pepper to a paste, adding a little water if necessary. Combine the paste and the coconut milk and then fold in the fish. Divide the mixture into fourths. Lay the banana leaves out flat. Lay lettuce leaves atop the banana leaves. Spoon the fish portions onto the leaves. Wrap each portion snugly in the lettuce leaves. Wrap the lettuce leaf packages in the banana leaves and secure with kitchen string or skewers. Bake in a moderate oven or grill over coals for 30 minutes. Serve with Lover Sauce (see recipe).

Yield: 4
Heat Scale: Medium

MICCHA TRONG KROENG (DECORATED FISH)

This recipe was originally published, before the days of darkness, by Princess Rasmi Sutharot.

2	dried chiles, such as Thai or piquin, stems removed
1	tablespoon sliced lemon grass
1	tablespoon chopped fennel bulb
7	cloves garlic
6	shallots
1	tablespoon galangal
2	tablespoons grated coconut
2	kaffir lime leaves
	Salt and pepper
6	tablespoons vegetable oil
1	pound catfish, cut into bite-size pieces
1	chopped fresh dill for garnish

Combine all ingredients except the fish, oil and dill in a blender or mortar and reduce them to a paste. Heat the oil to medium high and fry the fish till golden. Transfer the fish to a platter. Add the paste to the hot oil, reduce the heat and cook, stirring, for about 15 minutes. Correct the seasoning with salt or fish sauce. Add the fish pieces and shake the pan till they are coated with sauce. Garnish with chopped dill.

Yield: 4 Servings
Heat Scale: Medium

LAMB CHOPS CAMBODIANA

Sidney Ke and his wife Bopha of the Cambodiana's restaurant in Berkeley, California, belong to a school of cookery that draws a bit more from the French side of their national cuisine. They use butter and wine in their cooking, and their menu is arranged by sauce type. In this dish, rather than a slow burn or an intense flame, the chile is delivered in sparkles of flavor-heat that dance on the tongue. It is important that the cooking heat be medium, lest the spicy coating become a bitter, carbonized crust.

1	cup fish sauce
1	cup water
1	cup sugar
	Pinch salt
¼	cup minced fresh lemon grass
6	lemon leaves, crushed
4	cloves garlic, minced
2	shallots, minced
4	tablespoons paprika
4	teaspoons turmeric
1	teaspoon galangal, powdered or minced
16	lamb chops
4	tablespoons garlic/shallot butter
2	tablespoons minced parsley
1	red jalapeño, stem and seeds removed, very finely minced

Combine the fish sauce, water, sugar, and salt and bring to a gentle boil for 3 minutes, or until the sugar has dissolved and the liquid begins to thicken. Add the lemon grass, lemon leaves, garlic, shallots, paprika, turmeric, and galangal, return to a boil, then remove from heat and let cool.

Dip the chops in the cooled liquid and grill them over medium heat, turning once. When they are half done, dip them into the liquid again and continue cooking until they are glazed. While they are cooking, quickly brown the garlic/shallot butter. Drizzle chops with the browned butter and sprinkle with parsley and jalapeño.

Yield: 4 Servings
Heat Scale: Mild

SMOKY EGGPLANT COUNTRY-STYLE

The following is a very typical Cambodian dish. People who roast their own chiles will appreciate its distinctive flavor. When I tasted it near the town of Udong, I was unable to get the recipe, but Sidney and Bopha Ke were kind enough to give it to me.

1	**large eggplant**
½	**pound ground lean pork**
1	**scallion, sliced**
1	**clove garlic, minced**
1	**tablespoon fish sauce**
1	**tablespoon soy sauce**
1	**tablespoon oyster sauce**
4	**large cooked shrimp, peeled and chopped**
	Salt and pepper
	Sliced scallions, chopped chiles, basil leaves for garnish

Pierce the eggplant several times with a fork to prevent its exploding. Holding the stem end with tongs or a fork, stand it up over hot coals (or a gas flame) until the skin on the bottom is thoroughly charred. Lay it down and continue cooking in this way, turning when necessary, to char the entire fruit on the outside and cook it through on the inside. Wash the black crust off under running water. Tear the eggplant apart into manageable pieces and set aside, keeping warm.

Combine the pork, scallion, and garlic in a skillet or wok and quickly brown. (Use a dash of oil if necessary.) Add the fish, soy, and oyster sauces and bring to a boil, stirring. Stir in the shrimp to heat through and correct the seasoning. Pour on top of the eggplant. Garnish with sliced scallions, chopped chiles and basil leaves.

Yield: 6 Side Dishes or 3 Main Dishes.

SONY SOK'S HONEY SOAK FOR QUAIL

All kinds of birds, large and small, are eaten in Cambodia. This recipe was provided by Sony Sok, owner of San Francisco's Angkor Palace restaurant.

3 tablespoons honey
3 tablespoons soy sauce

3   tablespoons sugar
3   tablespoons oyster sauce
1   clove garlic, crushed
1   pinch salt and pepper
6   quail
2   cups vegetable oil
    fresh basil and mint leaves

Combine all the ingredients except the quail, vegetable oil and the basil and mint leaves to make a marinade.

Wipe the quail clean with a damp paper towel. Place them in a bowl and pour the marinade over them. Refrigerate overnight. Remove the quail from the marinade and drain. Heat the oil in a wok or deep skillet to medium high and deep-fry quail until they turn golden, about 5 minutes. Serve on a bed of basil and mint leaves with Cambodian Black Pepper Sauce (see recipe) on the side.

Yield: 2 Servings
Note: This dish requires advance preparation.

MINCED PORK ANGKOR

This dish is simple and superior. The taste is unique, and I was quite unable to identify the seasonings. Finally, Sony Sok let me in on the secret ingredient: anchovy. It's not enough to taste like anchovy, just enough to alter the flavor of the dish.

1½ pounds ground pork
2   cups Red Curry Cambogee (see recipe)
1   anchovy, mashed

Quickly brown the pork and drain off excess fat. Add the curry and anchovy and cook, stirring, about 5 minutes. Serve with steamed rice and basil or mint leaves.

Yield: 4 Servings
Heat Scale: Medium

THREE CAMBODIAN CONDIMENTS

Condiments for dipping, drizzling, and delighting are critical to Khmer cookery. These are the ones I encountered most often.

Cambodian Black Pepper Sauce:
2   tablespoons lime juice
½   teaspoon black pepper
½   teaspoon salt
1   pinch sugar

Combine all ingredients. Use with any kind of shellfish or fried fowl.

Yield: 2½ tablespoons

Lover Sauce:
1   tablespoon chile paste
2   tablespoons lime juice
½   teaspoon salt
½   teaspoon sugar
2   tablespoons fish sauce
12 basil or mint leaves

Heat all but the leaves in a saucepan over medium high heat until the mixture thickens into a syrupy consistency. Stir in the leaves and serve hot. Makes a superior sauce for fried catfish.

Yield: ¼ cup

Salt and Pepper for Fruit:
¼   teaspoon finely minced red chile
¼   teaspoon finely minced green chile
1   tablespoon salt
1   pinch sugar

Combine all ingredients. Brush lightly on any kind of tart fruit: fresh pineapple, green apples, gooseberries, green mangoes, grapefruit, and even, yes, durian!

Yield: 1¼ tablespoons

CHAPTER 13

A FEAST OF BROTHERHOOD:
BACK TO VIETNAM

*A*ND THE LANDS OF THE SOUTH CHINA SEA CALL ME *through the voice of history to a table of reconciliation.*

"*T*HERE IS A TIME TO KILL, AND A TIME TO HEAL...*a time of war, and a time of peace...and there is nothing better for a man than that he should eat and drink and enjoy the good of all his labor.*" —Ecclesiastes

My last glimpse of the jewel city of Saigon in 1975 was by the light of bombardment. During the night of April 29, the Army of North Vietnam had reached the outskirts of the city and began hammering Tan Son Nuht airport with rocket and mortar fire. The staccato lights of hundreds of shellbursts flashed through the darkness, ripping the night to shreds and illuminating brief, ragged images of the skyline. The ground rumbled like kettledrums. We laid low, waited, and watched. The next day the enemy would gain most of the city, and by dark, the entire nation. And a long darkness it would be for beautiful Saigon.

For the next decade and more, Vietnam would turn in upon herself, refusing commerce with the outside world. The rulers of the newly unified nation would throw a cloak of silence over the land, so that the only voices we heard from it were those of the fleeing boat people. Vietnam was going into hiding.

As for me, leaving the mouth of the Mekong River behind in the last hours of the war, I bitterly cursed the enemy, and I even cursed the land. I cursed the war and defeat and all the politicians and generals on either side. I swore I would never return. Although veterans often visit their old battlefields later in life, I vowed I would not. I would leave behind forever the land I had come to both love and hate.

But while I might leave Vietnam, she would not leave me. For nearly two decades, the Land of the Ascending Dragon had invaded my dreams. I awoke from them with the stink of cordite in my nostrils and cries in my ears. A friend has told me that I sometimes walked in my sleep, uttering Vietnamese words that have long faded from my conscious memory. In the town where I lived, Vietnamese restaurants sent their culinary siren call wafting through the streets, never letting me forget. They awakened a thousand sensual memories of the living fragrance of chile and the florid bouquet of lemon grass and garlic; of the streets of Saigon a-clatter and a-sizzle with the joyful, orderly chaos of cookery; of steam billowing from little noodle shops and the taste of life eagerly lived in the face of an evil war.

During the early '90s, the government of Vietnam decided that they were foolish to hold the world at arm's length, and by degrees, eased travel restrictions. For my part, I walked Vietnam in my sleep for too long. And for a man whose life is so much a pursuit of the savory and the sweet, bitterness can have only its portion and no more; balance must be observed. Finally, I had a great void to fill: the distractions of war had made it impossible for me to explore the culture and cuisine of Vietnam as thoroughly as I would have liked. My daily fare had been C-rations and mess hall chow, interspersed with occasional culinary bliss in the city. For my return, I was determined that I would eat my way through the whole country. From Saigon in the south to Hanoi in the north, I would rediscover Vietnam in a gastronomic tour de force, my only weapons this time being knife, fork, and chopsticks.

I did not return to Vietnam without some trepidation. Although it had been a place of the most bewitching loveliness, it was there that the ugliest scenes of my life had been played out. Amid culture, refinement, and delicacy, cruelty had been a fact of daily life. Now as I returned, I was hopeful with anticipation, and yet, full of foreboding. I knew that each pleasure I might find could cost me a pain. But I was sure that, unless things had changed very remarkably, the pleasures would outweigh the pains by just enough.

Paul and Bruce Harmon and I had to send to Mexico City for visas and take a circuitous route through Thailand and Cambodia. We finally arrived in Vietnam by car from Phnom Penh. I told my buddies not to let anybody know I was a veteran. "I have no idea how people will react," I said. As we crossed the border, the dusty Cambodian flood plain gave way instantly to green, irrigated fields. The rutted and nearly empty Phnom Penh highway gradually smoothed out and was filled with trucks and small cars hauling goods and crops, and people buzzing around on countless motor scooters. As we approached Saigon at thirty miles per hour, two young men on a motor scooter pulled up alongside, smiling and waving.

"Hello!" the one seated on the rear shouted. "Hello. Are you Americans?"

"Uh...yeah...yes we are," we shouted back.

"Veterans?"

Before we could respond, the bike's driver swerved to miss an onrushing truck. Three days would pass before I told anyone that I was a veteran.

Although we had a long and tiring journey in reaching Saigon, even greater efforts would have been worthwhile; she is a queen of cities, with a sensuous carnival atmosphere like New Orleans. She is busy, bustling, and pulsating with life. Trees by the thousands grow everywhere, cathedral tall and stately. Jacaranda, palm, and cypress form a vast canopy of green supported by wooden columns. Elegant French colonial buildings and grand hotels with terraces and curved corners blend easily with Chinese-inspired temples, schools, and theaters. So many motor scooters clog the wide boulevards that we laughed to see the occasional "motor scooter gridlock."

Although the city is obviously maintained with pride, there is a great shortage of cash in Vietnam, leaving many of Saigon's buildings in need of paint and trim. Plaster needs fixing and walls need shoring up. But then, the city is not as garish as she once was either. There is little or none of the wretchedness that used to be so common. Desperate poverty and malnutrition are nearly gone. Violent crime is almost unknown. What few police one sees go unarmed. They don't even carry night sticks! The city is like a lovely woman who needs to put her makeup on, as though she has just risen, hair in confusion and sleepy-eyed. But as soon as she is made up, she will dazzle the world.

On our way to Vietnam, an American diplomat in Thailand told us that Vietnam will be the economic lodestone of Southeast Asia when relations are normalized between Washington and Hanoi. People sign up by the thousands for courses in English. Their teachers are imperfect speakers who haven't used the language since

1975, and the graduates are nearly incomprehensible, but they forge on, undaunted. Already the city bristles with English-language advertising—a capitalist city in a communist country. A student of economics at Saigon University told me that in his first semester he studied John Kenneth Galbraith and Adam Smith.

"When do you study Marx?" I asked him.

"Oh," he said, "we don't study Marx very much. Maybe in the last semester, as an elective. But only the sons and daughters of party members take the course."

Saigon is a commercial carnival; everyone is hustling, hustling, hustling. Everyone is buying and selling: tour packages, mineral rights, tee shirts, investments, food and drink, joint ventures, arts and crafts, books, stereos, and TVs. If they have nothing else to sell, many will sell their bodies, seemingly just to be a part of the frenzy of commerce. Even hotel chambermaids will knock on the door and ask a man if he wants anything extra: "You lonely, mister?"

Saigon is a blending of first world and third world; East and West; old and new. She is stepsister to both Paris and old Shanghai: one cheek pink from a virgin's blush, the other from a harlot's rouge. Cleaner streets are not to be found in the U.S.A., Japan, or Europe. Neat, well-scrubbed children troop to school in the morning. Industrious artisans and mechanics work steadily in dim, close shops. If they have no shops, they set up operations on a street corner or carry their tools in old American ammunition boxes and go from house to house. There are no graffiti and no litter. Dark streets are safe at night.

Although cops and robbers are rare, pickpockets abound. Taximen, beggars, and vendors are maddeningly persistent. Restaurateurs, desperate for a customer, will nearly drag you inside, and if you don't like the menu, they'll get you something else and negotiate the price.

"You! Where you go?" the merchants demand. "What your name? You buy!"

At midday and in the evening, many people put their labors aside, and a graceful and refined cafe society emerges. Cafes in Vietnam are deep and narrow, no larger than a two-car garage. As though they were set in a Doonesbury cartoon, the word on the sign outside is often spelled "Ca Phe." They open completely onto the street, and all the little tables and reclining canvas chairs are arranged in neat rows facing outward. They call to mind the fuselage of an airliner flying to the street. My buddies and I came to call them "747 Ca Phes."

The patrons relax and sip tea, coffee, and beer and watch their city go by. Music is constant, loud but not thundering, often seeming to compete with the cafe across the street. Latin beats, disco, Viet-pop, at least half in English and mostly from the seventies, it nearly drowns out the sounds of the clamorous streets. The river of Saigon life rushes by to the music: lithe women in limpet hats and *ao-dai* dresses; porters in black "VC" pajamas bearing baskets balanced on bamboo poles; pedicabs, bicycles, motor scooters, pedestrians out for a walk. All these people are busy-busy-busy, hurrying past the monuments, markets, egg-carton-and-tinkertoy apartment blocks white with green or gray trim. Beggars, vendors, and whores insistent, people urging, "Hello! Where you from?" The music of the cafes makes of it all a pageant, a film scene, something to lose yourself in. These are neighborhood places, not downtown hot spots. The real people are here, leading their real, everyday lives.

The people and their lives have grace and poise. Women are well formed and supple, studies in style and comportment. Men are formal and courteous. But the Vietnamese also have a boisterous, in-your-face aggressive side. Beggars need to be firmly shooed away. People will insist on practicing their fractured English on you, even when you want to be left alone. The whores flirt roughly, with many pinches and blows. And, never make eye contact with a souvenir seller; you won't be free of him till you buy. It's no wonder that the Vietnamese were able to contend with Uncle Sam for years, with the French for decades, and with the Chinese for centuries.

I had expected some anti-American feeling in Saigon, but our reception was just the opposite. When I told people I was a veteran, I was patted on the back or saluted. South Vietnamese veterans eagerly showed me their old military ID cards and medals. More than once I was offered food as though I were a prodigal son returning.

Food sellers and restaurants are so numerous in Saigon that the city fairly screams that she is a monarch of cuisine. Those wonderful aromas that have kept my memories alive all these years were so thick on the streets that I thought I might eat the air. The Vietnamese currency is called the *dong*, and a dollar buys ten thousand. So upon arriving, we each exchanged one hundred dollars for one million *dong* and, leaving the bank as millionaires, went looking for food.

Vietnamese cooking is heavily influenced by China, especially in methods of preparation and kitchen equipment. Philosophically they share the concept of "The Five Flavors." The cook strives to balance salt, sweet, sour, bitter, and hot. A dish may be dominated by one or two of the five, but usually the others will play a pleasing harmony in the culinary tune. Stir-frying is a common method of preparation, but the Vietnamese use very little oil, reflecting a general de-emphasis on fats. The frying is more of a gentle simmering. Lightness and freshness are the goals. As in China, vegetables play a central role, but in Vietnam they are raw as often as cooked. Varying textures such as crunch and chewiness are prized at the Vietnamese table. An indispensable seasoning is fish sauce (they seldom use soy). Like a judicious splash of Worcestershire sauce when cooked into a dish, fish sauce buries itself in the flavors of the food and gives it a greater dimension without altering its basic character. Equally important are the firespices, both chile and black pepper. Normally they are not cooked into the food but are served as condiments—as commonly as salt.

We found Saigon's two most memorable restaurants to be Maxim's and the Hung Kim. The former has been a bastion of French cuisine since 1963, and the latter is a hole-in-the-wall with a clay floor. At Maxim's, 15 Dong Khoi Street, I was served the biggest, tenderest, juiciest filet mignon I ever touched with a fork. The service was eager and efficient, the decor plush, and a string quartet played Chopin. I brought my own California wine, just for the occasion. The bill came to about eight dollars.

As grand as Maxim's is, it was the Hung Kim we kept returning to. Though it sits across the street from the luxurious Rex Hotel on Nguyen Thi Minh Khoi Boulevard, it is wholly unremarkable from the outside. Its interior is dim, narrow, and deep, like a dusty cave. The tables rise only about twelve inches from the floor. The little stools are eight inches high and so small that it sometimes feels as though you're sitting on a golf tee. But this is a place that loves and respects food and honors the act of eating. It is almost as much a sacred grotto as it is a restaurant. The votaries of the muse of cuisine that operates the Hung Kim lay out some two dozen colorful and tasty dishes on a crammed buffet. They speak no English, but all you need to do is point to the dishes that most catch your eye, and they'll serve them up with big smiles.

The braised vegetables are especially good, but my favorite is Fish with Ginger Salsa (my own name for it, as I can't pronounce what they call it). A whole fish is steamed in a shallow plate of sweet/savory marinade scented with fresh basil. The fish is napped with a mixture of shredded ginger, red chile, garlic, and lime juice. It's a dish both straightforward and elegant, a characteristic I often noted in the Saigonaise.

A meal at Hung Kim, which includes soup, rice, vegetables, and a platter piled high with lettuce leaves, bean sprouts, and garnishes, costs about forty cents—twice that with a pint of beer. And beer is one of those pains that balance the pleasures: Vietnamese beer is thin, pale, barely effervescent, and never cold!

When the temperature is ninety degrees in the shade, it's worse than water. If you will have your beer cold in Vietnam, you will have to have it on ice and hope that the tropical microbes the frozen water may contain have not survived the chill. In Saigon the brand is Saigon Beer; in Danang it's called Danang Beer; in Hanoi...you get the picture. I cannot not drink beer. Despite a sojourn in England, I have never learned to drink it warm, so through a thousand miles of cities, jungles, highlands, beaches, and rice paddies, I drank bad beer on the rocks and took my chances. I never came down with anything worse than an unfamiliar longing for Coors Light, but I know that others have not been so lucky.

After several nostalgic and gustatory days in Saigon (only the government calls it Ho Chi Minh City), it was time to move on. We caught an early morning bus that took us to the highland retreat of Dalat. It was here that the French governor general of Cochin-China had his residence. Except for a few neo-Stalinist monstrosities put up in the '80s, most of the buildings looked like they were shipped in from a French village. During the American war, Dalat served as a getaway for U.S., South Vietnamese, and Viet Cong officials. Each had their own villas, and the tacit truce that allowed them to share the place was never broken. "Disrupting the peace in Dalat," I was told by an American veteran of those days, "would have been like shooting the piano player in a Western."

Though Dalat is not far from the sweltering heat of Saigon, its elevation makes it cool enough for jackets at night. And as the terrain and climate change, so do the people and their food. The Dalatois may lack the style and sophistication of the Saigonaise, but they also lack their frenetic city life style. Life in Dalat is quiet; the people are warm and hearty. In the chilly air of the evening, the sidewalk cafes serve a unique style of *congee*. Anywhere else, *congee* is little more than rice gruel or porridge, nourishing but bland. In Dalat the congee is rich with pork broth and chunks of meat, redolent of garlic and ginger, with a sheen of red chile oil floating on top.

The hefty portions are garnished with fresh bean sprouts and cilantro and a good pinch of coarsely ground black pepper. There was never a better remedy to the sting of the cold mountain air.

Our stay in Dalat was brief, for we had a long, long way to go. Travel in Vietnam is a pain, a slow pain. It's rather like military travel, except that it never departs or arrives on time. The only reliable transport between cities is by bus. Unfortunately, due to the great cash crunch in the country, the roads are in uniformly awful condition, and the number of buses is far too few. They try to depart as early as possible in the morning, usually about dawn, to compensate for the slow going due to the roads, and they are jammed to the rafters with people.

We left Dalat for the coast on a minibus that seemed comfortable enough to start, but we kept stopping to pick up more people and more people and even more people! And they all smoked, constantly! Halfway to the coast, the little bus, which seated twelve if they were small, had eighteen chattering chain-smoking people and their luggage inside and two guys standing on the rear bumper trailing cinders from enormous cigars. I thought I had been wise to sit in the front seat, but the boxes on the floor took up my legroom, my knees were wedged against the dashboard, and the driver's wife was sitting in my lap. She had given up her perch on the center console to passenger number eighteen, who wore a tee shirt proclaiming that "! Three Bear Boys have a top sense feeling!" I turned to the rear and hollered through the blue tobacco haze to Bruce and Paul, "How you guys doing?" Over the bumping, sweaty press of flesh and multicolored cottons, I could only see the top of Bruce's head and Paul's hand held aloft in a shaky high sign.

"How much longer to the coast?" I wearily asked the lady in my lap.

"Oh, two hour, maybe three hour," she replied nonchalantly.

"No more passengers?"

"Maybe one, maybe two."

"Maybe more?"

"Maybe."

As we bounced down the pockmarked excuse for a road, the driver blithely slipped yet another cassette of nerve-jangling Viet-pop music into his ancient stereo and cranked up the volume. He and the missus and the Three Bear Boy sang along lustily. Good morning, Vietnam.

Upon reaching the coast, we changed minibuses. This time we took a lesson from passengers we had seen on other vehicles: we rode on the roof, and we stretched out and relaxed in the sunshine and sang "Rawhide" and other television themes till we reached the beach resort of Nha Trang. There we found a seafood restaurant so good that an Israeli soldier on leave, a kosher Jew, confessed to us that for the first time in his life he ate prawns. The Hong Ngoc Restaurant, at 272 Thong Nhat Street, is owned and operated by Mr. and Mrs. Nguyen (the most common Vietnamese surname). As a former officer in the South Vietnamese Army, Mr. Nguyen found it difficult to make a living after the war. He knew only soldiering, but the victors wouldn't have him. Inheriting a small house from his mother, he and his wife taught themselves cookery and business and opened Hong Ngoc.

I had to have those seductive shellfish. I called them Delilah Prawns. They are cooked, in the shell, very simply in a little oil, lots of garlic, and a sprinkle of salt and pepper for about twenty-five minutes. The shells become thoroughly crisp and crunchy, and their flavor permeates the meat. There is no need to peel Delilah Prawns—just eat them whole. Mr. Nguyen sat and talked with us as we dined and eagerly shared his theories of cooking.

He told us that he puts red food coloring into the prawns because: "The power of color is great. Food is everything, not only taste. You must have something to see and hear and feel and smell." Then he wrote out the recipe for me, in Vietnamese, and I had it translated when I got home.

From Nha Trang, we made our way north through Danang and China Beach to the old imperial capital of Hue near the Seventeenth Parallel, the former DMZ. That bit of our journey was the worst experience I have ever had in Vietnam. Most of it was aboard a smoke-filled instrument of abuse we came to call "the barf bus." I'll say no more about it, except that when we got off the vile vehicle, I earnestly proclaimed that wartime was more fun.

Having been dumped in an unlit part of town in the dead of night, we shouldered our gear and trudged toward a distant glow, like three men following a star. Near the left bank of the Perfume River, we found the source of light to be the Lac Thien Restaurant at 6 Dinh Tien Hoang Street. While most of Hue closes by about 10:00 p.m., the Lac Thien stays open as long as anyone wants to eat or drink. Of the large family that operates it, all the adults but one are deaf, though none of the children are. We arrived late, dirty, smelly, and looking thoroughly disreputable, yet, to them, a wondrous apparition. Within minutes we were seated, awaiting the local specialty of Happy Crepes, and each of us had a child on his lap. The kids sang "Frere Jacques" and taught us several verses. We taught them "Ol MacDonald." I tried to teach them the theme from "Rawhide," but it proved too difficult for them. The only part they got was the whipcrack sound and "Yah!" I did teach them the head-rubbing noogie, though, and boasted that I had "brought the noogie to the Nguyens."

The Happy Crepes we were served that evening were in a way the quintessence of Vietnamese cookery. They employ the five flavors; yield a complex bouquet of aromas; have the textures of crunch, chewiness, and crispness; are as pleasing to look at as a still-life painting; and the sounds they make when cooking or breaking under a fork are almost musical. In fact, they are sometimes known as "Singing Crepes." They are made by pouring a rice flour crepe batter into a very hot pan. The hot side forms a crust, while the cooler upper side cooks to a tender chewiness. They are filled with a stir-fry mixture of ham, shrimp, onions, and bean sprouts and are served with a rich and spicy sauce.

We made the Lac Thien our headquarters while in Hue because it is a place that brims with love. The adults constantly caress their children and pat their customers on the shoulder. The kids have no fear of any adult and are as eager to give hugs as to get them. There is a telling little monument in the open kitchen one does not often see any more: a traditional Vietnamese hearth of three bricks laid in a triangle with the fire in the middle.

The legend of the hearth is that by misfortune a woman was separated from her woodcutter husband. In the course of time, she married a hunter. One day the woodcutter reappeared while the hunter was in the forest. The astonished wife had no time to react before the hunter came home with his catch, a deer. "Quick!" she said to the woodcutter, "hide under the haycock!" As the woodcutter hid, the hunter set the haycock alight to cook the deer. Seeing her first love go up in flames, the wife leaped into the inferno to join him in death. The hunter, thinking he had somehow driven his wife to suicide, leaped in after her.

The Jade Emperor, that is, The Creator, took pity on them because they had all died for love, and he appointed them deities of the kitchen so they could be together. Their togetherness is represented by the three bricks that form the triangle. They seem to put their heads close to one another against the fire. Every year the kitchen deities report to the Jade Emperor whether the kitchen is a place of love or strife, and the family is rewarded or punished accordingly. At Lac Thien, the Jade Emperor always smiles.

Throughout the south we three Americans were received like old friends returning. Outside Hue, the entire village of Thuan An turned out to greet us when we arrived with letters from relatives in California. In the center and north, we were greeted cordially and with respect, quite in contrast to the scorn reserved for the few remaining former Soviets. The people in the north seem to regard the Americans as true foes, and the Soviets as false friends, there being honor only in the former. A popular story was making the rounds with the few Western tourists in the land: Two Americans were chased through the streets of Hue by an angry mob shouting "Lien Xo!" (Soviet!). The Northerners' attitude toward us reminded me of the John Wayne movie *McClintock*. In it, the Duke and an old Indian chief had fought each other in the wars of their youth. Now, as elders in peacetime, they greeted each other warmly as "honored enemy."

Everywhere in the Socialist Republic of Vietnam, we saw capitalism and Americana displayed, worn, sung, and praised. People wear hats with American flag logos. Tee shirts with English words are hugely popular. It doesn't matter what they say or if they make sense, as long as they are in English. Typical messages are: "Sentiment Boy = American Dream Staff," the very popular "Inmutation is your sweetness: U.S. difference of information." And the vaguely socialist-sounding "Aspire to be physically fit!"

Hue, the citadel and the old imperial seat, had been a symbol of Viet Cong resistance since the Tet offensive of 1968. Now, a souvenir shop in the audience hall sells facsimiles of U.S. military rings. All the service academies and numerous divisions, air wings, and ships are represented. When I confusedly asked why the citadel would carry U.S. military facsimiles, I was told, "Because we ran out of the real ones." They still have real dog tags, though. I almost bought "Jerry A. Royal, Type A, Lutheran" and "John F. Truschke, Type A, Catholic." But I didn't know if they were alive, and I didn't want dead men's tags.

At first I thought all this American iconography was being worn like war trophies, but the people simply like Americana. "People want to have style," the ring and dog-tag sellers told me.

In the north the single most popular icon of any kind, more than Marx, Lenin,

Ho Chi Minh, or Jesus, is the Marlboro Man. People cut his image from magazines and tape it up on walls, doors, windows, and inside automobiles as though all the folk were Catholics and he their patron saint. I have even seen his manly gaze directed to his votaries from the ceiling.

One evening, I noticed him regarding me from the window of a small cafe. A familiar fuzz-tone guitar riff reverberated through the open door. Looking in, I saw people of many ages drinking bootleg Pepsi at tables in front of a big-screen TV showing a video of the Bangles playing "Walk Like an Egyptian." In my pocket, I had a copy of the new constitution of Vietnam, purchased from a souvenir stand. The document enshrines the right of foreign capitalist enterprise to do business, make a good profit, and be free from seizure.

My mind went back to the first week of May, 1975, as we sat for a few days off the coast of Vungtao waiting for refugee transport to Guam. I struck up a series of conversations with Captain Long of the late South Vietnamese Air Force. In a wistful moment, tongue only partially in cheek, he said, "You know, you Americans did it all wrong."

"I guess so," I said, "since we lost."

"That's not what I mean. Instead of sending Hanoi bombs for years, you should have sent them Coke and Levis and rock-and-roll albums. Then they'd be begging to join you."

As the Bangles played and swayed, and the seated patrons articulated their arms in King Tut poses, I wondered awhile if Vietnam had defeated U.S. policy only to be swallowed up by our culture and economy. Of course, there is no way they can play the hermit kingdom. If they don't strive to be a part of the world economy, they'll become a poor, backward vassal of China. They have to engage the world, and that includes Uncle Sam. So, by degrees, they are opening up and encouraging partners and investors. They do invite us, the Americans, to do as they do: consign the war to history, and become, at the least, proper neighbors.

Not all is right and rosy in Vietnam. It is a very poor country, partly due to its own government's follies and partly due to ours. Corruption is common. The only good highway is the one leading to the Cambodian front. Dissent is punishable. There is peace and order, no one starves, its principal cities are jewels, and the nation deals with the world more on its own terms than ever before.

In the interests of time and a desire to avoid another ordeal by bus, we decided to fly to the end of our journey at Hanoi; however, it was still a painful passage. Vietnam Airways is known for two things: falling out of the sky and a two-tiered price structure. A ticket to Hanoi for "capitalist tourists" costs $80.00. Locals pay $21.00. As a "rich American," I am used to paying a little extra, but this disparity was almost enough to get me back on the barf bus. Almost. Teeth clenched in both fear and anger, we flew to one of the last communist capitals in the world.

Hanoi was the French capital of Indo-China, and their architects were given free rein. It is a demi-Paris. Ornate monumental buildings line the shores of little lakes. Men dressed in corduroy jackets and berets recall the Parisian Latin Quarter. Everyone eats French baguettes. It is a sober city, though—a Boston to Saigon's New Orleans. Its people are industrious, disciplined, and reserved.

Although we had encountered no anti-American feeling in the south, I was sure we would find it in Hanoi. It seemed inevitable. We dropped more bombs on Hanoi and its environs than any other patch of ground in the history of warfare. Bomb craters are still a regular part of the landscape. While nobody evinced any overt hostility toward us, I wasn't sure if the degree of their reserve was the norm. People were polite, but whether with a natural cool or a cold shoulder, I couldn't tell.

One day I wandered the city alone, and I found myself in a little restaurant eating delicious, chewy sausage balls wrapped in tangy *la-lot* leaves, just grilled to crispness. The place was like the Hung Kim, but bright and airy. Beautiful silk paintings decorated three of the walls and the buffet colored the fourth. A Vietnamese man purchased his lunch and, though other tables were empty, he sat down with me. I judged he was about my age, or a little older, and wore his hair in a military cut. He smiled a greeting, but said nothing. We each ate in silent company, smiling politely now and then. It was clear to me that the man wanted nothing more than to eat with me, although I could not fathom why.

Finishing his meal, he pointed to one of the silk paintings, a still life of a table set with food and what I took to be a grace written beneath. He smiled again and spoke, apparently trying to explain the painting to me. I nodded and smiled, but he was insistent and got up and pointed to the words under the picture. He gesticulated and gestured and explained. I finally took out my notebook and copied it down, and he seemed satisfied. He even patted the notebook as I put it back in my shirt pocket.

He went his way. I put the inscription in a pouch along with the recipe for Delilah Prawns and other things to be translated in a few days when I got home and forgot about it. The Vietnamese neighbor who did the translating smiled when he saw the scribbled notes.

"An old, old proverb," he said. "In food, as in death, we feel the essential brotherhood of man."

FISH WITH GINGER SALSA

This dish is elegant, easy to prepare, and looks beautiful on the table. If whole fish is unavailable, use fillets cut into 4- by 2-inch pieces and arranged on the plate in a pinwheel, interspersed with lemon wedges and scallions.

¼   teaspoon salt
1   teaspoon sugar
½   teaspoon black pepper
4   teaspoons fish sauce
1   whole fish, any kind, about two pounds, cleaned
12 fresh basil leaves
1   tablespoon grated ginger
4   cloves garlic, minced
1   red jalapeño, stem and seeds removed, minced
    Juice of 1 lime

Combine the salt, sugar, pepper, and fish sauce and sprinkle over the fish. Marinate for 30 minutes on a plate spread with the basil leaves. Combine the ginger, garlic, chile and lime juice and spread evenly on the top of the fish. Transfer the fish, on the plate, to a steamer and cook for 30 minutes. If you don't have a steamer, cover the plate tightly with foil and bake at 350 degrees for 30 minutes. Serve with Nuoc Cham (see recipe).

Yield: 4 Servings
Heat Scale: Mild

NUOC CHAM

No Vietnamese table is complete without a dish of nuoc cham for dipping and drizzling. It is as ubiquitious as rice.

1-2 cloves garlic
1   red jalapeño, stem and seeds removed
2   teaspoons sugar
¼   fresh lime
2½ tablespoons water
2   tablespoons fish sauce

With a mortar and pestle, pound the garlic, jalapeño, and sugar into a paste. Squeeze the lime juice in. With a paring knife, remove the pulp from the lime and pound it into the paste. Add the water and fish sauce and mix well.

Yield: ½ cup
Heat Scale: Medium
Variation: For a real thrill, try this with an habanero chile!

CAULIFLOWER WITH STRAW MUSHROOMS

Braised vegetables are especially good at Hung Kim. This recipe is also good with other fleshy vegetables such as broccoli, bell peppers, or firm squashes.

1   tablespoon vegetable oil
3   scallions, sliced, white part only
1   cup cauliflower florets
2   tablespoons water
½   cup straw mushrooms
2   teaspoons fish sauce
1   pinch sugar

Heat the oil to high and stir in the scallions. Add the cauliflower and stir-fry for 1 minute. Add 1 tablespoon water, cover, reduce heat to medium, and cook for 2 minutes. Uncover, add the remaining water and the rest of the ingredients. Stir, cover, and cook for 2 minutes.

Yield: 2 Servings

MULTICOLORED VEGETABLE DISH

Mr. Nguyen, the Warrior Cook of Nha Trang, would say that it is as important to eat with your eyes as with your mouth. This dish would find instant favor with him.

The Sauce:
½	cup water
2	teaspoons cornstarch
1	teaspoon fish sauce
1	teaspoon oyster sauce
1	pinch pepper
1	pinch sugar

Combine the sauce ingredients in a bowl and set aside.

The Vegetables:
1	tablespoon vegetable oil
3	cloves garlic, chopped
1	small red onion, quartered
2	scallions, cut on the bias into 2-inch sections
2	bunches broccoli, stalks peeled, cut into 1/2-inch pieces
½	cup grated carrot
4	tablespoons water
1	tomato, cut into eighths

Heat the oil to high in a skillet or wok. Add the garlic and fry for 1 minute. Stir in the onion and scallions and cook for 1 minute. Add the broccoli and carrot and stir-fry 1 minute. Add water, cover, and reduce heat to medium for 3 minutes. Uncover and stir in the tomato and cook for 1 minute. Stir in the prepared sauce and cook till it thickens.

Yield: 6 Side Dishes

SAIGON STUFFED TOMATOES BRUCE

These are also a specialty at the Hung Kim and were a particular favorite of Bruce Harmon. Ordinarily, it's difficult to get him to eat his vegetables, but he always asked for more of these.

The Sauce:

1   teaspoon vegetable oil
1   fat clove garlic, chopped
1   tablespoon tomato paste
¼   cup water
1   tablespoon fish sauce
1   tablespoon sugar
1   tablespoon light soy sauce

Heat the oil to high in a small saucepan. Add the garlic and cook for 1 minute. Add the tomato paste and cook, stirring, for 1 minute. Add the water, fish sauce, sugar, and soy sauce and cook at a boil, stirring, for 2 minutes.

The Tomatoes:

6   ounces ground pork
4   cloves garlic, minced
2   shallots, chopped
2   scallions, sliced, white part only
1   pinch sugar
2   tablespoons fish sauce
1   pinch black pepper
4   tomatoes, ripe but still firm
¼   cup vegetable oil

Combine the pork, garlic, shallots, scallions, sugar, fish sauce, and pepper. Mix well by hand. Cut off and discard the tomato tops and scoop out their cores with a spoon or melon baller. Wipe the insides with a paper towel to dry them well. Stuff them tightly with the pork mixture.

Heat the oil in a wide skillet to medium. Add the tomatoes, meat side down, cover, and cook for 5 minutes or until meat is completely done. Turn the tomatoes meat side up and cook, covered, for another 5 minutes. With a slotted spoon, transfer them to a serving plate. Pour the sauce over the tomatoes.

Yield: 4

Variation: In place of tomatoes, use small eggplants that have been cut in half and hollowed out.

VIETNAMESE FRIED CABBAGE

The humble cabbage becomes an elegant dish with this recipe. Try it for lunch or a light supper. It goes especially well with a dry German wine.

1   egg
1   teaspoon fish sauce
1   tablespoon vegetable oil
1   clove garlic, chopped
1   pound cabbage, finely shredded
2   teaspoons water
    Salt and pepper to taste

Beat the egg and fish sauce together and set aside. Heat the oil to high in a heavy skillet and fry the garlic for 30 seconds. Add the cabbage and stir to coat with oil. Add the water, cover and reduce heat to medium for 5 minutes. Uncover and sprinkle with salt and pepper. Drizzle the egg mixture over the cabbage and gradually combine by gentle stirring or folding.

Yield: 6 Side Dishes
Variation: Add a thinly sliced chile pepper to the garlic.

VIETNAMESE VEGETABLE PLATTER

A plate of crisp raw vegetables is essential to a proper Vietnamese meal. Arrange a mound of lettuce leaves (any kind but iceberg) in the middle of a serving platter. Around the lettuce place small mounds of mint and cilantro. Around those arrange a ring of cucumber slices. Serve with a bowl of Ngam Dam.

    Ngam Dam
1   carrot, peeled
½   cup water
1   teaspoon white or rice vinegar
¼   teaspoon salt
1   teaspoon sugar

Using a vegetable peeler, cut long, thin strips of carrot, or shred it coarsely. Combine the carrot with the other ingredients and marinate 15 minutes.

Yield: ¾ cup

CONGEE DALAT

This soup is filling, flavorful, and satisfying. I tried it at several different sidewalk cafes in Dalat and found that no two cooks prepare it quite the same way. Some add other meats such as tripe, heart, or liver. Some add vegetables like squash, bamboo shoots, or eggplant. Almost anything in the kitchen could do well in Congee Dalat.

2	tablespoons pork fat (or substitute vegetable oil)
1	tablespoon minced ginger
1	tablespoon minced garlic
1	cup sweet or glutinous rice
4	cups rich pork broth (or substitute 3 cups chicken and 1 cup beef)
½	pound diced pork
2	tablespoons fish sauce
1	tablespoon red chile oil
	Bean sprouts
	Cilantro
	Black pepper

In a stock pot, render the pork fat over medium heat. Add the ginger and garlic and cook 3 minutes. Add the rice, broth, pork, fish sauce, and chile oil. Bring to a boil, then reduce the heat and simmer till the rice begins to disintegrate, 30 to 40 minutes. Serve garnished with sprouts, cilantro, and pepper.

Yield: 4 Servings
Heat Scale: Mild to Medium

DELILAH PRAWNS

When I told the Israeli soldier I was going to call these Delilah Prawns because of him, he laughed nervously and made me promise not to use his name. "My rabbi would understand," he said, "but not my mother." I told him he looked a lot like Victor Mature in the movie Samson and Delilah.

1	pound prawns in the shell, well-cleaned
1	teaspoon salt
1	teaspoon pepper
1	teaspoon sugar
1	pinch MSG (optional)
1	tablespoon vegetable oil
1	tablespoon cornstarch

2　tablespoons white wine
2　tablespoons minced garlic
1　tablespoon paprika (for color)

Combine all ingredients in a bowl and let stand for 15 minutes. Heat a wok or skillet to medium, add the prawns, and stir-fry for 3 minutes. Cover, reduce the heat, and simmer 25 minutes, stirring occasionally. Serve with Nuoc Cham (see recipe).

Yield: 2 Servings

CARAMEL SHRIMP

The Vietnamese are very artful with any kind of shellfish. They could use them to seduce Jew, Gentile, or Philistine alike. Caramelized sugar is a common item in the Vietnamese kitchen. Cooks always make their own; it is simple and keeps well unrefrigerated.

The Caramel:
½　cup sugar
¾　cup water
1　teaspoon lemon juice

Combine the sugar and ¼ cup water in a small pan over high heat. Watch it closely and when it starts to turn brown, begin stirring. Keep stirring as it darkens and when a billow of steam forms above it, remove from heat, stir in the remaining water, then return to the stove and cook, stirring, 5 minutes. Stir in the lemon juice, then transfer to a jar and let cool.

The Shrimp:
1　tablespoon vegetable oil
1　clove garlic, chopped
½　pound raw shrimp, shelled and deveined
3　tablespoons fish sauce
4　teaspoons sugar
2　teaspoons caramel (see recipe above)
　　Pepper to taste

Heat the oil in a skillet or wok over high heat. Add the garlic and stir briefly, then add the shrimp and toss. Reduce the heat to medium and stir in remaining ingredients. Cover and cook for 3 minutes and then uncover. Half the liquid should be evaporated, and the shrimp should wear a most delicious-looking glaze.

Yield: 2 Servings

SUGARCANE SHRIMP

This is one of the most elegant Vietnamese dishes of any kind. Although it can be made with a blender, a better texture is produced by using a mortar and pestle. Serve Sugarcane Shrimp as an appetizer or as part of a buffet. You will reap many kudos. I guarantee it.

4	cloves garlic
1	pound shrimp, shelled and deveined
1	teaspoon sugar
2	egg whites, beaten to a thin froth, not stiff
1	teaspoon cornstarch
2	tablespoons melted margarine
	Salt and pepper to taste
1	12-inch section of sugarcane

Mash the garlic in the mortar. Add the shrimp, a few at a time, and continue mashing until all are reduced to a thick paste. Unless you have a large mortar you may have to do this in batches. Add the sugar and egg whites and beat together till incorporated. Stir in the cornstarch, margarine, and salt and pepper. The result should be a sticky but malleable paste. Peel the sugarcane and cut it into 4-inch lengths. Split those lengthwise into quarters. Take about 2 tablespoons of the paste in your hand and mold it into an oval shape around one end of a sugarcane stick, leaving about half its length bare for a handle. If the paste is too sticky to work with, coat your hand with a little oil. Continue till all the paste is used.

Broil the sticks over coals, or bake 30 minutes in a preheated oven at 350 degrees.

Yield: 12 Canes

HAPPY CREPES

These are good for breakfast, lunch, dinner, or a snack. They require a lot of work, but they are such a hit with guests that the effort is very well spent. If you have a large kitchen, invite your friends over and cook these as a group. The meal you enjoy together afterward will be all the more pleasant and memorable, and the Jade Emperor will be moved to smile.

1	cup rice flour
½	cup cornstarch
¼	cup wheat flour
2½	cups water
3	scallions, green and white parts sliced separately
½	pound ground pork
2	tablespoons fish sauce
2	cloves garlic, minced
½	teaspoon freshly ground black pepper
½	pound shrimp, shelled, cleaned and split
	Vegetable oil
½	pound bean sprouts
1	onion, sliced
10	white mushrooms, sliced
3	eggs, beaten

Combine the rice flour, cornstarch, wheat flour, water, and scallion greens to make a batter.

Combine the pork with half of: the fish sauce, garlic, scallion whites, and pepper. Combine the shrimp with the remaining fish sauce, garlic, scallion whites, and pepper. Arrange the above, and all the other ingredients, handily near the stove. Heat a small skillet or an omelet pan to high.

Add 1 tablespoon of oil, then 1½ tablespoons of pork and 2 or 3 pieces of shrimp and cook for 2 minutes. Reduce the heat to medium and add 3 tablespoons of batter, 1 tablespoon of bean sprouts, a few slices of the onion, and some mushroom slices. Cover and cook for 2 minutes. Uncover and pour 3 tablespoons of the beaten egg over the crepe, then cover again for 2 minutes. Uncover and fold in half, adding more oil if needed. Continue cooking, covered, turning the crepe from time to time, until it is very crisp.

Serve with Nuoc Cham.

Yield: 6 Crepes
Heat Scale: Mild

SAUSAGE BALLS WITH LA-LOT LEAVES

La-lot leaves are often used in grilling and to flavor soups and stews. If you can't find them at your local Asian grocery, grape leaves will make an adequate substitute. When I prepare these, I cannot shake the image of the man who sat down to dine with me that day in Hanoi. To serve these at my table, I feel, is to honor him and all who share his abundant spirit.

1	**pound ground pork**
2	**cloves garlic, minced**
2	**scallions, white part only, minced**
½	**teaspoon salt**
½	**teaspoon sugar**
½	**teaspoon black pepper**
1	**tablespoon cornstarch**
	***La-lot* leaves or grape leaves**

Thoroughly combine all ingredients except leaves in a bowl and let sit for 2 hours. To give the sausage balls their characteristic chewiness, take about 1½ tablespoons of the mixture into your hand and knead it vigorously, turning it over several times, for about one minute. Then form it into a ball and set aside. Repeat until all the meat is used. Wrap each ball in a leaf and skewer them, 5 to a skewer. Broil over coals or bake in a moderate oven, turning once, to the desired doneness. Serve with Nuoc Cham (see recipe).

Yield: 4 to 6 Skewers
Heat Scale: Mild

VIETNAMESE BARBECUED BEEF

Variations on this recipe are popular throughout Vietnam as street food. A pedestrian is never far from a lone vendor with a small grill doing a good business in barbecue.

2	**cloves garlic**
1	**tablespoon sugar**
3	**scallions, white part only**
1	**tablespoon fish sauce**
2	**stalks fresh lemon grass, chopped fine**
	Black pepper to taste
1	**tablespoon sesame seeds**
1	**tablespoon sesame oil**

1   pound lean beef, cut into thin slices
½   cup Nuoc Cham (see recipe)

In a mortar, pound the garlic, sugar, and scallions to a paste. Add fish sauce, lemon grass, pepper, sesame seeds, and sesame oil. Marinate the beef in this mixture for at least 30 minutes. Grill over coals for 3 to 5 minutes per side. Use the Nuoc Cham as dipping sauce.

Yield: 3 to 4 Servings
Heat Scale: Varies
Serving Suggestion: Serve with a vegetable platter. Using the lettuce leaves and herbs, wrap up a piece of beef into a roll and dip it into the sauce.

ASPARAGUS AND CRAB SOUP

Asparagus is one of the crops introduced into Asia by the French. The Vietnamese have always referred to it as "Western bamboo," for its resemblance to bamboo shoots. It's quite popular, especially in the south.

2½   quarts chicken or fish stock
1   pound fresh asparagus spears, lower third removed
1   tablespoon fish sauce
1   teaspoon vegetable oil
1   clove garlic, chopped
2   scallions, sliced, white and green parts separated
½   pound crabmeat
¼   teaspoon white pepper
2   teaspoons cornstarch stirred into 2 tablespoons water
1   egg
¼   cup chopped cilantro

Bring stock to a boil and drop in the asparagus. Cook till fork tender, about 4 minutes. Remove, cut into bite-sized pieces and set aside. Add fish sauce to stock and reduce the heat to a simmer. Heat the oil in a pan to medium high and cook the garlic and scallion whites for 1 minute. Add the crabmeat and pepper and cook 5 minutes, stirring and tossing. Raise the heat under the stock and return to a boil. Stir the crabmeat mixture into the stock and then add the cornstarch. Break the egg into the boiling soup and whisk it vigorously. Cook 2 minutes, then add the asparagus, cilantro, and scallion greens, and serve.

Yield: 6 to 8 Servings

HANOI MEAT AND POTATOES

After so many days of dining on wonderful Vietnamese fare, I started longing for the food from home. I longed for red meat, red wine, and white potatoes. A kiosk near our hotel sold a variety of bad wines from the communist and former communist countries of Eastern Europe. I took my chances on a Bulgarian Cabernet Sauvignon. According to custom, I dickered with the shopkeeper for it, finally paying $4.00. From there I wandered the streets until I came upon what looked like a beer garden near the old opera house. The place seemed empty, but I ambled in and an eager young man suddenly appeared from behind a screen. He was very keen to practice his English and tell me his story. I had barely sat down when he told me, "I live here, in restaurant. When people leave I make a bed by this table. In daytime I go to university. Study business," he said proudly.

"Aren't you a communist?" I asked.

"No, no," he said, searching for the right words. "Communist...communist all...finish. Now we get capitalism economy."

"You study supply and demand? You know that?" I asked.

"Yes, yes! Supply and demand. Very good!"

I told him of my demand and asked him if he could supply.

"No problem!" he announced. And he rushed off to the kitchen, eager to pass his first exam. Here are the results.

½   **pound beef, cut into thin, bite-sized pieces**
1   **clove garlic, mashed or pressed**
1   **tablespoon fish sauce**
1   **teaspoon black pepper**
¼   **cup vegetable oil**
½   **pound small potatoes, peeled and cut into 1/4-inch slices and lightly salted**
1   **onion, sliced**
1   **scallion, sliced thinly on the bias**

Combine the beef, garlic, fish sauce, and pepper and marinate for 15 minutes. Heat the oil in a skillet to medium high and fry the potatoes till they are well browned. Remove and set aside. Pour out all but 1 tablespoon of the oil. Add the beef mixture and onion. Stir-fry till the beef is well browned and fairly dry. Pour over the potatoes and sprinkle with the scallion.

Yield: An A+
Serving suggestion: Don't serve with Bulgarian Cabernet Sauvignon!

METRIC EQUIVALENTS

Liquid Conversion

1 teaspoon = 5 milliliters

1 tablespoon = 15 milliliters

1/4 cup = 59 milliliters

1/2 cup = 118 milliliters

1 cup = 237 milliliters

4 cups = 946 milliliters

4 quarts = 3.8 liters

Dry Conversion

1 teaspoon = 5 grams

1 tablespoon = 15 grams

1/4 cup = 57 grams

1/2 cup = 114 grams

1 cup = 227 grams

Weight Conversion

1 ounce = 28 grams

2 ounces = 57 grams

4 ounces = 114 grams

8 ounces = 227 grams

1 pound = 454 grams

INDEX

STIR-FRY

VEGETABLES

The Crossing Press
publishes a full selection
of cookbooks.
To receive our current
catalog, please call toll-free,
800-777-1048.